JAZZ SPOKEN HERE

JAZZ SPOKEN HERE

Conversations with Twenty-Two Musicians

WAYNE ENSTICE
and
PAUL RUBIN

LOUISIANA STATE UNIVERSITY PRESS

BATON ROUGE AND LONDON

Copyright © 1992 by Louisiana State University Press
Manufactured in the United States of America
First printing
01 00 99 98 97 96 95 94 93 92   5 4 3 2 1

Designer: Laura Roubique Gleason
Typeface: Janson Text
Typesetter: G & S Typesetters, Inc.
Printer and binder: Thomson-Shore, Inc.

Library of Congress Cataloging-in-Publication Data
Enstice, Wayne, 1943–
    Jazz spoken here : conversations with twenty-two musicians / Wayne Enstice
and Paul Rubin.
        p.   cm.
    Includes discographies.
    ISBN 0-8071-1760-9 (cloth)
    1. Jazz musicians—Interviews.   I. Rubin, Paul, 1951– .
II. Title.
ML395.E57   1992
781.65—dc20   92-6612
                                                           CIP
                                                           MN

The paper in this book meets the guidelines for permanence and durability of the Committee
on Production Guidelines for Book Longevity of the Council on Library Resources. ⊚

If they hear somebody talk, they might give jazz a chance.

—Charles Mingus

CONTENTS

PREFACE

J*azz Spoken Here* is a book written for jazz fans by jazz fans. Over a seven-year period we had the opportunity to record a series of detailed interviews with world-class jazz musicians. It was an adventure into the heart of what once seemed a closed society. *Jazz Spoken Here* documents that adventure.

The chance to meet and talk with these musicians was a happy result of our voluntary roles as guest producers and hosts of "Just Jazz," which was broadcast on KUAT FM, the National Public Radio affiliate in Tucson, Arizona. Since we arranged the interviews, our involvement with each musician inevitably extended beyond the formal setting of the recorded conversation. In almost every case, our informal meeting with the musician was enriched by some spontaneous, personal episode.

Some of our fondest memories include the time that Clark Terry invited us impromptu to an NAACP dinner party held in his honor and the time that Lee Konitz dedicated "I'll Remember April" to us during a set and later waved good-bye from the bandstand as we left the club where we had interviewed him earlier. Most bizarre was the time we spent listening to the Ray Bryant Trio in a Phoenix hotel lounge, since throughout much of that evening the two of us constituted the entire audience. Although we never quite got used to the way our four hands clapping rung hollow in that spacious room, Bryant seemed unfazed by the poor turnout (we learned later that his appearance had not been advertised—he was booked solely to entertain guests of the hotel). After a few hard-swinging introductory numbers, Bryant looked at us and asked, "You fellas have any requests?" "'Green Dolphin Street,'" we replied. So the evening went, with the two of us requesting numbers as we enjoyed our "private" performance by the Ray Bryant Trio.

Our goal in each interview was to explore the milestones of each musician's history and approach to playing. Although we tried to find fresh lines of questioning to provoke our guests into reminiscing in unanticipated ways, we began to realize how prominently geography figured into our success. When these musicians came to Tucson or other places in Arizona, they traded the big-city pressures of New York or Los Angeles (where most of them lived and worked) for the casual ambience and comparative tranquillity of the Southwest. We are certain that these factors played a role in getting our subjects to relax and open up.

We did not seriously consider writing a book until the importance of what we had collected finally became clear. Despite the delay between the completion of the interviews and their publication, the content of this book remains current and vital. This is true because the musical contributions of each of these jazzmen are enduring. Moreover, most of the musicians included in this book are still active today, and the influence of those who have passed is keenly felt.

The informal conversations in *Jazz Spoken Here* have been organized alphabetically by the subjects' surnames. No attempt has been made to provide the reader with a chronological or comprehensive history of jazz. Instead, *Jazz Spoken Here* may be defined as a type of "oral history" that corresponds to the rich legacy that each generation of jazz musicians passes on to its heirs.

The book as a whole offers a diverse range of jazz styles and personalities. The story that each of these voices tells has been transferred directly to the pages of *Jazz Spoken Here*. We have edited only for the sake of clarity, never at the expense of what the musicians had to say or of their particular ways of saying it.

It is our hope that the excitement we felt in getting behind the scenes and learning about the world of jazz from the musicians themselves will be conveyed, at least in part, to our readers. Similarly, we would be pleased if *Jazz Spoken Here* helps to make more accessible what has often been called America's "true classical music." Perhaps more than anything else, the conversations recorded in this book testify to the joyful commitment of these musicians to their chosen art form. That love, we trust, will be apparent as you turn the pages of *Jazz Spoken Here*.

As a guide to essential recordings by musicians included in the book, a selected discography follows each interview. The recordings for each musician are listed chronologically, with the date of the original session (where available) or release included.

We have chosen records that, in our opinion, represent the musicians' best work at various stages of their careers. We have not limited our recommendations to records still in print, however. It is true that many classic recordings, from even just a generation ago, have long been out of the reach of the jazz enthusiast. Happily, though, the spate of jazz reissues in recent years, particularly with the advent of the compact disc format, promises that most, if not all, of the recordings we list will soon be available again.

This book could not have been written without the help and support of the following people: Patricia McQuown, former station manager at KUAT, who initiated the "Just Jazz" program and encouraged us to get involved in this project; Bill Pitts and Dave Saddler, announcer and technician respectively at KUAT, who regularly went beyond the call of duty to help us; and Edward "Kup" Kupperstein, current KUAT station manager, who shepherded us around several technical obstacles. Our gratitude must be extended to Marie Enstice, who tirelessly and always with good cheer spent hours at the word processor preparing the manuscript, and to Kish Enstice and Beverly Ryan for lifting some of the research and editing burdens from our shoulders. We are indebted to Margaret Fisher Dalrymple, editor in chief, and Catherine Landry, managing editor, at Louisiana State University Press, for their expert guidance and unwavering belief in this material. We also extend our appreciation to Angela Ray for her thorough job of editing our manuscript. Finally, we offer our heartfelt thanks to the musicians for their grace and patience in our company and for playing the music that inspired us in the first place.

JAZZ SPOKEN HERE

MOSE ALLISON

Photograph by Peter Darley Miller. Courtesy Blue Note Records.

B orn in 1927, vocalist-pianist-composer Mose Allison has fused urbane, witty lyrics, a countrified, catfish funky blues delivery, and a rollicking, eclectic piano style into a music of disarming appeal.

Allison's first public performance was as an aspiring eight-year-old singer-pianist competing in a contest in his native Tippo, Mississippi. He performed a passable version of Fats Waller's classic "Hold Tight" but did not take first-place honors. Undaunted, Allison continued to soak up the blues-drenched sounds of the Delta and drew on personal favorites, like Sonny Boy Williamson, Muddy Waters, and especially Percy Mayfield, to nourish his evolving musical conception.

In high school Allison learned trumpet and played piano with a dance band at gigs around Mississippi. During his college years he worked weekends with a rhythm-and-blues group. After graduation and a stint playing piano in the army, Allison traveled the Deep South and Texas with his trio. New York City was the inevitable next step, and in 1955 he moved north. Hired as a sideman in bands led by Gerry Mulligan, Chet Baker, Stan Getz, and Al Cohn and Zoot Sims, Allison soon earned a reputation as an excellent accompanist.

In the late 1950s Allison started recording his own material for the Prestige label on such classic albums as *Back Country Suite* and *Creek Bank*.[1] His songs were wry, lyrical tunes that poked fun at the hard-luck-and-trouble brand of life and love but added an incisive, underlying message that probed the spiritual bankruptcy of American culture. His cool, dry delivery, stamped with an unmistakable rustic twang, reached an audience disaffected by the soporific Eisenhower years. At that time, Allison's piano style recalled various keyboard influences such as ragtime and boogie-woogie, as well as the modern conceptions of pianists Nat Cole, Erroll Garner, John Lewis, and Thelonious Monk. More recently, the sonatas and concertos of twentieth-century classical masters Aleksandr Scriabin, Paul Hindemith, and Charles Ives have encouraged clusters of dissonance in his playing.

1. Mose Allison, *Back Country Suite*, Prestige Records, 1957; Mose Allison, *Creek Bank*, Prestige Records, 1958.

Allison has been on the road for over thirty years and has recorded some thirty albums. Despite economic adversity and the fickle nature of the music business, he has not swerved from his own unpretentious repertoire or his down-home roots. To this day he performs such evergreen originals as the blithely cynical "I Don't Worry About a Thing ('Cause I Know Nothin's Gonna Be Alright)" and the mocking blues "Your Mind Is on Vacation." He has been celebrated in jazz circles since the sixties, and his audience and demographic appeal broadened briefly in the seventies, when rock stars like Bonnie Raitt and Leon Russell recorded his material. In 1987 the Blue Note label released Allison's *Ever Since the World Ended*, featuring jazz notables Arthur Blythe on alto sax and Kenny Burrell on guitar. Mose Allison's wit has never been more caustic than on this album, and seldom has it been better received by the critics.

Recorded 1978

WE: Mose, considering the humor and irony in a lot of your songs, do you feel any relationship to Mark Twain?

MA: That's been mentioned before. I've been related to Mark Twain a couple of times by different people, and I feel it's valid. It's flattering to me because I like Mark Twain. The irony I think, that's one of my main things. I don't have to search for irony—irony follows me everywhere. My life has been riddled with it, so that's one of my recurring themes; one of the things that motivates a lot of my songs is the ironical situation.

WE: Like "I Don't Worry About a Thing ('Cause I Know Nothin's Gonna Be Alright)"?[2]

MA: Yeah, that's the idea—contrarieties, ambivalence, and that sort of thing.

PR: You majored in English, didn't you?

MA: Right. I have a B.A. in literature from LSU. The literary thing is also part of my background. I absorbed the blues feeling and played blues and boogie as a child and heard the blues—the way the blues sounded and everything—and learned it. Then after I got into college and started taking aesthetics and literature and so forth I got a different viewpoint. I looked at it from more of a conscious point of view and realized the possibilities there for a universal sort of statement—using the blues and the literary background, sort of blending 'em.

2. Mose Allison, "I Don't Worry About a Thing," Audre Mac, BMI, 1962.

WE: Underneath the humor in your lyrics there's usually some pointed content. Do you want your audiences to come away with a message?

MA: Now, that's it. You just said it. That's exactly the sorta thing I aim for in a lot of my songs. It's humorous on the surface, but it has also a point to it. You smile, but it might hurt a little [laughter]. That's the sorta thing that appeals to me, you know. "Kiddin' on the square" I think is the phrase.

PR: Is it difficult to get a balance in your songs so the message doesn't get too overbearing or maudlin?

MA: Yes, it's definitely that. That's the reason I write so few songs, I suppose. It's a question of gettin' just the right phrase that has just the right connotations and tryin' not to go overboard in one direction or another. It's subtle, and it can get mediocre pretty quick, I suppose, if you go too far in one direction.

It's a cryptic sorta thing where you try to get a lot into a short phrase, and you use phrases and things that everybody can understand but on different levels. They have different meanings; like the sort of phrases that appeal to me that usually wind up as songs are things that you think you know what it means on the surface. But then if you think about it a little, it has other levels, other meanings as well. Words that have multiple connotations, that's the sort of thing that appeals to me.

PR: Do your songs cover a wide range of content?

MA: They fall into different categories. I have categories of songs, you know. I consider some of them as slapstick, pretty much out-and-out slapstick, you know, things like "Your Mind Is on Vacation," "Your Molecular Structure," those sorts of things. And there are other things that are more personal crisis sort of things, and then there's some that I consider public service songs [laughter].

PR: Do you ever have the urge to compose extended works?

MA: Well, I've toyed with the idea off and on, writin', you know, fictional or biographical sorta things, but I think I actually get more out of just the short song, trying to get a lot into a compact phrase. I sorta go for economy and conciseness and that sort of thing. Actually it turns out that, like, the blues feeling and the blues structure, that lament and that short structure to the songs, actually I think is pretty much what I'm really best at. I don't like to get too stretched out, too wordy, because I feel like the most touching things are actually simple, and they hit you. You don't have to have a lot of word power behind 'em if you just get the right thing, you know, the right combination. So I tend more to short things.

WE: Would writing sonatas or poems be of interest to you?

MA: Well, you know, poems have become so nebulous. I mean, anything's a poem now, almost. I consider some of my things as sorta poetic, sorta like a poem. [The sonata's] actually too—I don't do anything that strict, you know. Like, in my piano playin' I'm workin' more in, like, ebb and flow. You start with some statement, and you work it, and you go in different directions with it and so forth, but it's not in any structured form. You sorta look for, you allow for, mistakes or accidents or things that will throw you into somethin' that you didn't count on gettin' into in the first place. That's behind the improvisation thing on the piano, you know.

PR: Does the ebb and flow of your piano playing relate at all to your background in boogie-woogie?

MA: Oh yeah, boogie-woogie is definitely a part. I started out playing boogie-woogie when I was around ten, after I started picking out things on my own. I took piano lessons for a while, but I didn't learn to read music very well. I didn't enjoy the lessons, but when I started pickin' out things on my own, that's how I started playin' boogie-woogie. It's that eight-to-the-bar thing which is so prevalent now, you know. All the Latin stuff and all the rock stuff is all eight-to-the-bar. So that's how I started out with that eight-to-the-bar feelin'.

PR: Aside from boogie-woogie, were you influenced by the bop pianists?

MA: I was, but now I listen mostly to classical, so-called classical pianists. I listen a lot to piano sonatas and piano concertos to get—you know, after you learn somethin' you get the handle on it, and you know how it works and everything, then you sorta just go on to somethin' else.

So I listen a lot to Hindemith and Carl Ruggles and Scriabin and Prokofiev and Ives and people like that, and I learned what to do with my left hand. I try to learn how to utilize both hands; that's what I'm doin' right now, tryin' to play two-handed. You know, the bop thing's a one-handed thing, and I went through that, but the last few years I've been interested in trying to improvise with both hands, which is somethin' that—I can work on it the rest of my life, I'm sure, without gettin' too far [laughter]. But it keeps me interested, and it changes your style up a little. So right now that's what I'm tryin' to do, you know, use both hands into the flow of the line.

WE: What's the relationship between your singing and your piano playing?

MA: They're interwoven, and I feel that they complement one another, but the singing is—there are different things you look for, different guidelines in the singing than the piano. With the piano you're dealin' with improvisation, and then the singing you're not dealin' with improvisation, you're dealin' with tone quality and texture and intonation and things like that. And then in my particular case, I'm concerned with inflections, tones, and texture, tryin' to get as open a sound as I can, you know, and puttin' the material across.

Since I wrote most of the songs and chose the rest of them very selectively, the content is *there*, so I don't even think about that. Sometimes I don't even think about what I'm singin', you know. I'm thinkin' more about tryin' to breathe right, tryin' to get the right sound in a note, and so forth, the right phrase and that sort of thing. And so there are two different techniques there, really.

WE: So when you're singing it doesn't affect your piano playing?

MA: Well, I think that probably when I'm singin' my piano playing maybe becomes simpler, more melodic as the result of following the vocal, you know. The instrumental numbers that I start the set off with are more pianistic, I suppose, and more improvisational, so there is probably a difference. If I listen to myself a whole set, a taped set or somethin', you'll probably notice that the piano playin' becomes maybe a little more melodic and a little more blueslike because of accompanying the vocal.

PR: How were you first exposed to the blues?

MA: I was raised in the Mississippi Delta, which was a predominantly black society at that time, and there was a lot of blues. The grocery stores had jukeboxes with blues records in them; there were blues singers around. And just the whole pace and the cadence of the whole scene was sorta like where the blues came from. It's like one of the hotbeds, and a lot of top bluesmen came from that area: Muddy Waters, Johnny Hooker, and lot of people like that. So I got real familiar with the feeling of it at an early age.

PR: Blues numbers have a very definite structure, don't they?

MA: Well, the blues I play, I don't stick to the twelve-bar structure. The lyrics are usually pretty well within the blues frameworks and the blues structures, although sometimes there's slight chord changes, like alternate melodic things. But when I'm playin' I don't stick to a twelve-bar structure. I stretch things out, you know, extend certain chords. If I had to stick with [the blues structure] all the time it would be limiting, so that's the reason I get away from it on a lot of the things.

WE: What are you especially critical of in your singing and also in the work of other vocalists?

MA: Well, first of all let me say that I don't particularly enjoy listenin' to my own singing back. Sometimes if I really get it exactly right, I can get a certain amount of pleasure out of it, but a lot of my recorded vocal work I'm not really pleased with. But the thing that I look for and the thing that I admire and I try to achieve is a completely natural sound. That has to do with gettin' the air to come all the way up through your throat and out through your mouth without any contortions of any kind.

Singers sing from different places in their mouth. Some of them sing from the roof of their mouth, some of them sing from the top of their throat, and there's all sorts of ways of constricting the vocal sound that I don't like to hear. Also I don't like to hear any falsifications, I mean, any contortions or anything that's forced or strained.

So what I look for and what I like is an easy, flowing-type open sound, and that's not easy to get, you know. You have to always try to concentrate on it. I notice when I sing at nights it usually takes me a little while to get my chest and throat open so that I really feel like the air is coming out right. And another thing I think about—you know, I was a trumpet player for a while, and when I sing I just consider my body as an instrument. I try to get a flow of air comin' from my body just the way you would put a flow of air through a horn or somethin'. So that's what I'm interested in.

PR: Do you have to keep physically fit to do this?

MA: Yeah. There came a point where I had to start gettin' in shape, you know, because you can get run down pretty quick doin' this travelin' and playin' different places all the time. So I don't drink any whiskey, and I run three miles a day—not every day, but a few days a week if I can, if the weather's good and I can find a place to do it. And I do Chinese exercises, t'ai chi, which are good for centering and balance and so forth, and they have a flowing quality too. So I do a lot of things, and I try to watch what I eat and so forth. I'm a moderate health freak [laughter].

WE: Is there any comparison between the natural flow in singing and what a good storyteller does?

MA: I think so, yeah. You know about Kenneth Patchen? He's a poet.

He's from the West Coast. He died recently, but he's one of my favorite poets, and he wrote a couple of novels that I really liked. His widow recently sent me a record that he made that hadn't been released or hadn't gotten around much, and it's him just readin' some of his stories. And I was very satisfied to hear that his voice was just as good as his writing is, and I admired his writing for years. I was wondering what he was gonna sound like; and his sound and the way he was breathing and everything I thought was perfect, you know, for what he's doin'. So it does have a relationship to just speech and tellin' a story.

PR: Jerry Lee Lewis grew up in the same area as you. Do you feel any relationship to his music?

MA: I never heard of him until some of his hits started comin' on the scene, I guess in the fifties or somethin'. I don't know, that's a little different thing. He's sort of like out of the country-rock thing, I suppose, and the way those guys played piano and sang didn't appeal to me that much, you know. I like some of the real pure country singers like Lefty Frizzell and some of those guys. Their sound appealed to me. In fact, Lefty Frizzell, I really liked the way he sang, some of the things he sang, 'cause he had some of the qualities I just described about what I like in a singer, you know, a very loose, noncontrived sort of thing. And I like Charley Pride a lot too. I like his sound.

So I like some of the country singers, but Jerry Lee comes from that heavy, sort of forced rock style that, you know, I always sorta categorize that as the "show biz thing." And I came up through the jazz scene, you know, so jazz players always felt the show biz guys were always making all the money [laughter] and the jazz guys were always tryin' to get work, so . . .

WE: Where did you first break in?

MA: I played beginning in high school, you know. I played dances on weekends and things. In college I played with a dance band. I had a big Dizzy Gillespie–type band at the University of Mississippi; I wrote arrangements—bop arrangements and things. And when I went to LSU, I worked on weekends and so forth. So soon as I got out of college I had a group, mostly trios, sometimes quartets, and we would play sort of a rhythm-and-blues thing with whatever jazz we could get by with, playin' nightclubs and for dancin' and that sort of thing.

So for years I played down south, the Southeast, Southwest, Texas,

Louisiana, all around for about six years with that sorta format. I had a bass player then that played good, and we'd get a drummer, and we'd just go somewhere and get a job and play. I'd sing pop tunes if I had to, and I'd sing some blues, and we'd do some group vocal–type rhythm-and-blues things, things like the King Cole Trio, and bouncy things like Louis Jordan and his Tympany Five.

So that's what I did for about six years. I was always playin' jazz. And after six years of playin' in the clubs down south and everything I figured there was only so far you could go. So I went to New York and started playin' around and got to playin' with some of the jazz groups there.

WE: Did anyone help you out when you got to New York?

MA: Yeah. Al Cohn was my sponsor, sorta. I had met his wife in Texas, and she had heard me play, and she had recommended me to him. And so when I went to New York I had his number, and he sorta sponsored me around, and at that time, you know, it was sessions. I think that's all died out. I'm not sure, but at that time—it was in the late fifties during the jazz boom—there was a lot of jazz around, a lot of jazz records being made, a lot of clubs, a lot of bands, and a lot of sessions.

So you could go to a session every night, you know, somewhere. And there were some southern guys that had sort of a southern jam session down on East Thirty-fourth Street in a loft down there, and all of the Lester Young–type players used to come down there, like Zoot [Sims] and Al and those guys, and some of the boppers like Phil Woods and different people, so I hung out there a lot. I played around, and I got to meet the big guys.

PR: We really enjoy your piano playing. Have you made a solo piano album?

MA: No, I haven't, but I was approached about that just recently. In fact, the guy who wrote the book *Bird Lives*, you know, that Russell, is doin' some things now, and he's interested in just piano players, and he's tryin' to get a lot of solo piano albums.[3] He asked me about the possibility of doing one, but I couldn't do one right now because I'm still under contract at Atlantic Records. But it could happen, I suppose.

PR: You couldn't suggest it to Atlantic?

MA: I don't think they'd be interested. They've been tryin' to get me

3. Ross Russell, *Bird Lives: The High Life and Hard Times of Charlie "Yardbird" Parker* (New York, 1973).

to go the other direction. They're interested mainly in an album with dubbed-in backgrounds.

WE: They want to make you more marketable?

MA: Yeah, that's the idea.

WE: How do you respond to that?

MA: Well, I respond by evading it [laughter]. I've been evading it now for years. I'll probably be doin' an album for them soon. It'll probably be not exactly what they want and not exactly what I want. Somewhere between the two.

PR: Have you been satisfied with your albums in the past?

MA: No, not really. When you make a record, when you first listen to it, there're some spots that you might feel good about, and there're some spots that you feel awful about. You always feel that you could've done it better if you'd had more time and so forth or if the circumstances would've been better.

Most of the records I've made were done—you get your car, and you go into New York City, and you try to find a parkin' place, and you run up to the recording studio, and there's two or three guys there that you might never have seen before, and you got three hours to do so many tunes. So that's the way most of the albums were made, you know—it's a long way from being ideal.

So you never feel completely satisfied with a record, I don't think. You always feel like there's certain things you could've done better. And in fact, a lot of times you'll be playin' for twelve people in some insignificant cocktail lounge, and you'll get somethin' goin' that you feel is like your optimum performance or somethin', and when you try to get it in a recording studio it's hard to get the same sort of thing goin'.

WE: Isn't part of the problem that recording studios are so antiseptic?

MA: It's like an operating room, most places are. They have these hard surfaces and fluorescent lights, and you know, everything is completely antithetical to relaxing and openin' up, anything like that. So that's one of the things that you just have to learn to deal with in some sort of way.

I think that what should happen, you should be recorded secretly during your performances, and then you pick out what you like, say at the end of a week or something. But of course nobody's gonna take the trouble to do that, you know. They're all interested in investment return. They've got the studio, and they've got the technicians at the studio, so you have to go to them. Instead of bringing the technology to the music, the music has to go to the technology.

PR: Have you always had to compromise to some extent what you've wanted to do because of record company pressures?

MA: Well, it's been the same thing all the way along. When I started out makin' records for Prestige, they didn't care what I did, because they were gettin' me so cheap it didn't matter [laughter]. So the first six albums I did, I could do anything I wanted to; in fact, the cheaper the better. They didn't care what I did. But as soon as it starts gettin' a little action and people start takin' notice, then they figure there's some commercial potential there. Then it starts, you know.

So then the idea's always to persuade you to do what they think is most accessible based on what sold best last year. They've got these charts and graphs and things. And it's actually very uncreative and very shortsighted, I think. I mean, I've been doin' it for twenty-five years, and I'm doin' better right now than ever before, and it certainly isn't because of the record company. Because they haven't done any promotion at all, you know. Atlantic has done no promotion. In fact, Atlantic offices around the country, a lot of 'em don't even know that I'm still with Atlantic [laughter]. I go to a town a lot of times, and people will call up and try to get a couple of albums from Atlantic, and they won't even know I'm with 'em. That's happened in several places.

So certainly I haven't gotten where I am as a result of record promotion. What I try to put across is that if I'm doin' well with what I do, why can't they just record that and promote it? But they can't see it that way, you know. They have their assembly line, and they have their routines, and they have their charts and graphs from last year and everything, and they have all these vice-presidents and people in charge of certain things, so everybody's got to—they have to try to redesign you, you know, like "We're going to make you into a star" or that sort of thing. That still pervades the record business, I'm afraid. That whole thing. They're always trying to get you to do what they think is gonna be most successful, most commercial.

WE: Have you ever led larger ensembles?

MA: I have had a few, yeah, but mostly it's been trios. When I was workin' in the South, at first I sometimes had one horn or two horns, and I'd write out little charts for them, you know, but nothin' very extensive. The most arranging I ever did was when I was in college. I wrote an entire book for a fourteen-piece college band. Since then I haven't done anything like that.

WE: Would horns get in your way?

MA: I made one record with five horns, and I wrote all the arrangements. And it wasn't that they got in my way; it's just that when I got to the studio and these backgrounds came flooding in behind me, it made me force a little. I felt I had to compensate for it, which was a mistake, I decided later. And if I had it to do over again, I would know better how to do it. But since I was so unfamiliar with singin' with horn backgrounds, I was tryin' to sing like a lead trumpet player. I was forcin' it a little bit too much, whereas I should have sort of just gone on and relaxed and done my thing as I've usually done it and let the horns be a complement to it, you know.

PR: What kind of preparation do you go through for an evening's performance?

MA: There is no preparation [laughter]. There's no preparation really, no rehearsal. I've never rehearsed, I don't think, that I can remember [laughter]. But you allow for certain variables, you know. And you allow for the personalities of the other players, and you choose the other players either through having played with 'em on the job or else having been given a good recommendation from somebody you trust. So it's an accumulative thing. I don't carry the same players all the time, but I don't go around pickin' up guys like just anywhere either. So since I've been doin' it for twenty years, I know guys in all the areas of the country that I can rely on. And I keep track of the guys who do the best job, and I just keep usin' them whenever I can.

I actually like to play with different people sometime. It gives you a little different point of view on what you're doin', and it throws you into a little different gear. And just makin' allowances for different personalities—their strengths and weaknesses—it keeps it interesting, you know.

WE: Do you have arrangements?

MA: No, no, I don't have arrangements. Only thing I have is like a book with the harmony in it and some of the bass lines and just the chords to the songs. If a bass player is with me long enough he learns 'em, but otherwise I just bring the book along. And there's no music for the drummer. The drummer has the freedom, you know, within certain limits, of doing it the way he wants to do it. I give him certain things that I don't want, and I tell him the sort of pace that I want and the sort of textures and things that I'm lookin' for.

PR: What kinds of other things would you tell a drummer?

MA: Well, I just tell the drummer that I don't like a heavy two-beat and I don't like rim shots, and what I want is a flowing quality. And I don't like things that stick out—patterns that stick out. There's certain general things like that that I tell the guys, like the emphasis on a certain beat and things.

WE: Do you have a fairly large organization? A road manager?

MA: I don't have anything [laughter]. I don't have a road manager [laughter]. I handle—well, there's really no paperwork involved except just makin' up contracts. You know, I have contract blanks and a type-writer [laughter]. There are a couple of agents around that I work with that book things for me on an individual basis, but I'm not signed with anybody. And the clubs that I've worked over and over for years, I just deal directly with them, you know, just call them up or they call me. And a lot of the stuff, though, I have an agent in Washington, D.C., and an-other agent in L.A. that book me on certain things and certain places. So it's a loose operation.

WE: How about the clubs you work in? Do the owners try to rip you off?

MA: Well, let's put it this way: the clubs will rip you off if you let 'em. It takes a long time for you to really understand the mechanics of it, and when you first start out—at least when I first started out I was so enthused about playin', you know, I'd go in and play for nothin'. I did that for a long time. But eventually you start learnin' how to count, and then you start calculating what the person is takin' in. And so finally you arrive at what you figure is your fair share of that, and then you just try to get it, that's all.

So you find out how big the room is, and so forth, or if it's a concert you find out who's producin' it and what's it goin' for. You just have to sorta look into it a little. But it's not that complicated. You can estimate pretty easily what somebody is gonna make out of somethin', so you just try to get what you figure would be your fair share.

PR: Your reputation among young people has increased over the last five years. How do you account for that?

MA: Well, I know one of the reasons is that they've learned about me through their heroes, through people doin' songs of mine. You know, like John Mayall or Bonnie Raitt or people who have a big following. The Who did a tune of mine, and Johnny Rivers. A lot of people have done my stuff, and I think that's the way that a lot of young people heard of me first, and then that influenced them to find more out about it, I guess.

PR: How would you characterize your level of success?

MA: Well, I don't know. Right now I'm not a superstar, I'm not a big money-maker, but I'm doin' well. Whereas the first ten years I just barely got by. So you know, in the last ten years or so things have gotten a little bit better, year after year. And last year I did some concerts with Bonnie Raitt, and I did a couple of TV things, and I was astounded by the impact from the TV shots, 'cause it seems like people who live on the same block with me on Long Island and didn't know what I did all of a sudden knew what I did [laughter]. And my accountant didn't know; he'd never heard me. And he called me up—he'd seen the TV show. And you know, I had reaction from that all over. I guess it just shows, the TV thing puts you in a completely different bag. You know, it's the people who would never hear of you otherwise, they're exposed to you. It does a lot, I suppose, for your mass audience.

WE: Do you feel that you're involved in an important art form?

MA: Yeah, I think so—possibly, potentially. I don't know. I can't say for sure, who knows? But I think that the music that has influenced what I'm doin' is possibly of universal significance. And I think it's a world music, 'cause it absorbs elements from any society. Like the jazz thing has absorbed elements from all over the world, and it's still absorbing elements and will continue to do so. Therefore, since the world is becomin' smaller and all the cultures are merging and everything, why, I think jazz is actually the music that signifies that, you know, in which that's worked out.

SELECTED DISCOGRAPHY

Back Country Suite. Prestige 7091. 1957.
Creek Bank. Prestige 24055. 1958.
Mose Alive. Atlantic 1450. 1961.
I Don't Worry About a Thing. Atlantic 1389. 1962.
Seventh Son. Prestige 10052. 1963.
Hello There Universe. Atlantic 1550. 1970.

Western Man. Atlantic DS-1584. 1971.
Lessons in Living. Elektra 602374. 1982.
Ever Since the World Ended. Blue Note 48015. 1987.
My Backyard. Blue Note BLN–B1 93840. 1989.

ART BLAKEY

Photograph by David D. Spitzer.   Used with permission.

A true innovator on the drums, Art Blakey led one of modern jazz's most durable and influential combos, the Jazz Messengers. Blakey was a key figure in the liberation of the drums from a purely time-keeping role to that of a frontline instrument. He was every bit the equal of the soloists he stoked with his explosive press roll and patented rim shots. Despite his power and emotional range on the drums, Blakey considered himself first and foremost an accompanist. A critic once remarked that Blakey said more in pausing between beats than most drummers say, period.

Art Blakey was born in Pittsburgh in 1919. He never had a formal drum lesson but schooled himself by listening intently to his idols, Big Sid Catlett, Chick Webb, and Kenny Clarke. Blakey's pre–Jazz Messengers résumé reads like a Who's Who of jazz. In 1939 he played in Fletcher Henderson's orchestra, then joined pianist Mary Lou Williams' first big band. He also led his own small combos.

By 1944 Blakey had become an integral part of vocalist Billy Eckstine's big band, which included future jazz legends Dexter Gordon, Gene Ammons, Kenny Dorham, Dizzy Gillespie, and Charlie "Bird" Parker. Eckstine's band broke up in 1947, but Blakey never lacked for work. Except for several months he spent visiting Nigeria and Ghana, he worked constantly during the late 1940s, drumming for such bandleaders as Lucky Millinder and Buddy DeFranco.

Blakey led his own large ensemble, the Seventeen Messengers, from 1948 to 1950, but the era of the big bands was fading. In the early fifties he cofounded a quintet with pianist Horace Silver. Birdland in New York City served as the platform for the gradual ascendancy of this new group and the "hardbop" sound they originated, which combined the heat and harmonic sophistication of bop with more soulful, funkier, finger-snapping rhythms. By 1954 the first official edition of the Jazz Messengers was born, with personnel consisting of Silver, Kenny Dorham on trumpet, saxophonist Hank Mobley, Doug Watkins on bass, and Blakey as the glue and the galvanizing force in the drum chair.

The Jazz Messengers, in their various incarnations, were a vital unit for more than four decades. At their best, Blakey's bands set the standard for a finely tuned balance between collective and individual expression. The Jazz Messengers' small-combo formula of combustive horns in dynamic interplay with the rhythm section, along with varied and fresh contrapuntal ensemble writing, continues to spawn progeny into the nineties. The Harper Brothers and Wynton Marsalis lead two of the most notable new groups to come under the Jazz Messengers' influence.

Blakey's fame as a bandleader is second only to the profound impact he has had on modern jazz drumming. Two generations of jazz luminaries matured under Blakey's tutelage. A sampling of "graduates" from the Jazz Messengers includes Clifford Brown, Lee Morgan, Kenny Dorham, Donald Byrd, Freddie Hubbard, Wynton Marsalis, and Terence Blanchard on trumpet, Horace Silver, Bobby Timmons, Ray Bryant, and JoAnne Brackeen on piano, Jackie McLean, Hank Mobley, Johnny Griffin, Benny Golson, Wayne Shorter, and Billy Harper on reeds, and Julian Priester and Curtis Fuller on trombone.

As much jazz sage as jazz player, Art Blakey was a messenger in the truest sense. Steadfastly believing jazz to be an indigenously American art form deserving of wider recognition, he used his music to preach his message from bandstands internationally until his death from lung cancer in 1990.

Recorded 1976

WE: Art, you've been playing the drums professionally for decades. How did it happen that you chose that instrument rather than something else?
AB: I didn't intend to be a drummer. It's just a means of survival. When I came along I was very lucky. I came along in the time of the depression, and it was very rough. I went to school in Pittsburgh. You know Pennsylvania always had integrated schools, but in our schools, especially in the junior high school, most of the teachers were white, and most of them were bigots, and I couldn't learn anything. I could see right through that. I could see that the teacher wasn't teaching me.

You see, I was sort of an orphan, and I was rejected by my father's parents. My mother died when I was six months old, and I was rejected by his parents. And they even had racial prejudice in my family—on my father's side was mulatto, and my mother, who was very, very black. Her father—my grandfather—and my great-grandfather, who I knew were all descendants of Africa, were very black people. And the part of Africa where they come from was Guinea, West Africa.

My father used to sneak out—because my mother was very pretty, and he used to sneak out and see her. She lived out in the country. So I happened along. They had a shotgun wedding, you see. They had this big church wedding, and they came out and got in the carriage. My mother was carrying me at that time, and he rode two blocks and got out of the carriage and went into the drugstore to get some cigars, and he went out the back door and went to Chicago. And after sitting out there for four or five hours—she was so stunned about it—she was very stunned, very hurt, and really they say she really didn't care. She died of a broken heart. She just gave up [and] took about four or five months to die. Well, my father, he couldn't take me in his family, right? So that left me sort of on the outside. So my mother's friend—well, she sort of looked out after me. She let me stay there, and I always felt that guilt, and I always felt that I had to work. I would work and go to school.

Then I formed a group in school. I always played piano because there was a piano around the house, and I played by ear. I never had the money to get the lessons, and I wouldn't dare ask the woman who was helping me—who I was living with. I called her my mother. I took the band into a club called the Ritz, in Pittsburgh. At that time, Prohibition was on. In them joints you come late at night and knock at the door, "Charlie sent me," and you get in. But I had an eighteen-piece band—we had the best gig in town. And we wore tails. So I had a lot of kids out of the high school band working with me.

We made fifteen dollars a week, which was a helluva lot of money at that time. A room with bath and everybody had a car, and you drive to school, and you hear a teacher talking down to you, and you know better. So I rebelled, and I went to the principal about it and he says, "Well . . . " I didn't like his attitude either, you know, the way he talked to me. I didn't think it was fair. So I was thrown out of school for doing a report—what messed me up, really. I had to do a report in history class on Africa. They told me that Africans go around in grass skirts and they eat people and they're cannibals. So I went and got a thing on Africa and found out that the first university in the world was in Africa, found out that—ohhhh, I found out so many things, you know, so many lies have been told.

And I had stayed in this club about two years with the band, and they brought in a show from New York, called "Tondelayo and Lopez," and it had some music. It was a lot of piano music, and it looked like some flies had been all over the thing—I couldn't believe it! So instead of being honest with myself and honest with the guys—they all knew I couldn't read music too. But you know I'm not going to admit it, to myself, above all. I'm the bandleader; you can't admit, right? So I come in and run the brass down that part, run the reeds down, run the rhythm section down. I'd run up and show the drummer how to do something, to catch different things, because I had a little experience in the school band about the drums and I always loved them. So I said, "OK, let's play it." So the band run it down, so we got to the piano part, and the band said *pow* and stopped for the piano to come in, and I sat there and look, and I start perspiring, and I looked up and said, "You all know goddamn well I can't read."

So I got up and stormed out. And so the guy that owned the club—Charlie—is sitting in the corner. He had a big .38 on him, and he said, "Hey, Blakey, come here." He say, "What's happenin'." I say, "Nothing." I said, "I got it, I got it." I saw some kid in the corner who was sittin' over there. And he was looking. So he came over, and he says, "Hey, Art, do you mind if I try that?" I said, "Sure, go ahead." He had been listening to the records; and the band come down and played it so beautiful, and it come to the piano part. He played the hell out of it. Like it was made for him. Come to find out it was Erroll Garner.

We were kids at that time. Erroll Garner had such an ear for music, and I said, "Well, damn." This man, he could hear that and played every note, played everything. I said, "Jesus Christ!" I was kinda bugged, so Charlie said, "Come here." He said, "Why don't you play the drums?" So I said, "Hey, Charlie, why don't you mind your own business." He said, "Well, how long you been working out here?" And I said, "Well, a little over two years, I guess." He said, "Do you wanna continue working here?" I said, "*Sure* I want my gig." He said, "Well, you play the drums. You dumb bastard, you go up there and play them drums." I went up there and played. I've been playing drums ever since. I went back to see him one time before he passed, you know. He said, "I told ya, ya big dummy." So that's how I started playing drums—I had to survive.

PR: Soon you went on the road, and you braved the Deep South. Since this was the early 1940s, it must have been difficult.

AB: I was working at night and day and goin' to school. 'Cause I wanted to support myself and I wanted to help the woman who raised me, so I left there. And I took the band, and I went out on the road, and we worked. We had a ten-piece band, and Fletcher Henderson come through and took the whole band because of the war. All the musicians were going to the army, so he just took the whole band out with him. Wonderful musicians. And I later joined Fletcher, because most of my buddies was in his band. And we traveled all over the country. We drove to Albany, Georgia, and I had some problems down there with the police and got beat up. They put a plate in my head. Boy, we fought like dogs down there, and I'm lucky to be alive in Georgia at that time. You know, *very* lucky to be alive. And that time was about 1942. I was down there, and I broke a policeman's jaw. At that time the South was very rough.

And what the people went through in the sixties ain't nothing what we went through, man. We traveled through the South all day and have a pocketful of money and couldn't get a glass of water. And if you did, they'd sell it to you a dollar a glass. And it would be hot as panther piss. This is the way, man, that you had to go and survive. That's the reason I see things always looking better. I always can look back and see where things were always worse than they are today. There is definite improvement in every field, especially in the jazz field. It's a helluva improvement.

Well, after that episode down there with the police, I got very sick and ended up in Boston and met the band there. And I got sick, and I stayed—because of that blow in the head. I stayed there for a year or so.
WE: Then you met up with Billy Eckstine and company?
AB: That was the most fascinating time of my life when I met Dizzy, and I met Sarah Vaughan, and I met—oh my God—all the stars. The band, the whole band, anyone you pick out is one of the big top men—they're the giants. Boy, they could play! I never heard nobody play that. The only big band I ever liked was Billy Eckstine, 'cause everybody in that band could play. There was no first trumpet player, no first alto player, no first tenor player—any part that you get you play. If you make a mistake, you just make it loud. Next time you don't make it, you replace it with another note. Everything was committed to memory. And that was, in my eyes, a helluva big band. That is a *band*. Now, that is a jazz orchestra! I've heard a lot of big bands, and they sound good, perfect, but they sound too clinical, it's too perfect, it's not a good band, it's not good jazz. Jazz is not clinical. It's not like that. Jazz is born by somebody goofin'. So if you feel that band hasn't got that looseness, they're not creating.

In that band it was a pleasure; it was like working in a small combo.

But the rest of the big bands wasn't: Lucky Millinder wasn't, Basie wasn't, Duke wasn't. 'Cause Duke was set. He had this certain thing that you do. And if you go to play with Duke, whatever it is, you let the punishment fit the crime. Whatever it is: you don't go into Duke's band and play Art Blakey, you go into Duke's band and play Duke Ellington. You go to Count Basie's band, you play Count Basie. You don't go and try to stick your influence in there. The only way I had a chance to stick my influence is in Billy Eckstine's band, because it was that type of thing. It was like a combo. But the rest of the bands you're the timekeeper. You understand? Like Billy Eckstine's band, I could—like in most big bands, it's like fifteen musicians and a drummer. In Billy Eckstine's band, there were sixteen musicians, and everybody got to play, and that made a difference, and it's the same way in a combo. That's why I like a combo, because every tub's got to sit on its own bottom. And if it doesn't, it shows up.

And they liked me—the style that I was trying to develop—I didn't know why I was trying to develop that on drums, but I was just trying to do something different because I knew one thing: I always wanted to record, and I knew that I was playing what I call a bastard instrument, you know, it's not set—you know the piano's got eighty-eight keys, the trumpet's got three keys, and the saxophone has, et cetera. But the drum you add this, you add that; but . . . I knew I had to identify myself, and I had to play different.

And I heard and I watched Chick Webb, and I tried to take the best of him and Big Sid Catlett. I tried to take the best of these cats and try to incorporate it in what I was trying to do. And the most advanced of all of them—the drummer at that time—was a little young guy called Kenny Clarke. Fantastic drummer! He came back to Pittsburgh, and I just admired him. He sounded different from any other drummer. But I admired him—Sid Catlett and Chick Webb I took in. I heard Ray Bauduc—I liked him. And Gene Krupa came, and I heard him. At that time Gene Krupa was known as the Chicago Flash!

I learned, you know. You pick up things here, and you pick up things there, and you listen and learn. And I tried to just do it a little different. It did pay off by joining [Eckstine's] band. I knew why they wanted me there. Because it was a little different. The attack was a little different, the way I played. I think that's some of the most happy days of my life. And I guess we made about ten dollars a night. Didn't make no difference about the money, I was so happy just to be there. I heard all these great musicians, and I watched this music change the trend of all American music. I watched Bird and them cats change everything.

PR: You've spoken often about how your peers of that era never received the attention they deserved.

AB: My contention is, is to give the people credit who brought forth the idea. Now this is my problem. They never give them credit for it. They never give Louis Armstrong credit for what he did. They never did, man. And they never gave Duke Ellington credit for what he did—or King Oliver the credit for what he did.

They turn around and they name Paul Whiteman the King of Swing, you know, and the only way he could swing is from a rope. I didn't think that was fair. Then they turn around and name Benny Goodman the King of Swing, and he's playing Fletcher Henderson's arrangements note for note. I could walk into Benny Goodman's band and play every arrangement they had, because Smack [Henderson] did it—it's Smack's music. He didn't get the credit for it, see, and that's what hurt. And he died a pauper—up in Harlem—and it hurt. And I didn't understand why that could be.

Don Redman, I mean these great men who've really put it down in music—Charlie Parker and these cats—man! I mean, why should this be—Art Tatum. And I remember when Artur Rubinstein come to New York—if he had a concert in Carnegie Hall—and I was working in Café Society in the Village with Art Tatum. Well, Artur Rubinstein didn't make his concert; he canceled it. Sold-out house—he'd cancel and be sitting down there looking at Art Tatum. But yet we had to take money up to bury this man—that hurts.

That hurts, I mean, where is things going? What's happening? And nobody's paying any attention to it. Right now we just found out where Bird was buried, and now they just begin to build a thing over his grave just to show some appreciation; they name a street after him in Kansas City. But what's happened to Art Tatum? He never had a marker for his grave. What's happened to Fats Navarro? I buried him; the union wouldn't even bury him. I buried him in New York. Yeah, I just left his daughter up there in Seattle. She's a grown girl, and her mother's dead, and this girl up there struggling to get through law school. Struggling like hell to get through law school, and you got to pity. Now you know that the records that Fat Girl [Navarro] has made, has made *lots* of money, and it's setting there somewhere. And you know they won't give it to her.

That isn't fair. *That is not fair!* We need some kind of legislation going on. The jazz musicians—Fats Navarro, and Eddie "Lockjaw" Davis—those records they made like thirty years ago. They still sellin'!

And this proves to me that this is the music. You know after a quarter of a century and you turn around and hear your own records, I mean, it must be something. Because everything else is gone and flash in the pan has past and forgotten, and every time you turn on one of these records it's just as fresh. You say, "Oh, man," you know—it's just as fresh. So this proves to me that it's right, and I can't understand why these artists can't get their just due—*all* of them.

WE: Art, you are as much a spokesman for the music as you are a musician.

AB: You can't separate rock from the spirituals from the church—that's where it came from. You can't separate modern jazz from rock or from rhythm and blues—you can't separate it. Because that's where it all started, and that's where it come from—that's where I learned to keep rhythm—in church. Because they'd be in there singing and shouting and swinging *all* the time, no instruments but their hands and their mouth and their feet.

You know so that's where it started, so you can't separate it. It's all American music. It's just as American as apple pie, and we got to stop this foolishness. Tell the kids where it's at so they can get a chance to go back and listen to that. Listen to ragtime, listen to dixieland. And the proof of that is Eubie Blake. Here's a man out there, and he's damned near a hundred years old, and he's playing jazz like he did then, and he's good. And it all come from the same thing. Like Eubie Blake say, he learned—he was playing every night in the house of ill repute. That's where it started.

See, it doesn't matter to me about like Freddie Hubbard and all the cats who work with the Jazz Messengers—they may go off in twenty different directions, but they know where home base is. They know where they got to go—they always turn around and come back to the mother they always know. They know what jazz is all about.

Even the Japanese, even the Africans. Just our [American] kids, man, just don't know. You take those kids over there, they say, "Yeah! so and so and so and so Charlie Parker he was born in so and so and so and so." It's amazing. I say, "How old are you, fifteen or sixteen?" It's amazing. How did they know way over there? At a disadvantage, they knew.

And the Japanese, they weren't even brought into jazz until in the sixties, really. And listen to them. My bass player is a Japanese. The first time he ever heard jazz he was a little boy and I come to Japan. He was a little boy with his dad. His dad is a music teacher, and he said, "I want you to hear something," and brought him in. He was a little boy—eight years old. And he grew up, and he's working with me. You understand?

Same thing with Chuck Mangione's father. When I first met Chuck he was eleven years old—his father brought him. He said, "Mr. Blakey, some day I'm going to play trumpet." And I said, "Yeah, he will." And he did. Because his father said, "Listen to this, listen to that." He's a well-trained and well-rounded musician. And Mangione grew up knowing just as much about Dizzy Gillespie as he did about Harry James, as he did about anybody. He knew all about it because of his parents, you see.

PR: Showmanship seems to be a very important part of your approach. Tell us how you developed your own stage style.

AB: I told you I had this band and was playing drums—I got into this drumming thing. I had an act that I could do, and I always envisioned myself someday just coming out just playing and doing my little drum act and that was it. So I had an act. I had taken the sticks, you know; you put this paint on them and take the black light and shine the light up. Well, I had some gloves you put on and you paint the sticks a different color. I had one stick on the trap-set—at that time we had a trap-table with a table about this big, and the cymbals come up and you have temple blocks on it, call it a trap-table—and I have the stick laying on the trap-table. But I had a black string from the ceiling down to the trap-table and this stick. I'd be playing, and all of a sudden I change sticks and hit a loud rim shot on my left hand and throw the stick out of my right hand, and people say "Oooh!" and it'd come back and I'd catch it.

But all the time this is going on ain't nothin' happening—it is quiet. Everybody is sitting there, so I went back in, and Chick Webb said, "Hey son, can I see you a minute. You interested in them drums?" I said, "Yes, sir, Mr. Webb." He said, "Bring your snare drum back in the dressing room." He said, "Bring your sticks." I come into the dressing room; I set my snare drum up. Chick Webb come back, and he has a Chihuahua and a camel-hair coat and his cap. So Chick Webb say, "OK, kid, the first thing I want to tell ya: The rhythm ain't in the air; it's on the hides." So he said, "You can roll?" I said, "Sure, Mr. Webb, I can roll." He said,

"Well, roll." I grabbed the drums and eh-eh-eh-eh-eh. So he eased over to the door, and he looked at me [and] say, "Shit!" Bam! Slammed the door and left me standing there.

I started crying. I was so hurt. I went out there, and he said, "I'm sorry, kid." He said, "You be down to the theater in the morning. Come down to see me. I want to talk to you." Boy, I get up at nine, get down there for the first show at ten-thirty. He said, "C'mon." Went upstairs to his dressing room, and he had this valet set a snare drum up in a room—way up on top where they weren't using. So we went upstairs, and he brought a metronome. He set the metronome down, and he turned real slow. He said, "Now I want you to sit there at that snare drum, and I want you to roll 'til you get to one hundred, and I don't want you to break that roll, and don't think I'm not listening to you." I liked to busted my wrist.

Every day I go down, and he'd say, "Up in the room." I'd say, "I want to tell . . ." He'd say, "Ain't nothin' to talk about. Get up there and play, start rolling." I developed a press roll out of that. I wanted to learn. From that he helped me develop a press roll. Because I couldn't even roll on a drum. And that's what's happening today. A lot of drummers, they can't even roll. And that's the fundamental part about the drum. And that's what hurts: you see the young kids, you don't get a chance to help them. They got seven, eight, ten, twelve tom-toms around, two, three bass drums. What is that, for show? *Play!* Never mind the show. All them drums and you can't even play a snare drum. That's all you need.

WE: Like Webb, you've passed the touch to the younger drummers. That seems to be a major theme of yours.

AB: That's awful important. That's the most important movement there is. Not the modern musician, but the older musicians. What happened during that time from the swing era over into what they call the bebop era—most of the musicians in that time, they got so when they felt that everything they did was right. This is the wrong attitude, because all the music that we have been playing all our lives and what we have done, we only scratched the surface. Just like Charlie Parker just before he passed, he was talking about the only thing he wished in earnest—that the young kids learn how to play the blues, 'cause he was learning how to play the blues. A lot of kids think, "I don't want to play no blues." They don't want to play 'cause they can't. All has not been played yet. And like they asked Charlie Parker, "What's the best record that you have ever made?" He said, "I've yet that to make."

Because the young cats need the older cats to tell them so they can help them to direct their energies. If they don't want to use the advice, they don't have to. But at least they know. But most of the guys just cut off the young guys: "Ah, you don't know what you're doing." They form cliques and go out on gigs with each other and leave the young musicians out, or maybe if they couldn't find nobody, they'd take a young guy, and if he played too good they would fire him.

So I didn't want to be around the musicians, so when they got old, I just said, "Hell with them." I didn't hang out with them either. I hung out with the young cats. And I always come up with a young group. If they had a band and so I come with my group and just wipe them out. They say, "Well, goddamn, you don't know what you doin'," and I say, "Just listen to them—you don't know it all."

Some guys come in the band, and Freddie come in the band, and Cedar Walton come in the band. They'd write some music, and I'd go home. And Wayne Shorter, he writes some music, and I say, "Oh my God, what is this?" I wouldn't say nothing to him. I would say, "Yeah, that's nice," and "Why don't you do this?" You know I'd make suggestions, but I say, "My God, are we going to go out and play this?" But do you know, three or four weeks from that time when I said that to myself, the music begins to make a lot of sense.

Now Wayne wrote a tune they called "The Children of the Night." Freddie Hubbard was in the band. Now each instrument was playing in another key—each instrument! He made it all come together. The most beautiful piece of music I ever seen. And this young man got two degrees in music. I never knew it. And this guy would sit down and write, and they would say about his playing, at that time he and John Coltrane was practicing together a lot. And the guys are standing outside of Birdland one night—young musicians, and some of the older musicians. "Hot damn! Jesus Christ! Wayne, man, that stuff he playing, man, sound like *scrambled eggs.*" So John Coltrane come up and said, "That's not the point. It's the way he's scrambling those eggs."

PR: How did the Jazz Messengers start?

AB: We had a seventeen-piece group called the Seventeen Messengers. At that time big bands were on their way out. We were like diehards; we were just going to hold on. It didn't work, so we broke the band up, and I was hanging around New York, Monk and I.

So Horace [Silver] came by and say, "All right, let's get a group together. [I] have Kenny Dorham, I got Hank Mobley, and I'll get Doug Watkins, you, and myself. We'll put this group together and call it the Jazz Messengers." Well, I was very disgusted then because we had formed—I'd formed—a group, I just couldn't get it working. I was like the house drummer in Birdland, and I could get work there. But outside of that I'd get spot work, so I said, "Oh, well, to hell with that."

PR: How did you hire Clifford Brown for your band?

AB: Charlie Parker hired Clifford Brown in my band. I was going to the Blue Note to open up. He said, "I already got your trumpet player, so go on down." You know, I believed Bird, and I went down there. And I saw this little country boy down there with his hair plastered, part in the middle, and one of these big zoot suits on. I said, "Jesus Christ, who's this?" He had very bad feet, and he was slue-footed, and he's standing there. He said, "Mr. Blakey, I'm Clifford Brown." And I said, "Yeah, you are." So, Ike Quebec was working with me. Ike Quebec come in, met him, and he called me back outside and said, "Why didn't you tell me we are getting some farmer to play with us?" So I said, "Well, let's wait and see, Ike." So we got on the stage and opened up the first tune, and boy, Clifford took the first solo, and Ike Quebec turned to me and said, "You a wise guy, huh, you knew this guy could play like this." So I said, "No, you called him country."

Anyway, we took him to New York, and he played, he astounded the people. He just astounded them. So then after that happened all the leeches were right on him. And we recorded the *Night at Birdland* album.[1] And it wasn't nothing, we just got together and just ran on some few things and just played, just played. And it was a swingin' thing. We had a ball. Well, and after that gig closed and things went on, and I turned around and he had the record company—I forget the name of this record company, I should never forget it—they'd signed Clifford Brown up. Then I wasn't working, then Clifford went out with Max [Roach], which was a relief. I found he went with Max, he was working, and he was doing good. So that ended that there. And after Clifford, I was disgusted, and then we formed—Horace Silver and Kenny Dorham and Doug—[we] went out, and that group hit.

I was pretty lucky then. We had some people backing us, and we were very sharp. At that time it was clothes things, you know, appearance in

---

1. Art Blakey, *A Night at Birdland*, Vols. I and II, Blue Note Records, 1954.

jazz. They always named the jazz musicians as "funky," and we were playing funky music, it's true, but people took, especially in Japan, they
thought it means you stink. So we come out sharp. We changed clothes,
we had suits, two- or three-hundred-dollar suits on. And we'd run around
the country in Rolls Royces and Cadillacs and stay in big hotels. And
sometimes the contract would call for about three thousand dollars a
week, and the hotel bill would run over that! Because we were trying to
get it moving in a big-time way.

So then Kenny left and Donald Byrd came in, and we made another
thing. We got with Columbia, and everybody was excited. We got into
Columbia and made some records, and one thing went wrong and then
another. Then Clifford died. I started the group out as being a corporation, and everybody was supposed to share equal. But they wasn't sharing
equal in the work. Nobody wanted to do the work but me. So I said, "Hey
fellas, look, I'm trying to start this thing, I'm spending my money and
ain't nobody doing the work, just me and Horace." We were doing all the
business and doing the work, just me and Horace. We were doin' all
the business, and I said, "Something's got to be done."

So we agreed to disagree. I said, "Well, I'm just goin' on with the band
because I can't carry nobody like that." If I'm gonna share, I mean, I want
to see some work. I want to see somebody put their whole interest in it.
Not just lay up and get high, and "where we going next" and so and so.
So we decided to break up and get rid of that group, and I started to
organize other things. But the group all through the years has kept the
same sound, but that's what I was trying to get over to the people all this
time. The Jazz Messengers' sound—the whole thing—and the way it
plays—it still plays the same way.

WE: You thought very highly of Clifford Brown, didn't you?

AB: His father and mother were music teachers—right now today. He
was in an automobile accident some years before this fatal one. And he
was in the hospital, in traction, and he was blowing his horn—practicing.
You go to see him, and he's practicing. He had the curtain down, you
know, all around him, in his bed, and he was in there practicin', playing
"The Carnival of Venice." And you could hear it around the rest of the
hospital. He couldn't get up to play the piano, so he practiced on his
trumpet.

He was a fantastic man, and you go up to see him, and he'd have a
conversation going on with a bunch of trumpet players, and he's got a

game going on over there in the corner with Max Roach, and over __e's cooking! He's got all these things going—just a fantastic guy. So sweet, so nice, I never heard him use any profanity and no vices. I never seen a person like him. I didn't expect him to be here too long because he was too good. He was a good person—a *very* good person.

I'd come to Birdland, and he was playing—he had this raggedy horn—he was back there putting rubber bands on it and cellophane paper. I said, "Clifford, for God's sake, get up and go down to Manny's tomorrow and pick out a trumpet, any trumpet you want, pick it out, and I'll call them and tell them you're coming. And get anything you want." And he turned around, looked at me, and said, "Mr. Blakey, it ain't the trumpet, it's me." And he played that trumpet all through his career, and it was a Blessing. You never heard of a trumpet called a Blessing? He was buried with that horn. But I hate to see him go away from us that quick. I think he had a lot of things to say.

PR: What about Mr. Monk?

AB: Monk is largely responsible for me. When I got to New York, Monk would take Bud Powell and I around all the places where the cats were jamming, and at that time they had cliques in New York. Because jobs were very hard to find, so, therefore, most of the musicians cliqued up together. Certain guys get certain gigs. Monk wasn't that way. He didn't work unless he wanted to—not that he had any money. He was just independent. He would take Bud and I around and make the piano player get up and let Bud play, and some of the musicians would walk off, and he would say, "Art, you play the drums." And sometimes it was just me and Bud up there playing, and then we met Al McKibbon. There was Al McKibbon and Bud and myself or Monk.

Monk plays when he wants to, and he turns away from it because certain things he can't take. He just say, "Well, the hell with it, I won't talk to nobody," and he won't. He won't talk to his family, nobody. He just stays in his room, and he writes and he sleeps. He don't come out, and he don't allow nobody to come in. When he gets ready to come out, he comes out. But by doing so and acting that way and people putting him down, he has his choice, he can do anything he wants—he can come out and say, "I want to play a concert." He can do it and sell out. But he didn't do it that way intentionally. But it just happened that way because that's the way Monk is.

Wonderful person, very brilliant. You can't beat him. You know, like they said, he had a nervous breakdown, and he was sick mentally, but I never seen anybody beat him in chess. I never seen anybody beat him in cards; I never seen anybody beat him playing table tennis. He went in the hospital on the Coast, and it happened that Eddie Henderson [the trumpet player] was his doctor. And there are all the doctors around looking at Monk trying to do things, and Monk was walking around the hospital looking at 'em, and the doctors would be looking at him, checkin' him out, and he'd look up and say "boo." He says, "See that, I scared you. You're not sincere." So they would say, well, he was crazy, so Eddie Henderson say, "Man, let that man alone, release that man, there's nothing wrong with him. Just let him alone. It's you. You have the problem. He doesn't have a problem, just let him alone." So they released him, and he plays, right? He does what he wants to do. Fantastic person, man.

WE: Art, you told us earlier about your dream of opening your own school of the arts.

AB: What has happened there, we had a whole thing planned out, but it cost a lot of money. We had the building, we had the theater, and what I wanted to do was open up the Jazz Messengers' School. Not just music, but dancing. We want to have all the creative arts. And we had gotten the building and everything, and we were promised money from different foundations. I am not going to name them, but when the downturn in the economy came, everybody backed out of it. But we are going to get it going. It's not going to stop me.

The building is there; they haven't torn it down yet. Right in Times Square—we wanted this building, and they offered it—the city offered one of those big hotels they had gotten rid of to put the students in you know, coming from foreign countries, but we didn't want it because it becomes a political football. I didn't want anything from the city; we just wanted to do it ourselves. I say we will just stay here and try to get it together ourselves, no matter how slow, but we'll get it together, and all the guys are in it—Mingus and Max and all the guys. These guys are coming in and going to teach, and when they are not there they are going to teach via videotape.

We want to take the West Side. We want to take all the brownstone buildings and remodel them and have the students stay in apartments and let them walk to school through the community instead of being housed in dormitories and crap, and let them get used to the whole feel of the thing so they have a better chance of learning. We had a lot of students coming out of the Soviet Union, a lot of students come from Japan and different countries. That's what we wanted to do. That's still the idea, but the only thing that is holding us up is money. I would rather it come from a foundation. If it comes from an individual, the only input he can put in is money; you can't compare what Max Roach and those cats are going to put in it. So we want to do it the right way, and it's going to be hard, but I think we will get to it. I hope so, anyway.

SELECTED DISCOGRAPHY

With Horace Silver. *The Jazz Messengers.* Blue Note 5058. 1954.
A Night at Birdland. Vol. I. Blue Note CDP7465192. 1954.
Drum Suite. Columbia CL 1002. 1956.
Art Blakey and the Jazz Messengers with Thelonius Monk. Atlantic AT-1278. 1958.
The Freedom Rider. Blue Note 84156. 1961.
Free for All. Blue Note BST-84170. 1964.
Anthenagin. Prestige 10076. 1973.
Album of the Year. Timeless CDSJP 155. 1981.
Keystone 3. Concord Jazz CJ-196. 1983.
One for All. A&M 7502153292. 1990.

RUBY BRAFF

Photograph by David Lubarsky.   Courtesy Concord Jazz, Inc.

R euben "Ruby" Braff is one of the most respected trumpet stylists in jazz today. Despite occasional charges that his music is a mere throwback, Braff is no revivalist content to try to recapture the past. He has forged a vital personal style inspired by traditional values in jazz and modeled after such premodern figures as Louis Armstrong, Bobby Hackett, and Bunny Berigan. For Ruby Braff, beauty is the transcendent element in jazz, defying categorization and the caprice of the commercial music world.

Braff is also one of our most eloquent, if underrated, interpreters of the classic popular song. Most of his repertoire was written between the two world wars, when melody was king, by some of America's greatest tunesmiths, including Cole Porter, Irving Berlin, Harold Arlen, George and Ira Gershwin, and Duke Ellington.

Born in Boston in 1927 and essentially self-taught as a musician, Braff was technically proficient on the trumpet before he reached puberty. By the age of fifteen, he was working in Boston clubs for money.

Braff's career as a working musician was checkered in the fifties, in part because his "old-fashioned" swing roots even then were considered passé. Despite Braff's professional ups and downs, his early years were well represented on vinyl. His earliest recordings were on the Vanguard label, beginning with a Vic Dickenson date in 1953. Soon after, he made his first record as a leader, *The Ruby Braff Special*, in the company of Basie alumni Jo Jones and Walter Page.[1] His first big-band work came with Benny Goodman in the mid-fifties. During the same period he participated in the much-revered Buck Clayton jam sessions for Columbia Records.

Braff worked infrequently during the late fifties. Although he was associated with George Wein's Newport All Stars in the sixties and regularly toured the United States and Europe, Braff did not record again in the States under his own name until he signed with the Chiaroscuro label in 1973. His affiliation with Chiaroscuro coincided with the formation of what is regarded as Braff's most durable and consistently satisfying work-

---

1. *The Ruby Braff Special*, Vanguard Records, 1955.

ing group, the quartet he co-led with the late guitarist George Barnes. The Braff-Barnes band recorded six albums from 1973 to 1975 and won both critical and popular acclaim for its combination of good tunes and tasteful blowing propelled by a relaxed but infectious swing.

In recent years Ruby Braff has been in growing demand as a live performer, due in part to increased public interest in traditional jazz. He has recorded for a variety of labels, and his preferred duo and small-group formats have showcased his gifts for graceful, uncluttered melodic lines and the robust tone and deep feeling that characterize all his playing.

Recorded 1979
PR: Ruby, do you listen on a regular basis to other jazz musicians' recordings?
RB: I spent my whole life listening to recordings and still do. I don't know any other way to learn. If you haven't listened to anything, you have nothing to play.
PR: How about when you were young?
RB: I went to everybody's house—everybody had different record collections when I was a kid. One guy had a million Duke records. One guy had records of only those Chicago guys like Bud [Freeman] or Pee Wee [Russell]. Other guys had only Billie Holiday records. So we would just go to everybody's house and just hear all this wonderful music, and you'd hear everybody's point of view about it. They were all older than me. They all knew much—I didn't know anything, even though I was playing, you know. God knows what I was playing. So, but you learn by—they cultivated our tastes. That's what it was.
WE: When we listen to your records, we hear a sound that is individual, but we also hear phrases and runs that remind us of Louis Armstrong.
RB: Oh, sure, he's "the university of music." It doesn't matter what instrument you play, you're supposed to be listening to Louis Armstrong. It doesn't matter whether you write, sing, dance, or anything. If you haven't listened to Louis Armstrong, there's nothing, nothing going to come out of your playing that will ever please me, I can tell you that. Everybody I ever knew that was great was a student of Louis', you know.
WE: What is important to you in Louis' music?
RB: Everything. Everything he does is important. He's the ultimate sculpturer and painter in his music. Of course, when I was a kid and I

heard him for the first time on the radio, you know, I'd been hearing all these other people play on the radio, different trumpet players, and trombone players, and clarinet players, and everybody said, "Have you heard Louis Armstrong yet?" And I said, "No, who is he? I don't know anything about him." They said, "Well, you'll get to hear him someday." I said, "That's nice."

And one day on the radio—there was one show that used to have fifteen minutes of each artist, you know, that was very good. And then they said, "Now the music of Louis Armstrong." And I heard this sound, even though I didn't know why it was all so good, you know, it takes a long time to know that, but immediately this *sound*, this bright, lovely, orange sound came over the radio. And it just grabbed me, I mean, even though I didn't know anything, I just knew that there was something very different about this person than anything I ever heard. As I said, it's such a beautiful sound itself that he makes that even an idiot has to say, "God, that's beautiful!" You can listen to one Louis Armstrong record for the rest of your life and never hear enough in it. As you grow you hear more of what Louis is playing.

WE: You said you heard an "orange" sound?

RB: It felt like a big, warm, orange sound [laughter].

PR: Aside from Louis Armstrong, are there other trumpet players in the past or present who have had a strong influence on you?

RB: Well, no, not in the present, very definitely not in the present, no. But *of course* in the past there have been people I loved, all kinds of players.

You see, don't think of Louis Armstrong as a trumpet player, though he was the most unusual virtuoso that ever lived on that instrument, relative to jazz. Nobody is ever going to catch up and do the daring things he did because they can't even begin to think that way. However, I said before, he's a university of music, not merely an instrumentalist, so forget about that when you say "Are there other influences." No matter who or what I think about, Louis is behind it somewhere anyway.

All the people that learned from him were *all* individualists, they all played unlike him—all the great players. Bobby Hackett, he never played like him, you know. Clark Terry comes—everybody comes out of all these things. Clark Terry is an individualist, isn't he? Roy Eldridge? *All* these people played their own thing, and I listened to all those guys.

There were all kinds of exciting, interesting players, like, Frankie

Newton was very, very good, and, of course, way way before my days, but I got to hear him on record a lot. Bix Beiderbecke was an influence on a lot of trumpet players, you know. I think he influenced Bobby Hackett. I hear a lot of Bix Beiderbecke in Bobby Hackett as well as Louis' things. Geez, there was so many wonderful—Bill Coleman, Buck Clayton—tons of guys, so many of them, you know. But I listened to other instrumentalists as well. I liked listening to saxophone players a lot, you know, 'cause that's what I wanted was a saxophone.

WE: You started when you were eight?

RB: Yeah, something like that. Actually they bought me a horn in 1935. I remember it 'cause I saw the receipt there for years in that case.

WE: Is it correct to say that you are essentially self-taught?

RB: I don't know if there is such a thing. What is self-taught? I mean, don't you think you are studying when you spend hours and hours going over to people's houses that have record collections and they're giving you their thoughts and their feelings about these records and you discuss them? That's studying. I don't know if that's self-taught. I don't think anybody is self-taught. I know what you mean, though; I think you're thinking academia. Are you talking about formal education as opposed to nonformal education?

WE: Yes.

RB: Well, I didn't have formal education, but I don't think that means a damn thing. There is no college on this planet who can teach what I've been taught. And there's no college on this planet that's teaching today what I'd like to have them know about, have them learn to *fall* in love with melody. Which they're not doing. They're just falling in love with their instruments and making a lot of noise and playing a lot of *crap!* That's what's going on. They're not listening to great tunes by Cole Porter or this one or that.

America is so *rich*. We have the greatest composers in the world. And the whole world grew up listening to our sophisticated music. Did we come all that way through Cole Porter and Harold Arlen and Duke Ellington to revert back to idiot tunes with ugly sounds, ugly lyrics, rotten poetry, and bad-sounding horns? I mean, is that why guys learn how to play like Heifetz, like Benny, and Johnny Hodges, and Lester Young so that eventually you could sound like a fart on your instrument? Was that the idea? If so, it is very, very sad because that idea will never strike at me.

I believe in beauty, and there's got to be nothing but beauty in this world. And if you're not playing beautiful music that takes people and takes them to another plane, to a delicious place that they can't ordinarily go in their own lives every day and show them beauty—what do I want to hear ugly sounds for? We hear all kinds of ugly sounds in the street. Why do I have to hear that coming from someone on the stage? I want delicious sounds, and beautiful horns and beautiful music put together so it'll take me away on a dream. *Dreams.* That's what it's all about—dreams. Without that, what is there—there's nothing. I mean, who's some little moron who's been playing a half an hour to insist that I have to hear all of his regurgitation, everything he's got to throw up from his miserable experience yesterday? Who cares about his experience? You ever hear Duke Ellington throw up on the stage? Everything he gave you was *delicious.* Right at the minute they began playing you were away on a trip, on a beautiful trip with them.

Well, and it's reflected in the clothing. Look what they wear on the stage: hats, stupid-looking shirts, and sweaters. And it's befitting the kinds of music they play. I see a lot of them at concerts come on with hats and all kinds of—this is *freedom*, baby, *freedom!* Freedom to what?

PR: Are you talking about recent jazz musicians?

RB: I'm talking about so-called jazz musicians. And they are the worst—the worst. Terrible, terrible, terrible. They're the ones what usually stink up the stage and the world. They smell up the world of music and turn people off of music, and that's why our kids listen to rock and all those kinds of things because, at least, as ugly as it is and rotten and stupid, although there are some musicians amongst them probably that are pretty good, but at least they can cling to the beat, they could feel a beat going on somewhere. Whereas with some of these other things, they can't find anything. So they're turned off. You certainly can't dance to any of their crappy music, you know. And people like to be included.

Another thing was that the good music that I heard beckoned—it actually beckoned you. It said, "Come on, come on over here and listen to this. We like you, come on." This stuff says, "Get away, get away, leave us alone. We want to be alone!" And they should be alone. And why anyone pays to see them I don't know. To me it always sounds like a bunch of people practicing on the stage.

PR: Are you referring to so-called free jazz players?

RB: I already told you what kind of players. The so-called avant-gardists. They stink. That's what kind of players.

PR: *Free jazz* is a term that is sometimes linked with the advent in the sixties and seventies of what's commonly called "black music."

RB: What is "black music"? I never saw black music. What is black music? Would you mind telling me? What is black music? Are they referring to jazz? Jazz is an American product made up by all people in this country. It is not from Africa; it has nothing to do with Africa or anyplace else. It's American music made by American composers, and it just so happens that great pioneers of jazz, of improvised music, were the black people, the great black artists, who would turn over in their grave if they ever heard the way any of these guys are playing today. It's a horror show. It's terrible.

The people that are playing what they call black music, well, if they want to call it black music, call it black music, but don't call it jazz because it has nothing to do with anything that ever happened. Call it whatever you like, you know, but I think it's ridiculous to be separating music by colors. For years and years and years black people wanted integration in this society and to get together, and they got all these people to help them—white people, black people. Now are they saying that they want to be separated now? Or do they want to be separated in music but not in housing, in industry, in politics? Where is it? Where is it?

I never in my life thought of music or anybody's color. We played with people. If you asked me if there was black cats in the band, I couldn't even tell you. I'd have to say, "Who's black here, who's white." That's how little any of us give a damn. It became important, a very important thing later, because in society when the black people and their friends no longer could stand the kind of treatment that this nation was handing them, as second-class citizens, that's when the word *black* became very important, and it is, and it should be used that way. But it shouldn't be used for devious self-purposes, you know. There's enough bad things going on without creating bad things, you know. And to be using things like "black music" and "white music"—to me that's all destructive. It does not make for good relations between musicians, people, or anybody else.

And I'll never go to a place that says "black music." I want to go to a place that has rainbows in it. I'm sick of looking at black people *and* white people. I would frankly like to see orange people and shades of—there are marvelous colored people from darkest Africa, Nigeria or someplace, that are so black that they're almost like a bluish. You see them a lot in London. Very interesting color. And I'm very, very sick of looking at our pale faces and our so-called white faces and our so-called black faces. I want to see more reds, coppertone type of things, and oranges, and I would, if they had, I'd like to see someone that looks green, kelly green. That would interest me, and light blue would be a nice color for a person. I think that would be nice. I would enjoy that.

WE: Some have charged, for instance, that John Coltrane played nothing but scales onstage. And yet he also wrote what I think are beautiful songs, such as "Naima."[2] Are there pockets in the music of some of these people that you can relate to?

RB: Yeah. Well, John Coltrane. I knew John Coltrane; he was a very nice kid. He was a very mixed-up guy. He told me himself that he's very confused. He didn't know what to play, and I said, "Look, you made a record of 'My Favorite Things,'" and he had a semihit for himself.[3] See. By playing a nice little melody. I says, "So shows you." He said, "I want to play millions of those melodies, but," he said, "the guys I play with and my fans," he says, "they would boo me if I do that." I said, "I don't think you should go by that." I said, "I think you should go by what you know is right to do," you know.

He was quite mixed up. He was a very nice person, and he had things to say, and I think he did, it's unfortunate, I think he did a lot of harm, in a way, because so many people tried to use him as a point of departure, and that's the wrong one. Go back to music. You don't start with John Coltrane, and John Coltrane is not going to lead you [to] anything 'cause he really didn't lead himself to anything yet, you know. He never had a chance to—to mature and be himself, you know. He was an amazing person, a disciplined person that practiced all day long. And like I said, he told me himself, he said, "I don't know what to do," you know. And I think it would be more important for them to listen to Lester Young, who *did* know what to do at all times, always, you know.

WE: Many critics favor the "new" jazz represented by such figures as Ornette Coleman and Cecil Taylor. Are their opinions in tune or different from the realities of the jazz music world?

RB: Oh, it's completely different. The press knows nothing about anything. If they knew anything—I like the one Lennie Bernstein always says. He says, "I've been all over the world, and I've never seen a statue

---

2. "Naima," recorded by John Coltrane, on *Giant Steps*, Atlantic Records, 1959.
3. John Coltrane, *My Favorite Things*, Atlantic Records, 1959.

of a critic," and it's true. Every critic I ever heard of is a frustrated musician that couldn't play and eventually went bananas and decided to write
about it.

Now, at their very, very best, at their very sincerest, they don't know
what a practitioner knows. They never did, they never will, and they're
never going to. And they might as well face it and realize it. Good music
doesn't need those guys for anything. I have no personal gripes against
them; critics have always been nice to me. But I'm just saying, you know,
in the forties, in the thirties, and at all times, to go back to what I said,
when people are listening and dancing to music and having a ball, they
don't have to be told who played good and who didn't, because they were
part of the scene.

Every dancer was a better critic than any critic writing about music
today. I used to hear them talk in the poolroom and everything. They
say, "Man, went to hear Basie's band last night, sounds much better with
so and so playing lead alto, and although the trumpet section sounded a
little weak but the tempos were the greatest." They knew everything!
There's no critic that knows what they do.

Why do I have to listen? To go in a joint and hear a guy for twenty-
seven years, and they say, "Well, this is not his night. He does play pretty
things." I say when, when? When does it happen? I've been here for four
nights, and I haven't heard him play anything that is even remotely understandable by anybody. So if I don't understand it, nobody in the audience understands it either. That's a lot of baloney. How come no one had
any trouble understanding Duke Ellington?

PR: You mentioned that there are some rock musicians who probably are
pretty good.

RB: I was saying not every rock group is made up of morons. There are
some musicians in those things that can play. But they're making so much
bread that they just—look at the greatest guitar player I ever heard in my
life, the greatest jazz guitar player I ever heard, is George Benson. He'll
scare anybody to death in this world. But you see the stuff he plays. He
gets a lot of money to do that kind of stuff. George Benson should be
playing Cole Porter tunes. George Benson, wherever you are, come in
[laughter]. Come out of that stuff, play some Harold Arlen tunes and
Duke tunes.

PR: How about younger jazz musicians? Are many playing what you
think is appropriate?

RB: I don't find hardly any of them—there's only a few kids, young kids like Scott Hamilton, Warren Vaché, there's a few guys. There are guys, there are guys around, but not as many as I would like to see. Because the other young ones are afraid that if they don't join the other thing they will be shunned. You know what I mean? You know what I'm saying?

WE: There are musicians you haven't mentioned, Keith Jarrett, for example, who, I think, profess an interest in beauty and play a sort of neo-romantic music.

RB: They're interested in beauty? When are they going to play something romantic and beautiful?

I saw Keith Jarrett the other night. I stayed up to see him on this *Saturday Night Live* or one of those shows, you know, and what do I see—I'm waiting to hear a wonderful pianist—playing a semi–kind of a half rock boogie-woogie horror thing when he is standing up and sitting down and he's caressing—it looks like he's having sex with the piano. And the whole thing is staged for the rock people type of mentality, and this is what all his wonderful knowledge on the piano has come to? What I saw him do the other night? I don't want to see that.

I'll tell you what I just heard recently. I heard Herbie Hancock and Chick Corea, you know, every now and then they do some concerts like that. But they have a record that they put out, and a guy played me the first two tracks of what was "Liza" and "Some Day My Prince Will Come," I think. And there you heard something wonderful. You heard two expert, marvelous pianists who can play the hell out of that piano, and you saw where all their wonderful knowledges were put together, and they played wonderful, wonderful versions of these tunes that people could hang on to and love, and that's what they should be doing, playing all those wonderful standards with their wonderful wit and knowledge and show people how marvelously they can do things. Forget their own tunes for another forty-five years, you know. Wait about another forty years.

PR: Didn't you write jazz criticism?

RB: No! That was a little thing I did for *Saturday Review* that John Hammond sucked me into. And the reason I did that is 'cause they promised me I could keep the records. And I said, "Only give me good records." And I would, you'd only have, like, about thirteen records, and you'd have about two sentences to say about them. And whatever I'd say the editor would change and do what he pleased with it anyway. And it drove me crazy 'cause I had to listen to the records for *hours* to see if I really liked it or didn't like it, you know. I took it very seriously, but it turned out he kept giving me worse and worse records. Most of them I didn't even want to keep. I said, "I told you I am not going to do this gig if you don't let me have nice records." So I stopped.

WE: Since the heyday of swing, has jazz gradually drifted away from the club setting and become more of a concert music?

RB: Not really, not really. I don't know. Frankly, I don't mind doing concerts, but frankly I'm a saloon player. I'm a saloon instrumentalist-entertainer, you know. And I like the clinking of glasses, I like noise, I like people walking by with trays of dishes and falling down with them. I don't like people who don't like noise in clubs.

And I know concert artists—real classical concert artists—who don't like playing concerts. Artur Rubinstein, what does he know? What is he, ninety-five years old or something? He said, "If I had my way everybody in the concert hall would have a drink and a cigarette in their hand." He said, "I don't know how anybody sits and listens to me for two hours." He's wonderful.

I don't know, how is it that Duke Ellington, Basie, Benny, Pops [Armstrong], everybody that I ever saw, how is that they've all played in places, in clubs, and I never saw them unhappy that people were having a ball? And when something was soft and had to be listened to, people listened to it, and they behaved right, and everything was all right, and there was no one going "shhh, shhh, shhh." That's awful.

When a person is really outrageous, then someone should come up to them and say, you know, "You're making a pest of yourself. Either cool it or please sit someplace else or go away." But the ordinary talk—people talking softly to one another—why in the hell should anyone object to that? What do you do, you take a chick to a club to hear music, and then you're supposed to write notes all through the evening? You don't go there to go to a concentration camp. A club is just what it says; it's a place of sociability. And most of these guys that complain and say they should only be on the concert stage, they shouldn't be in a club or on the concert stage or anywhere. They don't belong anyplace. They're awful.

PR: The quartet you recently co-led with George Barnes had a very orchestral sound. Is keeping a small group together for a long period of time an ambition of yours?

RB: Well, I would love to be able to keep a group like that nice group you were talking about. We didn't do enough work. We had no one to worry about it, and you can't be rehearsing and all that and be making calls to people. Somebody should be doing this sort of thing for you, and we had nobody to do anything. Eventually it fell apart. It also fell apart because I couldn't get along with George Barnes. But it was a nice group. It was different. It had a nice little sound to it. It's a darn shame. But at least we did make a lot of nice albums with it and made a lot of people happy with it. We put out about six albums of that kind of a thing.

PR: When you said you couldn't get much work. . . .

RB: There was nobody to book us! We didn't have anybody managing us or doing anything, you know.

PR: Why was that?

RB: Nobody cared.

PR: You mean everybody was attending to other kinds of music that you aren't as fond of?

RB: Yeah. Right. The people who could do something for you were interested in music that would make a lot of money for them, like rock or some other kind of thing, you know.

WE: Are you tired of being on the road?

RB: No, I'm not on the road often enough. I wish I were on the road every week like Basie. I'd have a ball. I like it. I love going every place and playing for people. I'm a performer, I'm an entertainer. There should never be a night when I'm not doing that.

WE: What is your schedule like now?

RB: Oh, I work every forty-five or fifty years. I've been fairly busy this year. I've been doing a lot of things, but I could never be busy enough because I have a ball when I play, man, and when I'm not playing, well, the only things that keep me busy when I'm not playing is I try to write and I listen to music.

WE: Write music, you mean?

RB: Yeah, you know, things like that. And I go hear other people play. But I would prefer to be playing every night. But when you're doing that every night then there is a tendency to say, "Gee, I wish I could rest for a week." There's always a little—but it's better to feel that way than not do enough of it. That's very bad. That could be very, very bad. You must be out there playing. It's important.

PR: Earlier you said that no school could teach what you've learned. And yet jazz programs are proliferating in schools across the country.

RB: I should say no school *is* teaching that because they don't have the guys that made that kind of music teaching anybody anything. There's no Lester Young teaching anywhere. There's nobody like me to tell people what to look for in a chorus, in a record. And those things have to—taste has to be cultivated. You aren't born with taste. It's cultivated, and you have to be led by the nose and shown—who cares what you like. When you're sick in the hospital they don't ask you what kind of medicine you want. They stick it down your throat, and you get better, and you're grateful. And in jazz it should be the same way. You'd have to take people by the ear and by the nose and pull them over here to hear this kind of a record and talk about it.

To show you: I'll show you in what bad shape young players are in. This is the proof of it. Jazz is the only art that I know of that there is that is young enough—it's a baby, it's like eighty-five or ninety years old, whatever, give or take a few years. Almost everything recorded—almost everything that happened to jazz—is available from the twenties to the seventies. OK? Every record store has all these tons of wonderful things that they issue—*wonderful* things. There is no excuse for any youngster that claims he is interested in jazz not going to all these different sources and not listening to all this. Don't they know that there's a reason why they heard the names of Louis Armstrong and Duke Ellington trillions of times? Aren't they even interested, any curiosity in finding out who these people are? Maybe they're awful. But why don't you find out?

But in the so-called classical field, when a kid goes to college to study, major in music, with hopes of being on the concert stage, you know, as a symphonic player, he studies the music of people a hundred years ago. By the time he grows up and plays so-called modern music or anything, he's already had a full background. He knows where he comes from, and he has a right to step onto the stage. These guys do not. That's it. They don't know what happened ten years ago, let alone what happened thirty years ago or anything else. That's why their playing is so empty. It's full of—they got good chops, they can all read, run over the horn. Nobody is saying anything.

WE: You said that someone who wants to play jazz has to be sat down and told what to listen for.

RB: Of course!

WE: So if I played you a Lester Young piece, could you point out some special things about it?

RB: Of course, I could tell you without even hearing it. Anything that he played was distinguished by the most important thing of all. He was a master composer. He was so in *love* with the melody and the thing he was playing that he was delighted to paint another chorus of it. Paint you another picture. And if you listen to any one of them, you'll see they all build in the most interesting—and every four bars is a beautiful picture. And he never, never, never does anything less than that. Even in his sickest period when he was half dead and his mouth couldn't even get onto that saxophone mouthpiece properly, he played with better form than anybody that plays that's healthy. That's what a master composer he was on that thing. That's what you're doing when you're playing jazz: you are composing. The people that I hear today are decomposing. That's the difference.

WE: So Armstrong, Ellington, Lester Young—all the musicians you love are linked by a heritage of taste and beauty?

RB: You see, all the people that I love, all the great players that I love . . . I know instantly that if I were to take every single one of them and put them in a room, I would know right away what records to play that they wouldn't complain about. They'd all like it. If I played anything lovely and beautiful, they would be hypnotized.

You should never take up music, ever, no one should take up music if they are a person who can turn on the radio and hear something like "All the Things You Are" and move the dial. If they find that they can move the dial, if it's possible to move the dial, they shouldn't play music. That's how overwhelming melody should be: it should grab them and drive them crazy and love it. If they don't feel that way they shouldn't be playing music. It's that simple.

SELECTED DISCOGRAPHY

With Pee Wee Russell. *Jazz at Storyville*. Savoy 15014. 1952.
Holiday in Braff. Bethlehem 1034. 1954–55.
The Ruby Braff Special. Vanguard 8504. 1955.
Adoration of the Melody. Bethlehem BCP6043. *ca.* 1955.
Braff! CBS Records Portrait Masters Series RJ44393. 1956.
The Ruby Braff–George Barnes Quartet. Chiaroscuro CR-121. 1973.
The Ruby Braff–George Barnes Quartet Live at the New School. Chiaroscuro CR126. 1974.

Ruby Braff with the Ed Bickert Trio. Sackville 3022. 1981.
With Scott Hamilton. *A Sailboat in the Moonlight.* Concord Jazz 296.
   1986.
With Dick Hyman. *Music from "My Fair Lady."* Concord Jazz
   CCD4393. 1989.

ANTHONY BRAXTON

M ulti-instrumentalist and composer Anthony Braxton has been a major figure in contemporary instrumental music since the midseventies. A virtuoso on alto sax and clarinet, he is also proficient on the flute, percussion instruments, and such rarely seen horns as the sopranino and contrabass saxes. Increasingly valued as a composer, Braxton works in an idiom that straddles jazz and the classical avant-garde. The recipient of a Guggenheim Fellowship and a National Endowment for the Arts grant for composition, he has written a variety of works, ranging from scores for small and large jazz ensembles to film soundtracks, from pieces for dance companies (including Merce Cunningham's) to a chamber orchestra commission.

Braxton was born in Chicago in 1945. His first love was classical music, but the influence of "cool"-style saxophonists Paul Desmond, Lee Konitz, and Warne Marsh inspired his interest in jazz. Braxton studied harmony and composition at the Chicago School of Music; he also did graduate work in philosophy at Roosevelt University.

In 1966 Braxton was discharged from the army after a two-year tour of duty in Korea. He returned to the Midwest and joined the Chicago-based Association for the Advancement of Creative Musicians (AACM). The experimental AACM workshop offered a conducive environment for Braxton's personal explorations of new music spearheaded by free-jazz player Ornette Coleman and contemporary "classical" composers John Cage and Karlheinz Stockhausen.

In 1967 Braxton formed the Creative Construction Company with AACM cohorts trumpeter Leo Smith and violinist Leroy Jenkins, and he cut his debut album with them later that same year.[1] His groundbreaking recording For Alto, which featured Braxton on unaccompanied alto sax, followed in 1968.[2] Despite critical acclaim for both releases, however, Braxton soon learned that little financial gain was possible in the subculture of the "new" jazz. During this period Braxton often earned his living by hustling chess games on the street.

1. Anthony Braxton, *Three Compositions of New Jazz*, Delmark Records, 1967.
2. Anthony Braxton, *For Alto*, Delmark Records, 1968.

Seeking a more sympathetic audience for his music, Braxton, along with many of his AACM peers, moved to Europe in 1969. Soon he became associated with the European electronic music scene, playing with the Italian improvising ensemble Musica Elettronica Viva in 1970. That year Braxton also joined pianist Chick Corea, bassist Dave Holland, and drummer Barry Altschul to form the short-lived group Circle.[3] The empathy and brilliant improvising of Circle was recaptured in a 1972 date led by bassist Holland that featured Braxton on reeds and flute, *Conference of the Birds*.[4]

After Circle disbanded in 1971, Braxton found himself in demand as a solo performer in Europe, largely because of the delayed impact of *For Alto*. One measure of Braxton's burgeoning reputation at the time was the estimation of him as "the greatest living alto saxophonist," according to *Coda*, Canada's premier jazz magazine.

Braxton returned to the United States in 1974. Relocating in New York, he recorded several excellent albums over the next few years, reuniting with former AACM and Circle colleagues, among others, in small-combo settings (duets, trios, and quartets).[5] He also pursued his ambition to write for large ensembles, creating what many consider an early masterwork, *Creative Orchestra Music 1976*.[6] In 1978 he toured Europe with his own orchestra and released a three-record set that documents a Mahleresque aggregation of 160 musicians organized into 4 orchestras performing onstage at Ohio's Oberlin College.[7]

Through the eighties and into the nineties, Anthony Braxton has continued to record and tour worldwide as a solo performer and as the leader of disparate ensembles. He has conducted the Copenhagen Radio Orchestra and completed a series of 12 operas, and in 1985 he began a three-year appointment as professor of music at Mills College in Oakland, California.

---

3. A live performance by this group can be found on *Paris Concert*, ECM Records, 1971.

4. Dave Holland Quartet, *Conference of the Birds*, ECM Records, 1972.

5. Prime examples include Anthony Braxton, *New York, Fall 1974* (quartet), Arista Records, 1975; Anthony Braxton, *Five Pieces, 1975* (quartet), Arista Records, 1975; Anthony Braxton, *Duets with Richard Abrams, 1976*, Arista Records, 1976; Anthony Braxton, *For Trio*, Arista Records, 1978.

6. Anthony Braxton, *Creative Orchestra Music 1976*, Arista Records, 1976.

7. Anthony Braxton, *For Four Orchestras*, Arista Records, 1978.

Recorded 1978

WE: Anthony, what does the term *tradition* mean to you, especially as it applies to twentieth-century music?

AB: Well, one, I've always looked at my activity as being traditional, or within the tradition, but not just twentieth-century tradition. I've spent a great deal of time researching the progressional thrust of world creativity regardless of time zone, and I find that I'm interested in building from a traditional base and extending, and hopefully, you know, I'll be able to come up with something that's relevant for this time zone. Although my music is generally talked of as being somewhat *radical*, in fact it has a real traditional base. It's not like the concept of "free jazz" which solidified in the sixties, that being activity that moved toward anarchy or something like that. I've never really been interested in anarchy, but rather I've been interested in the initiation of alternative languages as a means to reconnect to what I call the metareality implications of world culture.

So for that reason, even in this period, I'm constantly researching the progressional thrust of the music, whatever form. Whether it would involve the initiations of someone like Fletcher Henderson or John Philip Sousa or Charles Ives or what we call in this time zone Indian music or Japanese music. I am interested in reconnecting to the information that used to exist, or the dynamic metareality of world culture as it was before some of the changes which took place in the physical universe level.

PR: In 1968 you made a landmark solo saxophone album, *For Alto*. What prompted you to make that record, and why did you choose the alto from among all the instruments you play?

AB: OK, my decision to move toward solo alto saxophone was motivated by several things. One, I've always been attracted to solo music, and I think in the early sixties especially to the music of Arnold Schoenberg and Karlheinz Stockhausen and Fats Waller. I was very influenced by that, and it represented a dilemma to me because I wasn't a strong enough pianist to move into solo music, and also I had another idea about what the medium could mean for a creative improvising musician.

Now I originally chose the alto saxophone because it was the instrument I was closest to in that period. And why couldn't I do it on the saxophone? That was like my original feeling. Why is it that a single-line instrument can't also function in a solo context? Now in that particular period when I moved into solo music, I think it was around 1966, it was that time when I began to look at which direction I wanted to move in the music and the nature of how I wanted to function. That being I was in that period attracted into functioning as a multi-instrumentalist and as a composer, and I also wanted to function within the entire spectrum of the music. So as an instrumentalist that would mean functioning in a solo, duo, trio, quartet, quintet to an orchestral context, and for a composer it would have the same meaning.

So I initially, you know, undertook concerts and started to build a repertoire of compositions for solo saxophone because the saxophone's a very flexible instrument, especially the alto is. There's a lot of areas which have yet to be tapped on the instrument. Even though in this time zone acoustic instruments are looked at as being somewhat unfashionable as far as the projection or spread of the music, I always thought that there was room to carry forth acoustic instruments into the next cycle of the music as well. And so I chose the alto saxophone.

The reason I never used other instruments as far as like a complete solo concert is that I guess I'm somewhat sentimental. I see the saxophone as *my* piano. It's the instrument that I was originally attracted to. I started on clarinet, but I went to the alto saxophone after I discovered the music of Paul Desmond and Konitz and Jackie McLean and Coleman, and so it has a special place in my life. It became my piano, and I just made the decision that I would not do solo concerts on the contrabass clarinet or flute or clarinet for this time zone because I just wanted to be involved with the alto saxophone in a special way. Although I do do solo pieces for the other instruments, but not whole concerts.

WE: Could you tell us something about the organizational methods you use to compose your music?

AB: As far as composition is concerned and methodology is concerned, I was more attracted to going back to deal with what is the significance of number, what is the significance of color and shape and dance and sound? And I began to collect information that would move to give me a particular organizational route to consider, that being, say, I'm a Gemini, and the note that accompanies Gemini is F-sharp, and F-sharp rules the head and shoulders, and the color orange is related to that particular zone, and so it's like I moved towards astrology. Later I moved towards studying the Egyptian philosophy, and then moving back into empiricism and some of the post-Webern techniques.

And so now I've evolved my own organizational routes. And each route would, of course, depend on what composition we're talking about. But I was not just interested in system, but rather system in a proper metareality and composite context. That being, say, what a given thrust would mean according to its empirical developments and according to its vibrational and its spiritual implications, et cetera. And also what a given thrust would mean with respect to the scientific investigation that would relate to that thrust. And how that would be manifested in, say, what we call medicine or sculpture or computer science or astrophysics. In other words, where we could look at, say, Anton Webern and his use of serialism, and we can see how that works. What I was looking for was like a methodology that would also dictate the nature of the language of the music as well as its functional and vibrational significance.

So that was what originally propelled me into the study of methodology and language, especially language. Because I found for myself each language, while as an instrumentalist it would give me new problems to deal with and new conceptual areas to explore, it would also align me with particular forces as well, which is to say the systemic dynamics of a given organizational route not limited to the empirical use of that route but also as it's related to certain forces. So it's like, I'm interested in, say, "language 506" because it puts me in touch with "forces 506." I've come to the point now where I participate in music as a means to connect with certain forces, and as such I don't see myself as a musician in the same sense that I used to think of music, because I see music as only being like a step to get to "zone 12," if that's the zone we're talking about. And zone 12 is what's important.

In this time zone for the most part, we generally come to look at music as something that you dance to, or you sing a tune. And of course, that's part of it, I mean that does exist, and that's beautiful. But there's another whole area of creativity that's been lost. And I'm interested in that area, that being creativity as activity having to do with the high culture cycle of a given culture, and my understanding being high culture is the optimum state for a group of people to be living in. High culture is defined to the progressional work that was done in Egypt, in India in its high cycle, and in Greece in its high cycle, although there was a lot of transfer activity happening. What we call "Greek philosophy" isn't Greek philosophy; I imagine you probably know that, so we'll skip over that. But anyway, high culture as a desirable goal to move toward—that's what I'm interested in.

PR: You are one of the major musicians to emerge from the ranks of the AACM. Could you describe the origins and early activities of that organization?

AB: Well, the formation of the AACM came about because of the work that was done by people like Cecil Taylor, Ornette Coleman, John Coltrane, what I call the transfer cycle in the music. And the fact [is] that when the music began to change it became very difficult to find one correct information about it, and it became also difficult if you were interested in the music and wanted to perform because there was a lot of opposition to the music. So I remember before I joined the AACM I used to always feel like I was crazy because I didn't have anyone I could relate to, and suddenly here was thirty to fifty people who were all interested in the music. And because of the unification of the musicians it [meant the] possible opening up [of] outlets for the music, performing outlets.

But that was just one aspect of the AACM, because the AACM would later move to establish communities to teach young people about the music. It wasn't about making any money or anything like that, but to bring young people into the organization and teach them about the various projections of the music. And also to connect with the community. Because as you know some of the projections which are developed from so-called bebop have moved outside of the black community, where at some point black people have come to view the music as being something outside of their reality. And there are a lot of reasons for that, [such as] the collective forces of Western culture, the sophistication which surrounds the media in this period, and the misdocumentation which surrounds various projections of the music. So one of the first tasks for the AACM was to integrate their activity with the community and to make it a part of the community, so that, one, it would not be viewed as something alien, and two, because that's the highest order of the way creativity is anyway. It should be related to the community.

WE: Could you compare that sense of community you had in Chicago with the scene in New York City, where you now live and work?

AB: As far as New York is concerned, well, of course, you know, it's very different. New York is, well, New York is something else, but I miss some of the unification that used to happen; the unification which took place in Chicago is not happening in New York. You have a more competitive type of mentality, and also the information scan is even wider because now we're not dealing solely with black people or white people or red people, we're dealing with a composite, you know, community of people. Which, of course, is what has to be dealt with.

But at the same time it's harder for any kind of organization to take place in New York, and also I'm getting older now. It's like the AACM solidified more than ten years ago. I'm married and have a family. I have to now think about performing as well, and so New York is the best place to be in this country, because you're closer to Europe and there's more opportunities to work for the *survivors.* And so on one hand, as far as my individual universe is concerned, I've been able to develop, and things have improved somewhat for me. But as far as the total context of the music is concerned, I miss the unification that took place in Chicago, which is not to say that it's over.

The AACM is still very much together, and there's another whole wave of young musicians, in fact, several waves who are functioning. The music school is still working, and on occasion when I get the chance I'm able to go back to Chicago and keep in touch with the organization. I mean, I'm still in the organization. Also there's a chapter now in New York, because the people who functioned in the sixties, many of them now have made the journey to New York. At some point they were *forced* to because there's not that much work in Chicago. And so the AACM is still alive and strong, but the situation has changed from the early formation of the group in the sixties.

PR: Are you able to make a living on your music in America in 1978?

AB: Well, I mean, I was able to make a living ten years ago, but I lived on Hostess Twinkies, and I didn't have a house, you know. It's like I lived in the street, and every now and then I stayed in one of my friends' houses and had a Hostess Twinkie or maybe a McDonald's hamburger or something.

Comparing that time zone to now, I'm in a better state. But I don't want to get in a position of saying "Well, I don't think I make as much money as I should make" or something like that. The fact is I've been able to survive; my situation has gotten a little better. By rock standards or by commercial music standards, I don't even rate. But at the same time I've been able to pay my rent for the past couple of years—well, I've been late a couple of times, but she's understood, my landlord. And I'm able to eat food in this period. So I'm just very grateful that I'm healthy enough, and I still feel very excited about participating in creative music, and I'd rather say that as opposed to going to my own individual situation because I could make it *very depressing* [laughter].

PR: How about the acceptance of your music? Sometimes what you play is portrayed in the popular press as difficult and lacking in emotion.

AB: Well, OK. As far as my music being perceived as somewhat cold, I picked up a *Down Beat* magazine a couple days ago, and there was Phil Woods again putting the same type of charges. It seems like whenever he talks about my music he mentions "hate," as if my music is a chief exponent of some kind of hate. There's no way I can probably deal with any of those charges, because at the bottom of those charges it's like a questioning whether or not my life is valid.

Now I realize that the vibrational content of my music could be perceived as different, especially with the way the media talks about music and all the distortions which surround the creative process. But I work as hard as I can possibly work at my creativity. I'm trying to learn, and I try to give as much as I can give in my music, and if it's perceived as not having any emotional content, well, there's nothing I can do. But coming from where I'm coming from, I mean being inside this body and talking about my relationship with my activity, I am doing the best that I can possibly do. Yet I admit that there's much more to learn, and I want to be a part of that. And so I have lots to learn. I'm not afraid of that.

But as far as the charges of me not having any emotional commitment to my activity, there's no way I can deal with that, because at the base of that there's some kind of attack on the validity of my life, and I am on the planet equally just like anyone else, and I'm very happy to be on the planet. Since I'm here, what else can I say? [Laughter.]

WE: Did the explorations of Marcel Duchamp and John Cage exert any influence on you?

AB: As far as Marcel Duchamp and John Cage, I am, of course, very familiar with their work. And on some level I have been influenced by their work, and yet I don't see my activity as being in the same zone as John Cage or Marcel Duchamp, because I see their activity as being an outgrowth of the existential type of affinity alignment which moved out of World War II.

I'm really interested in creating a spectrum of music that will be about something or have something to do with, how can I say it, spirituality. I mean, like for instance, John Cage, I consider him to be a functional racist regardless of how positive he's contributed on some levels. He's done everything he can do to distort the metareality of black creativity. I think he's a very sophisticated racist, but racist nonetheless. I've done a lot of reading about John Cage, I've met him, I've researched his work. But as a black person I can't just simply ignore his treatment of black creativity, his comments on anything that's connected to black high culture, and the sarcasm and the really alien vibes that he puts out when confronted with anything having to do with black people. And so, of course, there's a difference between us there because I *am* a black person.

Not to mention that John Cage has solidified a projection which, I mean, I don't know how to say it, seems to be relevant to the projectional growth of certain forces. So if we could look at, like, why people who vibrate to certain areas of information, I can see Cage's music being very relevant. Not just white people, black people too. At one time it was very relevant for me. But as far as carrying the seeds of something which could move to substantiate alternative culture, I'm not so sure if I see Cage's work as life-giving. I see Cage's work as being—it takes the Western existential vibration to the twelfth power and exposes many of the flaws in the intellectual arena that has helped solidify this time zone, and in doing that, I think that's valuable. But at the same time I don't think he replaces it with anything that can move to rebuild the seeds of a *new* culture. For me, I think his music is *interesting*, but I mean, you know, it could be uninteresting. Add three more words, four commas, and two paragraphs, and that's how I feel about John Cage.

PR: You have been quoted as saying that your work is allied in some ways to what Eric Dolphy was doing prior to his untimely death. Could you detail the similarities for us?

AB: Well, Eric Dolphy was one of the first musicians in that time zone to reopen the road of the multi-instrumentalist. Of course, he wasn't the first—there were musicians way before him. Yet his work on the flute, bass clarinet, and alto excited me and made me again think about multi-instrumentalism. Also he was interested in world music. I mean, at various points of his life, he functioned in many different contexts. He played Varèse's "Density 21.5" for flute. And he was not afraid to work outside the so-called reality of the jazz musician. Well, I was interested in that, because I've never understood what people meant anyway when they said "jazz." And Eric Dolphy was interesting to me because of his interest in composition, although he was unable to complete half of what he probably would have. He died when he was very young. The cosmics only knows what he would have contributed in the area of composition had he the chance. And he also had a profound respect for tradition, something which isn't popular in this time zone. I mean, the basic idea that floats around now is that we want to get away from tradition. Most people not even knowing what tradition is. And Eric was, first and foremost, a person who respected the tradition and wanted to extend the tradition or extend the creativity in accordance with the most positive aspects of what could be brought forth from the tradition. So I have that in common with him, or I learned that from him. What else? He was a schizoid Gemini just like me [laughter].

SELECTED DISCOGRAPHY

Three Compositions of New Jazz. Delmark DS-415. 1967.
For Alto. Delmark DS 420-421. 1968.
With Circle. *Paris Concert.* ECM 1018-1019. 1971.
New York, Fall 1974. Arista 4064. 1975.
The Montreux/Berlin Concerts. Arista AL 5002. 1975, 1976.
Creative Orchestra Music 1976. Arista 4080. 1976.
With Max Roach. *Birth and Rebirth.* Black Saint BSR 0024. 1978.
Performance 9/1/79. hat ART 2019. 1979.
With Richard Teitelbaum. *Open Aspects.* hat ART 1995/96. 1985.
With Max Roach. *One in Two, Two in One.* hat ART CD 6030. 1990.

BOB BROOKMEYER

Photograph by David D. Spitzer.   Used with permission.

Deep-toned and incisive, the playing of valve trombonist Bob Brookmeyer is one of the most unmistakable sounds in jazz. The only important jazz musician other than Juan Tizol to concentrate on the valve trombone, Brookmeyer is also an accomplished pianist and composer-arranger.[1]

Born in 1929, the Kansas City, Kansas, native studied piano and composition at the Kansas City Conservatory. He began his professional career as a pianist in the early fifties, comping for various bandleaders, including Tex Beneke, Ray McKinley, Louis Prima, Claude Thornhill (with whom he played trombone and second piano), and Woody Herman. Brookmeyer started doubling on valve trombone in 1952, and in 1953 he did a year's stint with the Stan Getz Quartet that included the Paris Jazz Festival. It was not until the spring of 1954 when he replaced Chet Baker in Gerry Mulligan's West Coast–style pianoless quartet, however, that Brookmeyer achieved national prominence.

Brookmeyer worked steadily with Mulligan's sextet and quartet until 1957, then finished the decade by playing with the Jimmy Giuffre 3 and free-lancing as a player and a writer in New York for a year. He toured with Gerry Mulligan's Concert Jazz Band in 1960, contributing charts and taking key solos on trombone and occasionally piano. In 1961 he found a kindred spirit in trumpet player Clark Terry, and the two began a five-year association co-leading a popular and critically well-received quintet. The series of recordings they made for the Mainstream label persuasively captured the solid, straightahead blowing, the fresh arrangements, and the contagious joy that were consistent features of this congenial unit.

Brookmeyer was a charter member of the famed Thad Jones–Mel Lewis Orchestra in 1965, dividing his chores between arranging and playing, and he found steady work as a band member on television's *Merv Griffin Show*. Beset by personal problems, Brookmeyer left New York in

1. Juan Tizol played valve trombone in Duke Ellington's orchestra from 1929 to 1944, and again from 1951 to 1953.

1968 to resettle in southern California. For the next decade he did some studio work but was relatively inactive as a jazz musician.

Bob Brookmeyer came out of jazz retirement in 1978. He returned to New York and in 1979 began a long-term relationship as composer-arranger and musical director of Mel Lewis' retooled big band. Although Brookmeyer has concentrated on writing over the last thirteen years (the American Jazz Orchestra premiered one of his works in 1986, making him the first composer to be so honored), he continues to tour and is particularly popular with European audiences. Since 1979 he has also released some memorable small-group recordings on the Gryphon and Concord labels, which demonstrate that despite this versatile jazzman's devotion to composition, his gifts as an improviser and his abilities as a technically dazzling stylist have not diminished.[2]

Recorded 1980

WE: We enjoy the humor in your music. Do you hear humor in today's jazz?

BB: Well, I think there's been a slight change. To me, there's a broader way to look at it. In the times, say, from the late twenties through the thirties and the early forties, we had a period of great individualists. We had Lester Youngs, Charlie Parkers, Thelonious Monks, Duke Ellingtons, and Count Basies, and I guess the magic of the gift made them very innovative in what they did. I think probably if you're extremely different you become very secure in what you do. So I would think that a sense of humor would be implicit in a way to face and deal with life.

In the sixties we had some very outstanding musicians, but we didn't have quite the individuals that we had before. I've talked this over with some friends of mine who are writers and who are painters, and I think there is a general, if you want to call it, a cultural malaise. I'm not looking down my nose at it—it's a comment—that we have *very* fine musicians now—great musicians—but the character of the timber of the land doesn't seem to be suitable right now for producing the great individuals of twenty or thirty or forty years ago. And I'm not one who looks back to the good old days; to me, today is a good old day. I think that maybe

2. One splendid example is *The Bob Brookmeyer Small Band (Live at Sandy's)*, Gryphon Records, 1978.

that's one of the reasons that the humor might be—if it is missing— might be missing.

PR: One reviewer once said that "of all the dropouts from the ranks of active jazz men in the sixties few left less conspicuously than Bob Brook-meyer or were more missed." How do you respond to that?

BB: Well, when I moved to California I was in the process of dropping out of life. I was fairly ill at the time, and I went to California a sick man. I spent ten years there, and I got my health back. So it wasn't "I'm fed up, I quit." It was a confused "I wonder what's going wrong" or "what's going worse," and everything seemed to go worse. When I got my health back, things began to dramatically improve, and I am glad that they missed me.

PR: What was it like when you returned to New York?

BB: When I went back to New York I hadn't been active there really for about fifteen years as a functioning jazz musician. So it was a new world to me. There were a whole generation of people around town who were playing and working that I had to get to know again, and they didn't care what I'd done. They wanted to know what I could do.

PR: Could you give us an example?

BB: I think the best example was Mel Lewis' band. They were all new to me. And I came down, and I was the old geezer who'd written some of the fifteen-year-old arrangements that they were playing. They could look at me and say, "Well, he did that," but that was no wedge for me in the door. I had to spend the first year and a half in New York getting to know them and saying, "Well, now look, here's what I do, what do you think of that?" So it was really reestablishing credentials, because not many people of the younger generation would say, "Gee, that's really great you played with Gerry Mulligan or Stan Getz." They couldn't care less, you know. If I'd played with maybe Herbie Hancock or Chick Corea or John Coltrane—those were people who were important to them. So it was a different set of heroes and a different set of judgmental values.

WE: Did the response of those young band members strike you as nar-row-minded?

BB: No. When I first started playing my life was Count Basie and Bill Harris and Woody Herman. I didn't like Duke Ellington. I thought the man was sloppy and out of tune. That's how much I knew when I was in my late teens. And so *I* had firm opinions. I used what attracted me; I didn't say, "Well, I *should* like . . ." I heard Stravinsky, and I liked that first, then I learned to like Bach, and then I learned to love Bach, and I learned to like Mozart and like Haydn, you know. You can't say to somebody, "This is the right way, read this Bible and you will feel better tomorrow." They have to find for themselves what they want.

WE: What do you think of young players that you meet in clinics?

BB: The general rap that I heard before I began to do any clinic work— and I've not done a great deal—is great ensemble, no solo. That has been somewhat borne up by my experience. Once again, I'm speaking from a very small frame of reference.

What I think is most needed now are some traveling improvisational teachers who can teach people to begin to play a song on a C-major scale or make up a melody with four notes and make up another melody on four notes. To learn to instruct your mind to become an improvisational organ. You know, it's a skill. And *then*, when you start writing songs, you would naturally, I think, go around Lester Young and graduate to Charlie Parker to hear how things get refined and broken up.

WE: Do you think that improvisation has become a lost art?

BB: Well, it isn't a lost art, really. I think people imitate what's before them, that they find attractive, and what is being imitated now is a refinement of a basic. I have some friends in New York in their early thirties I advised to stop listening to Cedar Walton and Bill Evans and to Richie Beirach and whoever, and go back and listen to Bud Powell. This person wanted to be a hot piano player, "hot bebop piano player," end quote. I said, "Well, go back to where it began." If you listen to all of these other people they are reflecting what they heard in Bud Powell. It's like listening to Phil Woods to try to find out how Charlie Parker played. Phil Woods is a fantastic saxophone player, but we all listened to Charlie Parker to learn that lesson. So go back to the source.

PR: Let's turn to your early years. Since you were born in Kansas City, did the jazz scene there have any influence on you?

BB: I was about eight or ten years old when I first heard Count Basie, so I wasn't gettin' around town too much then. My limit was about four or five blocks away from the house. The radio did [influence me], because we heard a lot of big bands. And I liked all the big bands. That was the closest thing to jazz music we could hear. I liked dixieland on the radio from Chicago.

When I got old enough to get around in the clubs, there was, I think at that time, a Kansas City sound from rhythm sections. It was a very smooth, fluid sound, much like Count Basie had. And I knew a few players that had been, say, with Lionel Hampton that played that way, and they were magical to play with. The younger, white players tried to play like Max Roach or Buddy Rich. But from the black musicians that I was around a lot, I got more of a good feeling about the music.

When Charlie Parker left, the soloists were all gone. Right before I left, I worked a bit with Ben Webster. He had come back to town when I was about twenty. He came back for a few months. But it was pretty quiet by that time, and it's been, I think, fairly quiet since then.

PR: We read that you began on clarinet and played some piano before picking up the trombone.

BB: Well, it's a little out of sequence. I went from clarinet to trombone. I was shanghaied into playing trombone by my parents and the band director that needed a trombone player. I wanted to be a trumpet player or a drummer, for which I'd saved money. So after being sold down the river, I didn't really care that much for playing slide trombone, and I learned quickly how to finger like a trumpet. That was my second choice of instrument, drums being first. I began to play the baritone horn all I could. And as soon as I could, I got a series of exotic valve trombones and finally, when I was eighteen, got an official one from Reynolds. So I wanted to be something else than a trombone player. I still do, but I would like to look like Robert Redford and sound like Walter Cronkite. So I'm a trombone player. That's my voice, I guess.

The piano came by accident, kind of. I wanted to write music also. When I was about thirteen I began to teach myself how to write. And by the time I was fifteen, I was selling arrangements to a territory band company in Omaha, Nebraska. I sent them a copied arrangement every other week for twenty bucks. And I then finally got a piano just before I was sixteen, so I began to learn officially how a piano went. And since valve trombone players didn't work too much in Kansas City, maybe one night a year, I began to learn how to play piano so I could support myself playing piano—which I did. I supported myself in New York for my first year largely by playing piano.

WE: Your trombone playing abounds with vocal references. What's the source for that?

BB: The biggest impact on me as a trombone player was Bill Harris. He was a very emotive vocalese-type player. That's the way I tried to play on slide trombone, and that has hung over. I would tell anybody that if you want to play something through an instrument that you should be able to sing it with some conviction and authority and pleasant feelings in your heart as you do it before you can play it. I think it's still a melodic singing process. Beating on something and singing are the things that we start with before we approach an instrument or a chord.

PR: Early on, you played with the Claude Thornhill and Tex Beneke bands. In your estimation, were those dance bands or jazz bands?

BB: I would consider Claude Thornhill very close to being a jazz band. Gil Evans had written almost the entire library, and we had Gene Quill and Brew Moore in the band, Teddy Kotick was the bass player, so we had a very good band. Tex Beneke was obviously a Glenn Miller–type dance band. I was playing piano, Mel Lewis played drums, and Buddy Clark played bass, so we had fun. We had a band within a band. I did a lot of other dance band work. My first road job was playing piano with Orrin Tucker for six months. I got to travel, and I was in Chicago for three months, and I met an awful lot of people there.

PR: How old were you at the time?

BB: Twenty. And in California I met some people, so my philosophy was then to take the first job you can get leaving town, and when you're on the road get out and play all you can. That's what we did.

WE: Let's talk about J. J. Johnson. He is credited in the media as having been the translator of bop for the trombone. Is that true?

BB: I'm a friend and fan of J. J.'s. Yes, he was the man, as probably Dizzy Gillespie was, and Charlie Parker. The transition to playing bebop on trombone was very difficult, and J. J. solved it, I think, probably about as good as you could at that time.

Obviously, you don't have the upper range that is still desirable as you do in trumpet and alto. The timbre of trombone is dark and muddy and gets swallowed up by the overtone series of the drums and the bass. So it's sometimes a fight for total survival—acoustic survival—down there. But he found really a good way to do it. J. still plays that way, and he plays better every year, so he found a true vein. He was an innovator. He's the Charlie Parker of his instrument, I think.

PR: You played with Woody Herman.

BB: Briefly, yeah. All these big band stints were brief. In my first year in New York were stints with six or seven bands, I think. I went through a whole bunch of bands in a hurry. I didn't like any of them. They were all bands past their prime, and I was looking for something, I guess. I'd had a chance to join Woody Herman a little earlier when I was in Kansas City, and that was the kind of band I wanted to be on—the one with Doug Mettome. The bands I was on were not that good, so I quit. I figured I'd find something else. And I did.

WE: In the early fifties, didn't the melodic emphasis in your playing and Stan Getz's run counter to the bebop mainstream?

BB: The group in New York, of which Stanley became known as the leader, I guess—he received the greatest notoriety—would be Al Cohn, Zoot Sims, and Herbie Steward. They were the saxophone players *I* liked, because my instrument was very close to the tenor, so I heard as a tenor player. So I became, I guess, a Lester Young–type player. Because that's what I liked. That's the way I liked to speak.

It's what we were attracted to. And I think most of the alto players that I was around liked to play like Charlie Parker. Very few Johnny Hodges alto players or Ben Webster tenor players in those days. We all, as now, we all rode the crest of what was popular. Those were the voices that we heard that we liked and understood. Much more than we'd have heard Chu Berry or Coleman Hawkins and said, "Oh, that really turns me on. That physically excites me." Lester Young physically excited us, and that process of making music was what physically excited us.

I was about ten years old when I first heard Count Basie live at the Tower Theatre in Kansas City. I heard six shows a day and saw a rotten movie five times [laughter]. It was the only time I ever cut school in my life: four or five times a year I spent seven days a week there. And in the morning for the first show the band would be behind the screen. And to hear the first note—it was the severest physical thrill I think I've ever had. Drugs and sex and all that stuff—it was just the most powerful thing. Playing still gets that way. It's still just viscerally the most thrilling thing that I can do, and most guys, I think, feel that way.

So this is to say that when you pick somebody to play like, it's not a selection process, like you sit down rationally and choose a car, it's what *really* moves you, and that man's playing *really* thrills you. And that's all there is to it—it's like falling in love. That's the woman you must have at all costs. So it's the same process.

WE: That seems to contradict something Lee Konitz told us. He said that he consciously avoided listening to Charlie Parker because at first the music was too hard and then later because Parker's influence would have been too strong.

BB: I'm speaking for most of us. Lee is an exceptional man. He's a great artist, and there is a big difference. Lee has been aware of the process most of his life, I think. Jim Hall is another one. Jim Hall is *aware* of what goes into his music, and he treats his musical life much as a classic artist would. He keeps going back, enriching and working on fundamentals.

PR: In the fifties, the term *chamber jazz* emerged in reference to, for instance, the pianoless groups of Gerry Mulligan and Chico Hamilton. Was that term just a media invention?

BB: Yeah. *Bebop* is a shorthand; *chamber jazz* is a meaningless phrase.

PR: We figured as much. We know that you worked with Jimmy Giuffre with no piano and . . .

BB: No drums and no bass. Just Jim Hall and Giuffre and I. We liked it. We stuck with that for a long time. The first three months we almost didn't make it. We were really scuffling in New York, and finally the booking got better. What I look back now and find is that we didn't know it then, but we were a truly avant-garde band. We played everything from folk-sounding music, which Jimmy was writing then, to—we used to improvise all the time. We had free improvisations every set.

And sometimes I played piano, and we'd sound like twelve-tone musicians. Sometimes we sounded like, I guess, a lot of the free music today, [we'd] bash and clatter about. There were different ways we liked to play. And not different ways we contrived to play so we could sound like somebody—these were just ways that we would play if we were let alone to play. So that was it. It was nice. There was no word for it. They just said we were the guys with no bass player and no drummer [laughter]. But the words like *chamber jazz* don't mean much.

PR: Are there any good recordings from that period?

BB: We made two records—one when we first started and one just before we broke up.[3] If we'd have had tape recorders then like we do now, we would have had a lot of good tapes. But we don't.

PR: Was that a popular band?

3. The Jimmy Giuffre 3, *Trav'lin' Light*, Atlantic Records, January, 1958; The Jimmy Giuffre 3, *Western Suite*, Atlantic Records, December, 1958.

BB: We did pretty well. My fondest memory is when we began to work in New York with the band we did eight straight weeks at the then Café Bohemia. And we started off, I think, against Wynton Kelly's Trio, and Wilbur Ware had a quartet, and somebody else—the dynamite was getting hotter. And the last two weeks Miles [Davis] was there with a roaring band with John [Coltrane], and Bill Evans had just joined. And we thought, "We're really going to get killed because they're goin' to scream through us," because we at times were very soft, and "They're just gonna love Miles." Max Roach was down one night, and we were talking. He was saying that everybody talks through Miles and listens to you guys, and it was the damnedest thing we ever heard.

I guess we were so soft and we were really serious about what we were doing that they'd stay quiet, I think, out of curiosity probably. But yes, I think people liked it, and they liked it not because we told them that we have a new way to play. They liked it because we sat down and played for them, and they appreciated what they heard. They weren't warned in front that it was going to be different. There weren't so many severe labels like they got to be later on. Like "this is really an eclectic experience" and "this is gonna blow your mind." Rock 'n' roll hadn't come into the merchandising yet. So we were still just a jug and country and string band gonna be in your town next week.

WE: About 1960 you joined Gerry Mulligan's Concert Jazz Band. How did that come about?

BB: Gerry came by early in that year and had a week at Basin Street East and wanted to know if I'd write an arrangement for him. We hadn't played together for a couple of years. And I think he was kind of depressed that I quit—I quit in '57. So we got to be a little tighter, and the one week at Basin Street East turned into a band. I saw the opportunity to be part of a band that I'd wanted since I'd been a kid. The band I couldn't find when I first came to New York. Every band I played in was dumb. I mean, this was not the way it was supposed to go. The bands I played in when I was a kid were OK, but they should have been better, and we always had final points we couldn't go beyond.

This was a chance to work with a supreme musician—Gerry is a great writer and player and a great leader—and it was a ready-made circumstance. So I really tried to keep his interest up as much as I could, and I got some people for him to listen to. We finally wound up with a great band—we had Mel Lewis, and Buddy Clark, and Nick Travis—a really excellent band. And that was an achievement, I think. We stayed together for about four years.

WE: Were you and Mulligan co-leaders of that band?

BB: I wasn't a co-leader. I played first trombone, and I did some of the writing. My investment was emotional. I *wanted* that band, more sometimes probably than Gerry did. That's what I lived for in that year. I wanted to keep that going.

WE: So it was a spiritual co-leadership.

BB: Yeah, I wasn't going to let it die.

WE: But the band folded in the midsixties. What happened?

BB: I think a lack of work and a lack of interest, and Gerry's interest was getting—it's a helluva responsibility to be a big-band leader. It's a mess. And my interest was getting scattered around. My personal life was chaotic—up and down. So with both of us kind of in and out emotionally and with the work situation getting hard, I think that we just decided to concentrate on the quartet.

We never talked about it much. Maybe we felt that we had gone far enough with it, I don't know. My feeling was that I wished we had gone further. After 1960 I wanted us just to keep on expanding and get new music from George Russell, get Gil [Evans] to write for us, and do all this stuff, you know. I'm quite childlike and enthusiastic about that, I guess. But realities kept surfacing. So we did four years, and that was our time.

PR: Gary McFarland wrote for the Concert Jazz Band. What do you recall about him?

BB: Well, Gary was just different. He was one of those people that just seemed to hear everything and translate everything differently. He called me in early 1961. Gerry's band had just started, and he wanted to know the personnel, and he asked me if it would be OK if he brought something in. I said sure and encouraged him to please do that, and he brought in that first piece, an arrangement of "Weep."

PR: Was he known at the time?

BB: I'd never heard of him. Just a little bit through John Lewis and the [Lenox] School of Jazz, where I taught for a couple of years. He brought it in, and it was quite successful and *very* different. So he did another piece for us, and people began to hear about him, and Creed [Taylor] heard about him at Verve and took the chance on McFarland's first album. I think it was *How to Succeed in Business*.[4] So that was it, and he was off. He was a very nice man; I liked him very much. We miss him now, because in my estimation what we're still looking for the most are good music writers. We have good soloists and good ensemble players, but we're still short on really good writers.

PR: Do you think that McFarland's recordings turned commercial during the last years of his life?

BB: I wasn't seriously around Gary after about the middle sixties. We shared some office space with a couple of other guys for a long time. He liked to socialize very much. He liked the Cary Grant–type of life—the cashmere coats and the cocktail hour and all that—as we all did but in varying degrees of assiduously persevering on it. He might have gotten turned, I think, a little bit to being something that would be a hit.

You know, it's a helluva thing. We were talking the other night with somebody about being true to what we do. If somebody were to come to me and say, "Here's a hundred thousand bucks, we'd like you to do this project," my only answer is that I've gotten myself down to such a place that I really wouldn't know what to do with the money. It would be nice to have, but it wouldn't change what I do. I've become, not monkish, but I've become pretty austere in my personal life. But it's a big decision.

If they say, "You wouldn't have to be that much different. Just do some of this, and just like that, just this one shot." And of course, that's a seductive druglike atmosphere—you find all these things are possible. You can go to here and there and wear this and bank this and drive this, you never could before, so just *one* more. It's the Las Vegas syndrome. I know people in Las Vegas that've been there twenty years that just went for six months to get some money together.

But it's a real-life situation, and you can't say that somebody denies their art to do it. It's too complex for that. A lot of people remain true to their art because nobody likes what they do [laughter]. But they keep doing what they do, and later on—a hundred years later—somebody finds out, hey, they were really good. They were pure artists. Well, I think that might've been rot. They just couldn't sell anything they wrote. So it's once again a real-life process, I think.

4. The Gary McFarland Orchestra, *How to Succeed in Business Without Really Trying*, Verve Records, 1961.

WE: You were signed with the Verve label in the sixties. There were so many Verve recordings in those days with basically the same roster of musicians. Were you all overrecorded?

BB: I think we recorded too much then, probably. The band you heard was what they called the "A band" in New York. They had the best jazz people, that they thought were the best, anyway, that they would get for all the records. One thing we had then that we have a severe shortage of now, we had some very good producers: Creed Taylor first at ABC Paramount, and later on at Verve, Bob Thiele did some good work. We had Jack Lewis in the early fifties and the middle fifties who did some great things at Victor and later on at United Artists. We had people to start projects for us and who had the funding. We have some people now with good ideas that have trouble getting money because the record business has become so catastrophic and such a really big business venture. But the producers then were really instrumental in giving us ideas. They'd think of a project and say, "What do you think of this?" And we would be off on it, so that was a great help.

WE: Have you done much studio work?

BB: Yeah, all my life until about two years ago.

WE: Did you find it stifling?

BB: Well, I'll tell you, in the fifties it was fun because they had jazz-type backgrounds. We had a Bobby Darin date, Al Cohn and Ralph Burns would write the arrangements. And we had a forty-five–piece band you could pat your foot to. But by the sixties, when rock 'n' roll really began to hurt . . .

As I went to California, I really felt I'd sunk into something because I went everywhere and nobody smiled, nobody joked or laughed, you never drank on a date. You never snuck out and got high or anything, you know. It was really serious business, and you were supposed to really act like you respected what you did. And for me, with my personality, it was just murderous, so I couldn't do it; I failed the studio work. A lot of people can do it—work all day with earphones and do rock 'n' roll and come out at night and play for five hours. They have my admiration and gratitude. I couldn't, you know. I just do what I do, that's all.

PR: In the sixties, we'd go to New York's Half Note one night to hear the quintet you co-led with Clark Terry and return the next night to take in the John Coltrane Quartet. Did you and the members of your band ever exchange views with Coltrane?

BB: Not really, not between John and us. My recent experience tells me that people who are now about thirty-five have a very reverential attitude towards those days, toward John and his music, because John is their hero, you know. The day after John died they ran a radio interview in New York, and Bill Evans was speaking of Miles's band and Miles's attitude towards Coltrane, which was supportive. Bill said the rest of us used to wonder why Miles hired him, because he wasn't playing too well. But Miles heard the true Coltrane.

So therefore, when I'd hear John, he'd play one tune for forty-five minutes, and he'd play an awful lot of notes. I'd enjoy it up to a point. So my ears were responding—I didn't feel reverential. He was another man in the same business. I probably should have been more reverential, but there wasn't cross-pollinating between us because John was much more advanced than either Clark or I were. He was consciously trying to advance as an artist, and Clark and I were doing what we did.

PR: Were there jam sessions in the sixties when younger players could get on the bandstand with you and test their mettle?

BB: No, I don't think so then. There weren't the chances. When I first came to New York, I was twenty-two years old, I played piano at a place on the Lower East Side, and it would loosely be called the Dixieland Place. And some nights the four or five horns would be Coleman Hawkins, Pee Wee Russell, Harry Edison, Buck Clayton, and maybe Warne Marsh and Lee Konitz. One night we had a rhythm section of George Wallington, Baby Dodds, and Pops Foster, and I played trombone. So I got to play with a lot of different people.

My observation on somethin' that was true then that may not be true now, I think, could be interesting. When I was in my early twenties and middle twenties I became friendly with the guys in Duke Ellington's band because we did a couple of tours together. I was with either Mulligan or Getz. They were very warm and supportive, and I established, I guess, what the psychologists would call a "father-son relationship," not quite that heavy. But they were fully grown up in my eyes: they were men, and they played like men and lived like men. I was very young, and they would come down gratuitously and say, "Now look," and we'd talk about stuff, rarely music. But we'd talk about the way to live your life or "Where you gonna settle in L.A.?" We'd rub each other, and we'd get warm over the process. So it was an older generation warming up a younger one, saying,

"It's OK, I approve of you, and I support what you do. Now, go out and do it."

They could have hated the way I played music, but they acknowledged me to be in their business, as John [Coltrane] and I, without saying anything, acknowledged [that we were] in each other's business. We didn't have to love each other's playing, but we were in the same area. There was no "He can't play," "He should play this way," or "He can't play at all." We were in the same business, and the guys in Duke's band taught me that, and Count Basie's also.

WE: Do you think that some of the younger so-called avant-garde players today, like George Lewis, are extending the jazz trombone tradition?
BB: Well, sure. I just heard a bit a couple of years ago of a solo trombone album. Obviously the man can play. I don't, as much as I used to, say "Gee, he really can't play, I don't like that." I don't care what I don't like, it's not important. I try to support what I do like, and what I do like are people who are trying to make things better, trying to find ways to expand the language.

In George's case, he is working hard at what he does. People could sit down and say that he doesn't swing. I say, well, OK. There are some jazz musicians who don't swing, and I'm among 'em sometimes, but what else does he do? Jazz is a language. It's now a way of thinking and writing. I'm beginning to write music for jazz orchestra that doesn't bear an awful lot of relationship to 4/4 swing, and it's going to get more and more that way. And I'm going to fight to have my music considered music by a jazz composer. 'Cause that's what I am.

If I were a classical—this is varying it a bit, but I think it's explanatory—if I were a classical composer coming in to write jazz, obviously I would be unsuited. I would say all classical composers are unsuited to write jazz music. That is not their experience. That is not what their feet say. My feet say jazz music, so anything I write I think would come that way because that's what I am.

If somebody comes along in my world and wants to make jazz music better, I say go ahead. I don't have to like it, but I do have to encourage them to keep on doin' it, I think. That's my job, because out of that, you see—I'll maybe explain something that I've come to feel, that all artists kinda work a general field, however big you want to make it in your mind. It's a field of earth. Our job is to go out every morning and work that field all day doing what we do. Once in a while, the musician, whoever it is, comes and drops a seed, and we get a Coltrane or a Charlie Parker or a Jelly Roll Morton or a Louis Armstrong. But the rest of us go out there and plow every day anyway. That's our job.

PR: Is your playing a way for you to find out more about your own identity?

BB: Yeah, well, it is for me, because I need to keep on top of things, you know. I'm a sober alcoholic, and I've been sober for about four years, and my penalty for not living my life in some kind of reasonable and advancing way is probably not living.

So my choices are clear-cut. I'm fortunate: I either live or die every day. It's not dramatic like that, but everybody's choice is life or death. So far, anyway, I opt to live, and my choices toward music are that way. And I've been, fortunately, given a clear-cut choice. A lot of people have the pull between "Shall I be rich today and rich and famous tomorrow" and then "Thursday I'm gonna cut out this nonsense and settle down and really work hard for a couple of days." It's not important because I'm almost fifty-one, and my time has become finite, as everybody's is. When you're twenty-one your time is finite, you know.

Yeah, I'm seeing things clearly, more clearly now for many reasons. That's why I explained the other thing—the alcoholism thing. So a lot of things are clear and getting clearer. I'm in a very fortunate position having been where I have been to get where I am. I think that was worth it. So yes, I try to get more control over me, because that's going to give more control over what I do. Like Lee [Konitz] was talking about. That's why I admire him very much, because he's been an artist and some people are born that way. They just see artistically. It's taken me a long time to even get close to that. Now I'm working probably to where he's been, mentally.

SELECTED DISCOGRAPHY

With Gerry Mulligan. *California Concerts.* Vol. II. Capitol CDP 7-648642. 1954.

With Bill Evans. *The Ivory Hunters.* Untied Artists UA-6044. 1959.

The Blues Hot and Cool. Verve 68385. 1960.

7X Wilder. Verve VG 8413. 1961.

Stan Getz / Bob Brookmeyer. Verve 68418. 1961.

Gerry Mulligan '63 / The Concert Jazz Band. Verve V/V6-8515. 1962.
The Clark Terry–Bob Brookmeyer Quintet. *The Power of Positive Swing-
ing.* Mainstream 6054. 1964.
The Bob Brookmeyer Small Band (Live at Sandy's). Gryphon 785. 1978.
With Mel Lewis. *Live at the Village Vanguard.* Gryphon 912. 1980.
Oslo. Concord CJ-312. 1986.

DAVE BRUBECK

Courtesy Concord Jazz, Inc.

P ianist and composer Dave Brubeck, one of the best-known figures in jazz, has been at the center of controversy almost from the start of his trailblazing career. Steady critical disfavor in the jazz press has accompanied his popularity with a wide circle of fans. Particularly in the fifties and sixties, Dave Brubeck embodied the wisdom that within the echelons of modern jazz nothing wears as poorly as commercial success.

Born in 1920, Brubeck grew up on a cattle ranch in northern California. Despite starting piano lessons at age four and leading his first band while still in high school, he began his university studies in veterinary medicine. After a year, however, he switched to a music major.

Trained in the classics by day at the College of the Pacific music conservatory, Brubeck played jazz in juke joints with local musicians at night. This seeming split in musical identity is symptomatic of Brubeck's affection for masters of both the classical and the jazz idioms. He feels as much at home with Bach and Bartók as he does with Waller and Ellington.

Brubeck first gained popular attention with the quartet he organized in 1951, featuring alto saxophonist Paul Desmond. The group recorded for the California-based Fantasy label until 1954, committing to vinyl some of Brubeck's most enduring work, especially two college concerts recorded live in 1953.[1] During this period, the Brubeck Quartet, along with combos led by Gerry Mulligan and Chico Hamilton, assumed a leading position in what was then called "West Coast cool jazz."

Dave Brubeck's appearance on the cover of *Time* magazine in 1954 accelerated his rise to fame. The period of his greatest public acclaim began after 1956, when drumming phenomenon Joe Morello joined Desmond and bassist Eugene Wright to form the classic Brubeck Quartet. Columbia released *Time Out* in 1959, and it became the first in a line of top-selling albums devoted to explorations of odd time signatures. "Take Five" and "Blue Rondo à la Turk" were excerpted from *Time Out* and issued as a 45-RPM single in 1962. The record sold a million copies, unprecedented at the time for a jazz instrumental.

Dave Brubeck dissolved his famous quartet in 1967 to concentrate

1. *The Art of Dave Brubeck: The Fantasy Years*, Atlantic Records, 1975.

more fully on his writing. The quartet reunited in 1976 for a concert celebrating the twenty-fifth anniversary of its formation and toured until Paul Desmond's death in 1977. Since the eighties, aside from performing his jazz-tinged cantatas and oratorios with symphony orchestras around the globe, Brubeck has continued to tour and record with a series of refurbished quartets, which at times feature his sons, Chris and Darius.

Recorded 1977

WE: Dave, what would it have been like to have been one of your high school teachers?

DB: Well, I was in a high school where there were less than ninety people in the entire school. I was raised in a small community, and I lived about three miles from town. The high school was mostly for farm kind of kids, although there were quite a few that went on to college, and you would have found me as one that didn't want to go.

My main interest was to stay right on the cattle ranch—my dad had a cattle ranch—and I didn't want to go to college, and everybody was willing to accept that except one high school teacher who said I should go to college. His main reason that I should go to college was because of the way I played the piano, not because of any interest in anything scholastically. I was just anti ever gettin' away from that small community, and then my mother insisted that I go to college, and the family made a bargain that I would go to college and study to be a veterinarian.

My first year at school [the College of the Pacific in Stockton, California] I was a premed with the idea of going on to a good veterinary school. But I was still trying to stay home, and I only went to college because of my mother. And the idea would be that when I was a veterinarian I could come back to the ranch.

Now the complication is that I discovered that I had to work *very* hard to keep up with the other students in science and zoology because I had come from a small high school that didn't have good equipment and not the greatest teachers, and on top of it, I wasn't naturally talented in that direction. So after a year of that, my adviser in the science department said, "Brubeck, you seem far more interested in what's goin' on across the lawn in the conservatory than what's goin' on here, and I'd advise you to go over there next year." So I was able to convince my parents that I was a very poor premed student, passing, maybe C average, and I could do most of the homework for the musicians that lived in the boardinghouse, and they were doin' most of my homework—the other science majors—gettin' me through.

So that's what happened. I switched over to being a music major. I had nothing there but natural ability, and I graduated from the conservatory without knowing how to read music, which worked until my senior year. And the last semester I had to take piano because you had to learn every instrument, and my ruse so they would never find out I couldn't read would be always learning a new instrument, and you didn't have to read much. So I learned cello and clarinet, a brass instrument—you had to learn one instrument of each family. But finally, you had to learn a keyboard instrument, and that's where they found me out.

And the dean went up in arms and said I was a disgrace to the conservatory, and they wanted to not graduate me and kick me out, and then some of the other teachers went to bat and said, "He's the most talented guy in school, and you're crazy if you kick him out." So the compromise was that I could graduate if I promised never to teach music [laughter]. Which I promised, and I graduated, and that's the way I got through school.

So you said, "What would it be like to have been one of my teachers?" It would've been an experience, believe me, because I was the worst kind of student possible, and I hated school. To this day anything that smacks of book learnin' and "the way to do it, the one and only way," I'm never very good at.

PR: During those years when you attended the conservatory, what kind of music were you playing on the outside?

DB: Playing jazz six nights a week when I could manage it and sleeping through classes. Because I thought that's where my education was—in the joints where I was playing with older jazz musicians that were good.

But there was a young teacher at the College of the Pacific, his name was J. Russell Bodley. And he was the one that would always go to bat for me. He was interested in jazz, and he had me in harmony and ear training. When no one else [in his class] would know too much what he had played in ear training, they'd wake me up, and he'd say, "Now Brubeck, do you know what just happened?" [Laughter.] I'd give him a roundabout answer, and he'd know I knew, whereas the other students didn't know.

But I never did get a conventional training. When I did graduate work with Darius Milhaud, I still couldn't read music. Which really shook up that conservatory. And it was Milhaud that kept me in the classes and said, "Well, he's got a lot of talent. Someday he'll figure out what to do with it." But I shouldn't have been in any of *his* classes. By osmosis is the way I learned, and that's not too bad if the osmosis is comin' from a Darius Milhaud, who's probably the greatest musician in the world.

WE: Were you exposed to music in your family?

DB: Both of my brothers, older brothers, were fine musicians. One is dean of Palomar College now, and the other is retired head of Santa Barbara High School music. Me being the third son, my dad claimed me for the cattle ranch, and we moved out there. And my mother moved out there too, but she hated every minute of it. And my mother was a piano teacher. Excellent musician. I was just listening to music all the time. I didn't really get involved myself, but I heard the best piano literature from my mother all my life.

WE: Did she play jazz?

DB: No. God, no. The oldest brother, Henry, played jazz and classical. The next brother played only classical, and he was Darius Milhaud's assistant at Mills College in Oakland. The one that's "Dean Brubeck" now. So I heard great music all my life, jazz and classical.

PR: Do you regret not having studied in a more conventional way?

DB: Almost all the guys I've known that've really been individuals have had a weird background. Like a [Erroll] Garner that never learned to read and the blind guys that have not studied in a conventional way, but studied. I would consider the greatest musical genius that I've ever met in my life was Art Tatum. I would put him against any American musician I've ever known. So there's a lot to be said for the people that do not come out of the mold, so to speak.

And I would say that so many great jazz musicians are guys that came out of playing in joints or in big bands. I just played a festival in Europe where there were two hundred jazz musicians, and all of us approach music in a different way. Whereas you take the average conservatory, and they come out of there like they're comin' out of an automobile factory. So let it be said a lot for the gypsies, the Django Reinhardts of the world, the Art Tatums who could hear anything once and play it exactly like he heard it and then turn around and improvise the rest of the day on it. They weren't the conventional types. Duke Ellington isn't a conventional type, Louis Armstrong wasn't the conventional type, just to name a few. And long live the individual who educates himself [laughter].

WE: Who were you listening to when you were playing those gigs six nights a week?

DB: Fats Waller, Teddy Wilson, Art Tatum, Duke Ellington. And then the unknown guys that are scattered all over the country. Last night at Lake Tahoe I was talking with a bandleader there, and he mentioned, "Did you go through the College of the Pacific in Stockton?" We were talkin' about it. He said, "One of my best friends went through that school."

And I remembered this guy. He was a great baseball player, and he was a natural musician with perfect pitch and total recall. So he pitched for the Chicago, would it be, White Sox? His brother also had perfect pitch, and I'm not talking about a baseball pitch [laughter]. He's still pitchin', or he's on the coaching staff of that team. They shoulda had fantastic careers.

Sometimes you can work in a joint, right here in this town, there'll be some guys playin' that, had they wanted to go out and stick with it like I did for thirty years, could've made it and been internationally known. That's why I always respect the guys anyplace I go, because the first guy I ever heard that scared me to death came out of Sonora, California, out of a mining camp. You never know where they're gonna be, but it's usually these people with a natural gift from God—perfect pitch and total recall.

WE: Do you listen to pop music with the same philosophy?

DB: You try to avoid it but keep an open mind, because the next record on a pop station nowadays *could* be Herbie Hancock [laughter]. Not too often, but you gotta keep an open mind to everything. My recordings of "Take Five" and "Blue Rondo" hit the pop charts, and it was a challenge to all the musicians.[2] So you can't say that something very challenging won't come out of the pop field.

Sometimes you'll hear a rock guitar player and know that he's fantastic. And it'll just be this natural raw talent. You'll hear it from a hillbilly-type band or harmonica player that's had no training, and you just look for those individuals, and they can be in any form of music—classical, jazz, pop, or rock and roll.

PR: Did your quartet widen the audience for jazz in the fifties?

DB: Well, the acceptance of "Take Five" and "Blue Rondo" really shook

2. "Take Five" and "Blue Rondo à la Turk," recorded by the Dave Brubeck Quartet, on *Time Out*, Columbia Records, 1959.

the whole industry up, and a lot of the myths about popular music, jazz music, were canceled out by that recording. But I want to mention that when I was in high school in this small town in northern California, the pop music of that day happened to be Duke Ellington, Glenn Miller, Tommy Dorsey, Jimmy Dorsey, Count Basie. A commercial thing would be Ella Fitzgerald doing "A Tisket, a Tasket." So what happened to those great days where the pop music of the country was really great art music, great American music?

I think that after the war, when I came home in 1946, that musically the country had been destroyed. I couldn't believe the transition. The big bands were on the wane, the music in the nightclubs, which was our rehearsal—the place we all grew to be musicians in—the atmosphere was terrible in the clubs; where it used to have been the most friendly, there was racial problems.

WE: Was your quartet one of the groups that helped rebuild the public's interest in jazz?

DB: With the things we were doing, the public did, I think, get led back into jazz, in a wider acceptance. Because the great bebop players had turned their back on the public. Now I don't want to take the credit alone, but the guys that came along at about that time were being more friendly with the public—my group, the Modern Jazz Quartet, Garner, [George] Shearing. Shearing's was very important as a group that was opening that up again.

When I put out the *Time Out* album, it was against Columbia's policy because it was all originals, it was all different. I wanted to use a beautiful painting for covers—that was unknown. So we did turn it around. We got what you'd call "concept albums" going. *Time Out* was a concept album where we were using all time signatures that were out of the usual.

PR: Were there other groups in jazz using unusual time signatures?

DB: Well, in 1946 I could have done an album like that, but the public wasn't ready, and no record company would've recorded it. And I don't think I would have done it as well then.

There was a group led by Max Roach in New York that was getting into time signatures, but he didn't know what I was doin', and I didn't know what he was doin'. And then we met in Detroit at a concert, and we both said, "Hey, your group's doin' something interesting." We talked, and we're still friends. But that's the only group I knew that was doin' that—getting away from 4/4, and 3/4, and 2/4.

WE: Turning back to the late forties, were you and your band members influenced in general by the new music of the time?

DB: As far as other people influencing me or the members of my group to do new things, no. Because we were isolated in San Francisco, and it was a city where nothing much was happening in the late forties and early fifties. And then all of a sudden it was a city where everything started happening. Like the first concert that Mort Sahl ever played was with me. I asked Mort, I said, "You know, you come on at intermission and see what happens, and don't consider yourself just a nightclub act." And he took this concert audience just by surprise. Here was a comedian with such an IQ and such awareness.

And also out of San Francisco at that time came the Kingston Trio and [Lawrence] Ferlinghetti, and other poets, and Johnny Mathis. Pretty quick you looked around and the strongest things that were happening in the whole nation were coming right out of the Purple Onion, the Hungry Eye, the Blackhawk. So you never know, you know. But that became a great period for us—all of us.

WE: Wasn't Stan Kenton involved in new time signatures at about that time?

DB: No, he wasn't, I don't think. He was involved in great things himself. I took my first big-band arrangement to Stan when I was twenty-one years old. And he said, "Bring it back in ten years." Which was a compliment. You know, he wasn't saying, "You're crazy, young kid." People didn't want to play my music, and they weren't ready for me when I was a kid. I don't say that I was great and accomplished, but I *was* ahead of my time.

PR: So the mid- to late forties were hard times for you?

DB: Sure. I rehearsed the Dave Brubeck Octet for three years without a job. We lived on, oh, maybe eighty dollars a month, my family, whatever the GI bill was paying at the time. But it was a great period in my life, because I was surrounded with great musicians like Paul Desmond, Cal Tjader, Bill Smith. Everybody from those starvation days made it in my eight-piece group, but we couldn't get a job. That's why I took the rhythm section from my octet and went into this period where we played only standards.

My first recordings were "Tea for Two," "Blue Moon," "Back Home Again in Indiana," and "Laura"—all big standards. And for the ensuing years I wrote nothing, and I developed a following with the trio. And then I started the quartet, and I wasn't writin' original music very much, and one night Paul Desmond said, "What we need is to hire somebody to write original music for us." And I said, "*Paul*, I can write two tunes before midnight," and this was after a concert. And I wrote "In Your Own Sweet Way" and a thing called "The Waltz" within a half hour or an hour. And from then on I started writing to the point where I was writing all original material again.

WE: According to some jazz scribes, your band with Paul Desmond in the early fifties was part of the West Coast cool school. Do you agree with that?

DB: No, it's absolutely wrong. Because I could play you old records where anybody who'd call my piano playing "cool," they're crazy. It was torrid [laughter]. And at the same time they're callin' it "cool." But it was called that because intellectually we looked cool. Paul Desmond and I always wore business suits; the whole group did, and we were in a framework that they weren't used to on the East Coast. And we approached playing with a different kind of attitude, and I think the attitude was cool.

But my playing has never been cool. Paul's playing might have a coolness in his beautiful clear tone. I could see why you could call Paul "cool," but at the same time you should call Lee Konitz "cool," and he's on the East Coast. Why ain't they callin' Lee Konitz "cool," then? I think he was classified cool, but then they got it mixed up with East Coast–West Coast. Geographically jazz has usually had a handle, like New Orleans or Chicago or St. Louis style, and we just got stuck with West Coast.

PR: Jazz critics have also commented that your piano playing is often heavy-handed, or too percussive. How do you respond to that and to what critics say generally?

DB: Well, they're usually wrong. To really criticize somebody like myself you should go on the road for about a year with me and hear what it's all about. I think the essence of what jazz is supposed to be is creative, or else why not play classical music?

But I couldn't tell you what style I play. I don't know what style I'm gonna play tonight, and when I finish one tune, I don't know what the style of the next tune is gonna be. But I can tell you where they've missed the boat is I probably played the most delicate piano of anybody playin' and the most severe, loud, and everything in between, and they've only heard, as critics, when I really used to get some strength goin'. And if a guy is a milk-toast kind of a guy he just can't take that, and that's what he would remember of the whole night.

Sometimes the piano wasn't big enough for me, you know, and I'd really lay on it and get some strength out of it. And when I hear what the rock kids are doing with all the amplification, I kinda realize what I was trying to do, only I wasn't amplified [laughter]. Sometimes I played a lot louder than anybody I know, but that's the way I wanted to play. Sometimes a lot softer. Those guys never seemed to have been around when I did "Koto Song."[3] They can hear a whole recording of mine, and maybe on one track it was loud, that's all they would remember. And percussive—the piano happens to be a percussive instrument.

WE: Paul Desmond died recently. Since you knew him as a musician and a human being probably better than anybody, could you give us some insight into what he was like?

DB: Well, *genius*, if we're in a hurry, covers him. Probably inadequately. And wit, beyond most people I've met.

WE: Could you give us some examples of his wit?

DB: Well, just the whole day might be spent without him saying much, especially before noon. We all knew to be silent, and if you're gonna survive for thirty years like Paul and I did, you give a lot of silence to each other. But there might be—like he made the statement he wanted his alto saxophone playing to sound like a dry martini. And his wit was like that. He would sum up something in one sentence that would just cut through a room.

If you ask me to tell you some funny things he said, it's very hard to recall 'em except every day there'd be a capper, so to speak. I can't think of any right at the moment that I could tell you. He had us constantly breaking up when he was playing, because the wit went into the solo lines that he'd be playin' on saxophone. And they were *so* far out. And we'd talk occasionally through themes—quote another song relating to what's going on in the nightclub or the concert. And we would talk back and forth by playing tunes in the middle of another tune that would tell what's going on that night.

PR: How did you meet him?

DB: When I was in the army in '44, I was going overseas. I went into the

---

3. "Koto Song," recorded by the Dave Brubeck Quartet, on *Jazz Impressions of Japan*, Columbia Records, 1964.

army in '42. I was goin' over as a rifleman in the infantry, so I was tryin' to get into a band at the Presidio in San Francisco. When I auditioned for the band, Paul was in that band, and we had a session after the audition. And it's often been quoted that he thought I was stark-raving mad, because harmonically he didn't know what I was into.

Then after the war we got together again, because he was curious. He'd sit in every night where I was playin' in San Francisco, and we discovered that we played very well together. And he opened areas for me, and I opened areas for him. We both loved Bach and Stravinsky and a lot in between. We would start improvising in the style of Bach or quote from Stravinsky or Bartók. Most guys I was playing with at the time didn't have the knowledge that Paul had.

Trying to get over Paul's death is very hard for me and for my sons. The last concert he played was with us. It's been a rough time for us. We were his family; he didn't have a family. He didn't have a family per se, but he had a whole family in the world that felt close to him, and he felt close to them. Nobody's gonna fill that void.

WE: One of our favorite recordings of yours is *The Real Ambassadors*, which is actually a full-fledged musical production.[4] Was this work ever produced on, for instance, Broadway?

DB: Well, it was only produced *once* live, and that was at the Monterey Jazz Festival. To this day they say it was the most moving thing that ever happened at Monterey. And I can believe it, because I was there that night, and to me it was probably the most moving thing in my entire career. With Louis Armstrong's band, my band with Eugene Wright, Joe Morello, Carmen McRae, and Lambert, Hendricks, and Bavan, the vocal group, it was a stage loaded with talent. And my wife was on a different stage, 'cause she'd written the show for Louis, where she was narrating what would have had gone on had we been on a Broadway show, say. But there wasn't time to do the whole production, and she would give the audience the background, which would lead into the next action onstage.

There were TV cameras there that night, and if I'd had the money that they wanted to do a taping—it was $750, which I didn't have and I couldn't get from anybody—I'd had this forever, and it would've been the greatest thing I'd ever owned, but it got away from us.

4. *The Real Ambassadors*, with Louis Armstrong, written by Dave and Iola Brubeck, Columbia Records, 1962.

PR: As you mentioned, *The Real Ambassadors* was written as a tribute to Louis Armstrong. Tell us about his performance that night in Monterey.
DB: Looking back on that night I could just tell you that Louis was inspired. Well, he was usually inspired, but that was one night where—he delivered the lines of the play with great conviction. If you listen to the album you can hear Louis almost crying where he says "really free." If you play that album someday and then know that that was in a studio and there *wasn't* an audience, but the way he delivered those lines in Monterey . . .

This was a play we couldn't get done on Broadway because the Broadway producers said you can't have a black and white integrated show in that period. There'd been way before and way later, but this was a time when nobody would risk that. You could have a show, an opera like *Porgy and Bess*, which wasn't successful either if you'll recall, where it was all black. But this country was way too long hung up on racial relationships, which is a disgrace of the country. And people like Louis helped solve them without saying much, just being Louis.

And this show hit at the racial relationships, but never hard—it hit at them in a funny way. I would use things from the Bible and try to show people how hypocritical it is to judge a man by the color of his skin. So I had lines that I thought would make the audience laugh, and Louis delivered 'em, and he made them cry. So that shows you how he was delivering the lines that night.

You see, this all seems like old hat, but there was a time when racial relationships were so terrible, like I couldn't be on television with my black bass player, on the *biggest* shows in this country less than twenty years ago. The compromise was that they would keep my black bass player so you couldn't see him, but you could hear him. I told them to forget the show. Now Duke Ellington did that show with an all-black orchestra. So they weren't against black people, they were against integration—less than twenty years ago. So we've come a long way here.

Now the reason we came a long way was because of Nat Cole, Louis Armstrong, and people like this that the public loved. Willie Mays, athletes, boxers. It shouldn't have been the athletes and boxers, it should've been the average citizen that was making us come a long way, but we were too prejudiced. It had to be somebody that got in the public limelight because they were so loved, like a Louis was loved by everybody. You could put words into the mouth of someone like this that the public loved, and then they'd listen. And this was what I was tryin' to do with this show.

And the line that I thought would make everybody laugh was—I used Genesis—"They say I look like God, and God is black, my God. If both are made in the image of thee, could thou perchance a zebra be?" Now I thought that that was gonna be a funny line, but the way Louis delivered it, there were tears—the sound in his voice, you know—and he kept doing that throughout the show.

I was tryin' to get the thing *light* so we could attack racial prejudice, and Louis was so emotional in talking about really being free. "Love to me is like a summer day." Do you remember that? The day Louis died they played that in New York on one of the stations, which I thought was a great tribute to Louis, and I was happy I'd written it. Happy my wife had written it. But the feeling in that show which I thought would be light was one of great love for Louis. We shoulda done that on Broadway; there shoulda been a movie made of it. It woulda documented Louis in many ways. I had considered I had written a Broadway show for Louis— Broadway-type show—and Louis said, "Brubeck wrote me an opera" [laughter].

So that's how he considered it. And to think that at his age—he was, I think, sixty-one when he did this—and on the road, one-nighters and everything, that he could get down into his mind all that music, 'cause he had to carry the lead in that show. Shows you what a great mind . . . And he couldn't read music in a conventional way. We'd write it out for him, and here again is what I'm talkin' about. He had me play all that stuff and put it on a tape, and he'd listen to it, and also the notes written out too, and the combination of that—he was the quickest study I've ever seen in a recording studio.

So what difference does it make whether he could read in a conventional way? If you talk to Bing Crosby or anybody else who's worked with him, they'll tell you the same thing. He did it Louis Armstrong style. His ear was phenomenal. He just didn't make mistakes. This old guy on the end of this record, he goes up and hits a high F about ten times in a row. The average young, strong college student that plays trumpet will tell you that that takes an iron man. Here he was over sixty years old.

WE: A last question. Since 1968 you've spent a lot of time composing oratorios, cantatas, and symphonic pieces. Does jazz play a role in these works?

DB: Yeah. It's always there, and it always will be there. And that's what Darius Milhaud told me: "If you wanna express this country, you will always use the jazz idiom. The people that are just going to Europe and studying and have a lot better background than you, they're not gonna say as much." He would always defend jazz. He'd say, "You know, never forget you're a jazz musician. Don't keep saying that it's nothing and putting it down," because, he said, "I'd love to be able to do what you can do." And I couldn't believe that [laughter].

SELECTED DISCOGRAPHY

Dave Brubeck / Paul Desmond. Fantasy F-24727. 1951–53.

The Art of Dave Brubeck: The Fantasy Years. Atlantic SD2-317. 1975.
Reissue of *Jazz at Oberlin* and *Jazz at College of the Pacific,* 1953.

David Brubeck's All-Time Greatest Hits. Columbia PG-32761. 1956–65.

Time Out. Columbia CG33666 CDCBS 62068. 1959.

With Louis Armstrong. *The Real Ambassadors.* Columbia Masterworks C5850. 1962.

With Gerry Mulligan. *Blues Roots.* Columbia CS9749. 1970.

With Anthony Braxton and Lee Konitz. *All the Things We Are.* Atlantic SD1684. 1973–74.

Brubeck and Desmond, 1975: The Duets. A&M CD3290. 1975.

Reflections. Concord CCD4299. 1985.

New Wine. MusicMasters 5051-2-C. 1987.

RAY BRYANT

Courtesy Fantasy, Inc.

P ianist-composer Ray Bryant is a compulsive swinger. At the core
of his hard-driving music are his affinity for the blues and his deep
roots in the heritage of jazz. Bryant is a vital contemporary link to boogie
and barrelhouse pianists, and his abiding respect for the stride legacy of
James P. Johnson is evident in his performances. Added to these prime
sources are his early experiences with gospel music and rhythm and blues
in Philadelphia, where he was born in 1931. Bryant also occasionally colors his playing with the Afro-Cuban rhythms that inspired one of his
most enduring compositions, "Cubano Chant."

Bryant's love for the blues form grew out of his early contacts with
African-American religious music, specifically his family's involvement in
the black gospel church. His first professional job was with Billy Kretch-
ner's dixieland band, based in his hometown. Following that two-year
stint, Bryant, then twenty-two, headed the house trio at Philadelphia's
Blue Note jazz club, where he accompanied a pantheon of jazz giants,
including Lester Young, Dizzy Gillespie, John Coltrane, Sonny Stitt,
Miles Davis, and vocalist Anita O'Day.

In the mid-fifties Bryant served briefly as a member of the reorganized
Clifford Brown–Max Roach Quintet after an automobile accident claimed
the lives of Brown and his pianist, Richie Powell. Bryant moved to New
York late in 1957, following two years on the road as Carmen McRae's
regular accompanist and a brief period in the Jo Jones Trio. He soon
established himself as a sideman in mainstream groups led by Coleman
Hawkins, Charlie Shavers, and Roy Eldridge and in modern units fronted
by the likes of Donald Byrd, Benny Golson, and Sonny Rollins.

Miles Davis helped arrange Bryant's recording debut as part of an all-
star group in 1955. In 1959 the tune "Little Susie," penned and played
by Bryant, was a best-seller, which gave him a boost in public profile.[1]
His reputation as a deep-dyed, full-keyboard blues piano player took on
added luster that year when John Hammond recommended him as house
pianist at the Newport Jazz Festival. Subsequently, Hammond signed
Bryant to a recording contract with Columbia Records.

1. Ray Bryant, *Little Susie*, reissued on Columbia Special Products, 1973.

The commercial success of "Little Susie" enabled Bryant's trio to get steady bookings on the club circuit. After Bryant left Columbia, however, some unfruitful associations with other labels saw his popularity decline in the United States. But his stature rose in Europe and Japan, initially on the delayed influence of his essential 1958 recording, *Ray Bryant Alone with the Blues.*[2]

Since Bryant joined Pablo Records in the seventies, his records, on that label and others, have been dependably excellent. Although he tours constantly and is a particular favorite with audiences at European jazz festivals, he remains underappreciated in the United States. This is particularly tragic since, at age sixty, Ray Bryant is one of the few remaining genuine heirs of the classic blues and jazz innovators of the past. Recent testimony to his credentials can be found in his EmArcy release *Ray Bryant Plays Basie and Ellington* (EmArcy/Polygram, 1987), in which Bryant again swings deep in the tradition.

Recorded 1978

WE: Ray, considering your gifts as a pianist and your longevity as a jazz musician, why is it that you are not well known in the United States?

RB: Well, that's a hard question to answer [laughter]. Actually in some places I am pretty well known, such as in Europe and so forth. I was on the Cadet label for three or four years, during which time some of my albums were maybe a little misguided, because Cadet was a more or less commercially oriented record company. And they sort of influenced what I recorded, even though once in a while I think we managed to get in somethin' that was pretty good. But for the most part they were lookin' for records which would reach a much broader segment of the listening audience, as they put it.

So those years with the Cadet people were more or less lost, you know. And before that I was with another company by the name of Sue, and we did some things there which were not among my best recorded efforts. Before that I think my best things were done on Prestige and Columbia and like that. So anyway, I'm with Pablo now and, as some people seem to think, back on the right track [laughter]. At any rate, with Pablo I have the freedom to do *exactly* what I want to do.

2. *Ray Bryant Alone with the Blues* has been reissued as Ray Bryant, *Me and the Blues*, Prestige Records, 1974.

As to why I'm not better known, like I say, in some parts of the world I *am* much better known that I am here in the United States—Europe and Japan, you know. I do tours of Japan *and* Europe and mostly on the strength of things I did many, many years ago—the Prestige *Alone with the Blues* solo record. It's been reissued maybe three or four times since it was recorded originally. And things which I've done with other musicians, as a sideman, with Sonny Rollins, Max Roach, and so many others. So it's on the strength of these things, I guess, that the general jazz public knows me. But it just happens that, I don't know why, more people in Europe and Asia know about me than here in the United States.

PR: A new generation of pianists has come to the forefront in recent years led by the likes of Keith Jarrett, Chick Corea, and Herbie Hancock. In your own mind, how does your style compare with theirs?

RB: Well, I'll tell you, I don't get a chance to listen to Keith Jarrett or Chick Corea too much, but from what I do hear they're doing things which are sort of aimed at the fusion jazz listener, whatever fusion music is—I guess that's a sort of mixture of pop and jazz rock or somethin' like that, you know. Whereas I guess the things I do would appeal more to the traditional jazz listener, like the Europeans, who are more interested in solo piano, so to speak, and the real two-handed approach in the style of a Fats Waller and Earl Hines.

The kids today are more interested in the things that Keith Jarrett would be doing or Chick Corea. And in the United States this is listened to. I guess it has to be since it's played so much more on the air. I mean, you very seldom will hear an Earl Hines record on the air or a Fats Waller, you know, except on special stations. Whereas in Europe you very seldom will hear a Chick Corea or a Keith Jarrett record on the jazz stations.

I think that the more down-to-earth, deeply rooted style of playing is much more listened to in Europe and Asia and places like that than it is in the United States simply because the jazz over here has been sorta swallowed up by the pop and rock influences, you know. The record companies see the chance to capitalize on this and use the jazz musicians' creativity and ingenuity to their advantage. And the guys like Chick Corea and Herbie Hancock and guys like that have, of course, recorded in that idiom, and of course, they've gained much more acceptance than a guy who's playing the things that I play.

WE: As you mentioned, the roots of your playing go deep: James P.

Johnson, Art Tatum, and Teddy Wilson come to mind. In your travels do you meet many people who are informed about past greats of the music?

RB: Well, I feel sorry for the ones who really don't know about the old musicians. But there's a reason that they don't know, and the reason is because they've never been exposed to it. They've never heard these people. You'd be surprised how many people I run into who've never heard of Art Tatum or Teddy Wilson. But if you mention Herbie Hancock, they know who he is, or Chick Corea, or the other guys, they know exactly who they are.

WE: Were you influenced at an early age by past greats of the keyboard?

RB: I really can't explain exactly how *I* came to play this way except for the fact that Art Tatum has always been my piano hero, and Teddy Wilson. I always list these two guys as my main influences, you know. And then when the bop era came in, I listened to Bud Powell. And I like playing solo piano. I like playing the old tunes. I like playing the blues, and I understand that there aren't too many guys who can play the blues [laughter] like that, you know. It's just my way of playing. But I also like the more, if you will, modern things; I always include things like "Django" on my program, you know.

I guess it's just what struck me from a very young fellow, you know. When I was twelve or thirteen years old I was playing with the older guys. Guys who were maybe forty, forty-five, fifty, sixty years old, you know. Or it may have something to do with the fact that I come from a gospel background. My mother is a minister, and I guess one of my earliest influences would be gospel music, which is very closely associated with jazz and blues and things like that. It's just a feeling amongst musicians and people, like Coleman Hawkins, you know, I can relate to what he was saying. Lester Young and Charlie Parker. They all had a part of this immense mass spiritual thing.

PR: Do you feel that your playing embodies a different heritage than may be found in many other prominent jazz pianists today?

RB: I guess it depends a lot upon your early experiences. Like I said, my early experiences were with rhythm-and-blues men, mostly. I mean hard-swinging rhythm-and-blues guys, you know, and I guess I stay with it because I figured this is the way it should be, this is jazz, swinging profound music.

And I've never gotten away from the belief that jazz is 4/4 swinging music, you know, one, two, three, four, one, two, three, four. Course guys have carried it in different directions, 5/4 and 3/4, and this, that, with the rock beat and so forth. But actually when you turn on a jazz program in most cities now it's hard to find any of the good old-fashioned 4/4 swinging jazz. They very seldom put on a Lester Young record or Coleman Hawkins record. They put on the fusion stuff now, you know, with the rock beat and so forth like that. But to *me* when you say "jazz," it's the 4/4 swing. That's the way I see it.

WE: Is playing solo the supreme test of a pianist's abilities?

RB: Playing solo piano is a challenge in itself, you know. The piano, it's all there, and the piano player should be able to play it alone, and it's gotta swing too. That's a challenge with just two hands, and as far as I'm concerned nobody swung it like Fats Waller and James P. Johnson and those guys, you know. And even though I've never made a conscious effort to imitate them or even try to be like them, I guess I've definitely been influenced by those guys through, well, definitely through Tatum, because he's the one that I listened to most and he was definitely influenced by Fats Waller and James P. Johnson and all those other guys, you know. And that to me is piano playing. That to me is playing the piano. All those notes are there, and it's a complete instrument unto itself, and you should be able to play it alone and make it sound full and not miss anything. Of course, the drums are not there, and the bass fiddle's not there, but you should be able to play the piano without that.

PR: Did you ever meet Art Tatum?

RB: I met him one time, one time. And it almost killed me. I was maybe fourteen or fifteen years old, and I was playing in a nightclub in Philadelphia where I really had no business being because I was too young, but they always let me in to play anyway. One night the door opened, and in walked Art Tatum. I knew who it was. So right away I became all thumbs, you know. And I'll never forget at intermission I made it a point to meet him, and he says, "That was nice." And so that really made me feel good. That's the only time I ever really got that close to him. Of course, I heard him play a couple concerts in Philadelphia prior to that meeting. But that's the only time I really got close to him.

PR: Your playing is so much more spare than Tatum's. Is there a certain pianistic way that he influenced you?

RB: Well, he was the most logical pianist I've ever heard. If there were two or three different ways of, like, in the course of playing a song, you know, there are sets of harmonics which go with the melodies. Now there are alternate ways of playing. We call 'em "substitute changes," you know, like that. But it always seemed to me that the harmonies and harmonics that Tatum would select to play were the best that could be chosen. He was very, very precise. Everything was where it's supposed to be.

And a lot of people say, "Well, he made a lot of runs, but they didn't make any sense." But that's not so. Every note in every run had a reason. Every note had a reason, and there was nothing that would have sounded any better in that spot but that run that he made. I don't play that way, because I don't have the technical proficiency to do the things that he did, nor would I want to, I guess. I just don't think like that. Even though I feel that he's the best that ever did it, I don't try to imitate him or anything like that. I just feel like he was the best, you know. Harmonically, he was impeccable, and when he played a song it was played, and there's just no better way to do it.

PR: Tatum played dozen of standards. If he played them to perfection, doesn't that set up an obstacle for you when you want to play those same pieces?

RB: No, it doesn't. I don't know why not. I can't tell you why it doesn't [laughter]. Even though I might be that crazy about the way he did it, I still wouldn't want to do it that way. This may sound contradictory, but I still feel like I have my own way to do it. No, I mean, that that would lead to complete imitation, you know. It's like I enjoy listenin' to lots of guys, lots of piano players. I'm a great listener. That's my hobby, you know. I like to go and hear other guys play. Just go and listen to them, you know. Tommy Flanagan, Cedar Walton.

WE: Were you influenced at all by the so-called free jazz of the sixties?

RB: I don't think so. No. I listened to it. It was there. It seems to have receded a little now, I would say, you know. But even though, that did leave its mark on music. Of course, I enjoyed some of it—I enjoyed quite a bit of it. But it never occurred to me that maybe I should start doing that as opposed to what I was doing. That *never* occurred to me.

And John Coltrane, I can put on his records now, especially the things that he did in the late fifties, early sixties. Miles Davis had the group with Cannonball [Adderley], remember that? And also in the early days of Coltrane's own group after the Miles Davis thing, you know. I can enjoy every note he plays. I can hang on every note he plays. The same with Miles Davis, you know, from a certain era there. Of course, I had the opportunity and the privilege of playing with all those guys. I worked with Coltrane around Philadelphia. I've worked with Charlie Parker, Dizzy, *everybody*.

But I know what you mean. There was a certain period they called the "freedom period" or somethin' like that, right? When you'd just play anything, and that's what it sounded like [laughter]. That never did bother me too much, you know.

WE: In what direction is your music growing?

RB: I know that having lived through the fifties and sixties some of the ways that the guys went are definitely not the way I'm gonna go or anything like that. I feel like this part of jazz—the basic down-to-earth jazz—*that* wasn't explored enough.

I like to develop my thing harmonically but not in the way that some guys are going, like with the modal things. There's a different way to go, which I hear, I don't know exactly, I have no name for it or anything like that. But once in a while when I'm playing I do something, and I say "Yeah, I think I'm getting a little closer to it," you know.

But this involves, you know, it's never going to leave the basic swinging foundation thing. Which is where I think lots of young guys now who start out playing or who want to play jazz are at a disadvantage because they're never heard or experienced the rudimentary things of the Lester Youngs, and the Chu Berrys, and the Art Tatums, and like that, you know. Those guys were definitely headed in the right direction, and who knows where they would've ended up had they lived longer. And I want to go along somewhat in *that* direction.

But I wanna take it a little farther than that, you know. Charlie Parker started, and he went a little farther. Then I think Coltrane was heading in the direction which I liked, and then he veered off and went someplace else. I don't know exactly where [I want to take it], but it's not headed towards atonality or anything like that, 'cause, you know, I don't try to confound anybody when I play. I don't try to confuse anybody or snow 'em or anything like that. But at the same time I want to progress as far as I can harmonically and technically also. I just want to play that piano to the best of my ability and go as far with it as I can in the direction that I feel is right, and so far I really haven't found anybody who is going in the direction that I would really like to go in.

PR: Nobody on the scene now?

RB: No.

PR: So you're pretty much alone. Do you ever get together with other musicians just to talk jazz and listen to records?

RB: Well, I guess the closest I come to something like that would be if maybe Harry Edison might invite me to his home, you know. So we invariably end up putting on some Art Tatum records. And every time we listen to these records we hear somethin' different, you know, and so we just listen, and Tatum does somethin', and we look at each other, and we know exactly what he meant. So we communicate like that. Most of the guys that I feel I can talk to and relate to, like that, they're mostly the older, seasoned musicians.

See, one of the guys that I think I would have liked to have been associated with on a lifelong basis, had he lived, a guy like Clifford Brown. He's one. I don't know of many pianists that I would just like to collaborate with, and be with, and exchange ideas with, and so forth like that. I can't think of anybody right around now. I guess I go more or less my own way.

WE: Are there opportunities for you to jam with other musicians, or have those sessions pretty much disappeared?

RB: That's the way it is generally now. There just isn't too much more the jam-session thing going on. In the first place, more guys now find themselves involved with having to make a living, and we don't have time to jam, you know. And most of the guys now when they play they have to be paid, because they don't have too much time to play for just fun.

The closest we get to a jam-session setting now would be like in a festival, like the Nice Festival or something like that, when the festival just happens to bring together eighty-five or ninety or a hundred musicians. It's like I myself, if I'm at home, like I very seldom say, "I'm gonna go out and just find a jam session and play," you know. It's been years since I've even thought like that. And I think that most of the guys, you know, don't think like that anymore because it has become something like a business too. It's hard to explain. You have to be sort of, well, schizophrenic. I mean, we love it as an art, and I would definitely not want to do anything else, but still it's your living too. You know, we're not subsidized or anything like that, and we don't do anything else.

PR: If jazz is an art form, is there a conflict between the serious side of the music and the fact that people often come to clubs to be entertained?

RB: No. Even though it's an art, it's an art which can be enjoyed, and it should be enjoyed. It swings, and it moves people. This doesn't detract from the artistic qualities of it. I like to play and see people enjoy themselves, you know. I play in places where people drink and so forth like that, and talk sometimes, but I also play concerts sometimes, and in most cases, I play the same things. So it's something that an audience can listen to seriously, and I'm serious when I play it too, you know. I'm just as serious when I'm playing for a drinking crowd as I am when I'm playing for a concert audience.

PR: Is it frustrating at times when people don't pay attention?

RB: Well, yeah. But the music itself is just so broad, you know, it encompasses everything. You can't say that this is only for listening, it's only for people who are musically educated, who can analyze it and take it apart and see exactly what it is. It's not only for those people, you know. It's for the guy who really doesn't understand, but that's where this deep spiritual thing comes in. The fellow who is just listening, who really has no musical knowledge, he can get that too. It comes through to him—from *you* to *him*. Somewhere in all your complicated notes there's a definite message going out to this guy, and he *gets* it.

Like guys used to come up to me and say, "I like what you did there. You inverted the third, and you suspended that," and so on. And I say, "Oh, I did." So fine, he can get that from that because he knows the music. But then another guy will come up to me right after him and say, "That was beautiful, that really moved me, you know, that was nice." And he doesn't know anything about music. So that's very gratifying. You get to everybody.

WE: How old were you when you had your first gig?

RB: I started playing when I was around twelve years old for dances and things like that, you know, along with little small bands.

WE: Did you start with piano and stay with it?

RB: Yeah. I played a little bass fiddle during high school, that's only because, like in the orchestra, the classical orchestra, there was only room for one pianist, you know, and that chair was taken long before I got there. Of course, in a jazz band in the school I occupied the only piano chair in that, you know. So I played a little bass fiddle—classical bass fiddle. Played tuba, sousaphone, things like that. But it was only just in passing; I was never serious about it. Piano has always been my main concern.

WE: How old are you now?

RB: I'm forty-seven.

WE: So from ages twelve to forty-seven you've been playing piano pretty much continuously?

RB: Yes, I have, yeah. I mean, I don't practice five hours every day or anything like that, you know. It's become a way of life—it's part of me—it's a way of life. That's why I don't think I could become musically frustrated or anything, because the whole spectrum is just so big, you know, and you have to realize that you're never going to be able to encompass it all. The piano's somethin' that I live with. I play the piano, and they say, "Well, Ray Bryant plays the piano." I'm a piano player. As far as I know I've always played the piano. I started taking lessons when I was five or six years old, and as far as I know I will play until I die.

It's like the skin on my body. I know that my skin's gonna be with me, hopefully, as long as I live, right? And the piano's gonna be with me as long as I live, and I'm gonna be with the piano as long as I live. And if I do things which people might deem to be great in this process, fine. But I will always be serious about it and love it and want to do it to the best of my ability. There've been years when I was maybe going through some emotional crisis or some difficulty in my life when I didn't play as much as I have in other years. But I never worried; I knew that that piano was there just like the skin on my hand, and it wasn't going anywhere. I wasn't going to leave it; it was not gonna leave me.

PR: You spoke earlier of playing with so many great musicians. Do you have favorite memories of some of those people that you could tell us about?

RB: I have little stories to tell about most of the guys I know that I wouldn't repeat here [laughter]. But OK, take for an example, like this finger here, the index finger. Every time I look at this finger I think of Lester Young, because it just happens that Lester Young was appearing in Philadelphia at a place called the Blue Note, and I happened to have the house trio. In that capacity I and my trio would provide accompaniment for any musician who came to town alone. So that's how I met most of the guys that I know: Lester Young, Charlie Shavers, Dizzy Gillespie, Sonny Rollins, Clifford Brown, everybody, you know, who came to town alone and we would play for them.

Anyway, one night we just finished working, just finished playing, and we were gettin' into the car to go home, and my finger got caught in the door, got squashed in the door. And so Lester Young—we were going to drop Lester Young off at home—and so anyway Lester Young went to the hospital with me, and he would not leave until he was sure that my finger was going to be OK. You know, he was a lovely man. So every time I look at this little scar on my finger I think of Lester Young.

Now Dizzy Gillespie [laughter]. One time I was in Europe, couple a years ago, and we went to a restaurant. It happened to be up on the second floor where they come down on an escalator—no, the escalator was not running. So it was on the second floor. We got finished eating, and we were walking down, walking down the escalator steps which were not moving. Dizzy was all the way down at the bottom, so he looked down and saw the button, and he looked back and saw me walkin' [laughter], so he pressed the button, and the escalator started going—up, right? I'm walkin' down and goin' up, right? [Laughter.] It was a big joke, you know, but every time I see an escalator from now on I'm goin' to think of Dizzy Gillespie [laughter].

But all the guys that I've played with are really special—every one of them. I have nice memories from all of them. Charlie Parker, a very nice guy. We had the opportunity to play with him two times in Philadelphia. As a matter of fact he had—we were gonna make a record. He said, "I want you guys to be on my next recording session." And then he passed away before that came about.

WE: A last question. Do you feel that the kind of jazz you love is flourishing?

RB: You know, I find that playin' in clubs in the States, I find that the audiences are gettin' younger. The kids come in now, and they're comin' to hear this swing jazz music, which to them in some cases might be something brand new. Really. And some of these kids are, should I say, survivors of hard rock music, you know. And those of them who can still hear after all those decibels want to hear something else, and they hear about jazz, and once they hear it they like it, and they're comin' in.

SELECTED DISCOGRAPHY

Me and the Blues. Prestige P-24038. 1974. (Reissue of *Ray Bryant Alone with the Blues* and *The Ray Bryant Trio*, 1957–58.)

Little Susie. Columbia Special Products JCS-8244. 1973. Originally recorded 1959.

Con Alma. Columbia Jazz Masterpieces CJ-A4058. 1960.

With Sonny Rollins. *Sonny Rollins on Impulse.* MCA Impulse MCAD
    5655 JVC 458. 1965.
Ray Bryant Alone at Montreux. Atlantic SD1626. 1972.
Here's Ray Bryant. Pablo 2310 764. 1976.
Solo Flight. Pablo 2310–798. 1976.
Ray Bryant Montreux '77. Pablo Live Deluxe 2 308 201. 1977.
Ray Bryant Plays Basie and Ellington. EmArcy/Polygram 832 235-1. 1987.
Trio Today. EmArcy/Polygram 832 589-1. 1988.
Blue Moods. EmArcy/Polygram 838 368-2. 1989.

LARRY CORYELL

Courtesy Concord Jazz, Inc.

G uitarist Larry Coryell, a leading figure in the jazz-rock movement during the sixties and early seventies, remains one of the
most eclectic stylists in contemporary jazz. His daunting technique and
intense, blues-tinged style have been featured in a wide range of musical
contexts from fusion to mainstream acoustic to free jazz.

Coryell spent his first years in Galveston, Texas, then moved with his
family in the late forties to a small town in the state of Washington. When
Coryell was twelve, his grandmother bought him a ukulele, which quickly
gave way to a guitar. Soon the young Coryell was imitating his early
guitar idols, Chet Atkins and Chuck Berry.

Jazz lessons as a teen inspired Coryell to take a different direction. He
devoured the conceptions of a new set of guitar heroes, including Charlie
Christian, Tal Farlow, Joe Pass, and Barney Kessel. But Wes Montgomery
was his favorite. Coryell became entranced with Montgomery's single-
note wizardry, chord substitutions, and innovative use of octaves on the
guitar.

Coryell moved to New York City in 1965. Venerable drummer and
bandleader Chico Hamilton hired Coryell the next year for several gigs
and a recording session.[1] At the same time, Coryell's discovery of rock
guitar phenomenon Jimi Hendrix, as well as other cult idols of the idiom
such as Bob Dylan and the Rolling Stones, led him to form Free Spirits,
an early crossover band with a revolving-door membership of young musicians who had jazz chops and an ear for rock and roll.

Coryell gained more national visibility in 1967, when he joined a band
led by popular jazz vibraphonist Gary Burton. Several of the recordings
he made with Burton on the RCA Victor label, including *Duster*, *Lofty
Fake Anagram*, and *A Genuine Tong Funeral*, hold up today as remarkably
original efforts in an era dominated musically by saxophonist John Coltrane and the Beatles.

At the forefront of the jazz-rock movement, Coryell left Burton in
1969 to start his own groups. He had perhaps his greatest impact as a
jazz-rock pioneer when he cofounded Eleventh House with drummer

1. Chico Hamilton, *The Dealer*, Impulse Records, 1966.

Alphonse Mouzon in 1973. Eleventh House featured Coryell's high-volume, meltdown pyrotechnics on the electric guitar, replete with feedback and heavy-metal distortion techniques. The quality of the Eleventh House recordings is mixed, but efforts from the same period on the Vanguard release *Spaces*—with British guitarist John McLaughlin—provided listeners with vintage Coryell in a straightahead jazz setting.

As the popular appeal of jazz rock waned in the later seventies, Coryell began touring and recording in duo with other guitarists, including Steve Khan, Philip Catherine, and the late Emily Remler.[2] Coryell disappeared from the music scene in 1981 to battle alcohol and drug abuse but returned to the jazz fold the following year. Since then his work has remained stunningly diverse: he returned to his Wes Montgomery origins with an acoustic rhythm section, he headed a reunion of Eleventh House, and he even completed an album of Stravinsky compositions for which he transcribed the music.[3] Through it all, Larry Coryell has held on to a faithful following of fans and is extremely popular on the international jazz festival and club circuit. He also has contributed a regular column to *Guitar Magazine*, dissecting the solos of his peers, past and present.

Recorded 1981

WE: Larry, could you relate some of the struggles you had in forming your musical identity?

LC: Struggles? Well, I was so dedicated to being original I never had that problem. Well, no. In the beginning the only thing I was capable of doing was imitating my heroes like Joe Pass. Then when I discovered that I was doing a very poor job of imitating, and also I had some friends around me who advised me to do your own thing, and I didn't know what that meant, but I found that if I could be original people would notice me and I might get more jobs. So I really dedicated myself to getting my own identity.

But I don't think I could have established my own identity without having first tried to learn everything that was already there. That's important for me—to learn the past. To see where it came from in order to

2. Larry Coryell and Steve Khan, *Two for the Road*, Arista Records, 1976; Larry Coryell and Philip Catherine, *Twin House*, Elektra Records, 1976; *Larry Coryell–Emily Remler: Together*, Concord Records, 1985.

3. Larry Coryell, *Pétrouchka/Firebird Suite*, Philips Records, 1982.

take part in contributing to where it is going. And I felt compelled to study everything that emanated from Charlie Christian in jazz guitar—you know, Charlie Christian, Django Reinhardt. I felt that this was required for me. And I think I did the right thing. Because to know it I don't necessarily have to play it. But the knowledge of it strengthens my own attempt at the continuation of my identity. The continuity of the identity is essential to survival, because if you only go so far and don't grow, then you stagnate. I find that very important.

PR: You mentioned studying other jazz guitarists. Do you mean that you listened to records and played solos note by note?

LC: Exactly. Especially Wes Montgomery. To learn his solos gave me an idea how he thought. And that just opened up a door. I fed all these informations into my computer, as it were, and when you feed enough of it in there eventually what comes out is your own.

[At this point we played Wes Montgomery's version of "I've Grown Accustomed to Her Face."⁴ Coryell responded while the record played.] I *love* him. Sometimes I want to cry when I hear him play. Especially 'cause he's dead. It's really funny; a seventeen-year-old Kiss fan—I have no idea how they would react to this music. They might identify "Oh! this is the kind of music I hear in the cocktail lounge where my mother works," you know? Oh! if they only knew. That's a nice thing about being old, you know.

[Coryell listened intently to the record, then laughed.] Used to work in a lot of bands that played in nightclubs every night, you know, seven nights a week. 'Cause you're with each other every night you start getting these corny jokes, you know, between sets, like we called this song "I've Grown a Crust upon My Face." Really corny, you know these corny puns. The thing I like about him is the way he reharmonized these pieces. He doesn't use the same chords that were rendered in the Broadway show. He knows them, and he finds, like, nice substitutions to literally jazz it up. That's the positive meaning of *jazz* to me, is to improve a piece—improvisation. That's a great opportunity we have as improvisers.

PR: You can even take a mediocre composition and turn it into something beautiful.

LC: Exactly. I've heard the great improvisers take "Happy Birthday," or

4. "I've Grown Accustomed to Her Face," recorded by Wes Montgomery, on *Full House*, Riverside Records, 1962.

they read from the Tucson phone directory, and it came out sounding like the opera!

[The recording of "I've Grown Accustomed to Her Face" finished.]

WE: Before we started taping, you mentioned that you met Wes Montgomery and had the chance to play guitar for him.

LC: Yeah, right about the time of the release of that record [1962]. I had the good fortune to be in Seattle, Washington, where I was going to school, and he came up there to play. And it was like, you know, the Beatles are here. God has arrived! Jesus is here! Because I was just *mad* for him—followed him around the whole time. I was a groupie before the word was even coined.

WE: How did he respond when you played?

LC: He loved it because I played his solo from "West Coast Blues" note for note. He was flattered. He gave me his blessing.

PR: You said earlier that you copied his solos note for note to find out . . .

LC: How he thought! 'Cause I had no idea how to think in those terms. Yeah, because I knew he had to play the changes, but I didn't know how to make statements. Ah, let me see. I knew all the scales. Here's what it was like. When I was playing alone, when I was practicing, I really felt like I had something together. And I was really shocked when I went to play with other people. I realized that I didn't know how to play with other people—I didn't know how to keep this dialogue going. And I can't explain how difficult, rather how different it is to play alone and to play with other people. It is completely different. Because when you're alone you have to do everything yourself, but when you play with other people it's kind of done for you and you just kind of do your part. And I love that—I mean, I love playing solo, but it's really different when you play with other people.

WE: It always seemed to me that Montgomery's phrasing was unique.

LC: Yes, he had some phrases that he used quite a lot that were his trademark that nobody else apparently had done before.

WE: He was a natural conversationalist on the guitar.

LC: Yeah, that's what I was trying to say earlier. I really didn't know how to speak. I didn't know how to make that conversation, you know; I didn't know how to use the language. I knew the vocabulary, but I didn't know how to use the vocabulary. That's what it was, 'cause I spent all those years practicing by myself, and I had vocabulary, up the, you know—I had plenty of that—but let me see, to use a parallel, I was very poor in grammar. And he was a prime example of a man who really used the language well. Beautifully. And it's only now that after having played for years and years that I'm finally getting to a point where I can do that.

When I first learned a solo off his second Riverside album, it was a blues. "D-Natural Blues" was the title.[5] When I was learning it, you know, as I would learn each phrase, I would say, especially as he came to the eighth, ninth, and tenth bars of the piece, I said, "God, will I ever ever grow enough to understand *this*." 'Cause I couldn't believe what he was doin'. I couldn't really believe that he had soloed *that*. 'Cause the changes are basically D-seventh, G-seventh, two, five, one, a D, and bang. But he would play a whole lot more changes and going places; I was never at that place, and he was at that place, and it gave me the feeling—wow! if I could ever think like *that*, you know, it would be amazing, really amazing. It took me years just, for example, I was talking about the blues—it took me years to really play the blues right. I didn't know how to play a blues; I thought I knew how to play a blues.

I think the ultimate is where you reach a point where you're not even thinking about what you're doing. You just let it happen. Originally, like I'd go to a jam session, the cat would call a tune, and as soon as the tune would be going on I'd be, you know, playing along and thinking, "OK, what comes next? what comes next? what comes next?" you know, thinkin' of the changes. And that made it hard, to have to think. But if you know it, basically if you keep doing it for years and years and years, especially if you're familiar with the material like a tune like, ah, oh, anything—"A Night in Tunisia" or "My Favorite Things" or "Just Friends"—you play it enough times you really get familiar with the changes, then you get *completely* free.

In other words, you have—what's the word, what's the word—you've done something with the structure. I can't think of it. What is that thing where you—shucks! What is that, I can't think of it. Where you have the structure so much—assimilated! You've assimilated the structure completely where it enables you to be completely free within the structure. That is freedom. That's what I was trying to say. And that is the thing that attracted me to this music. I was overwhelmed by how much I

5. "D-Natural Blues," on *The Incredible Jazz Guitar of Wes Montgomery*, Riverside Records, 1960.

couldn't comprehend it. I didn't know what it was, but I knew that that's what it was. I went crazy. I dreamed of it, man, I ate, breathed, and slept, and went to the toilet nothing but music. And that was my goal, man.

PR: You talked about the blues. Did you know that Mike Bloomfield died?

LC: What! What! When? Oh, no! Oh, no! no! no! Tell me it's not true! Oh, that's terrible. I don't believe it. What happened? I'm in a state of shock. I hadn't seen him for years.

PR: He was one of the main people in the sixties.

LC: He did for me what, oh, I can't tell you what he did for me when I was hanging with him. There was a point in my life where I saw him every day—*every day*, man. I mean, that was one of the most wonderful times of my life when I was with Mike Bloomfield in New York City. I mean, he opened the door for me in blues. Oh God! I mean, I used to go and watch him play and just—man, I really loved it. And it was nice because he was crazy about my playing, you know, because I could do stuff that he couldn't do. You know, the technique. Oh, I'm sorry, man. I'm sorry. Forgive me, it blew my mind. I'm surprised I didn't hear about it before—in San Francisco? God, I had some good times with him.

WE: How do you learn to project feeling in jazz?

LC: By learning basic blues. That's the only way I can answer that question, you know. I don't know how to say it any other way—by going back and learning how to phrase with emotion. In other words, I took the same attitude that you have when you play the simple blues and complicated it. Is that possible? Or made it more complex. I didn't complicate it, I added, oh, I see what I'm saying, I developed more complex forms, but I never lost sight of the original motive which was to project feeling. I think I've always projected feeling. I think that's the difference between me and players who are more in the mind. A lot of cats are mind players, and I'm fascinated by that. But it comes from my thing, I think; it comes less from my mind and more from this area right below this—see where I'm pointing—it's kind of in the viscera.

PR: Have you had the opportunity to play with older black musicians and learn from them?

LC: Oh definitely, most definitely. You know, that was my dream when I was first starting to play was eventually to get good enough where I'd be hired by my heroes.

PR: Charles Mingus? Sonny Rollins?

LC: That's what I was thinking about. Oh, those two experiences, man, for me was among the greatest.

WE: How did you get hooked up with Mingus?

LC: I got to play on the record *Three or Four Shades of Blues*, and then he called when he was going to make the next one, *Me, Myself an Eye*.[6] He called me for those sessions too.

WE: Was he still playing at that time?

LC: He played on *Three or Four Shades of Blues*. He played bass on that. But the second session, by then he was in his wheelchair.

WE: But he was in charge?

LC: Oh yeah. Oh yeah. He sat in his wheelchair, and there was no question who was in charge.

PR: When we interviewed Mingus, he said he wasn't interested in using electronics to make music. He said any electronic sound can be made with acoustic instruments if you know how to voice them.

LC: This is true, but I tell you, in especially the *Me, Myself an Eye* sessions, he encouraged me to turn up. I was really surprised. He said, "Turn it up." It was great, and I'm almost sad that I never played as well on my own records. You see, he made me play way over my head. In that situation I was just a wide-eyed little boy, man, who couldn't believe that I was privileged enough to be in the same room with not only Mingus but with all these other giants that he had hired. And the ego was not—my ego, I left it in the bus, you know. It was just—I didn't get high or anything—I just went in there and kept my mouth shut and concentrated on what I was supposed to do, and man, gosh, the only time I ever played that good on my own records was very seldom in my opinion. Of course, I can't be that objective.

PR: How did he treat you?

LC: Oh, he *loved* me; he treated me like a son. He didn't mince his words. If he didn't like what I was, you know, you know, he gave me everything—the plus and the minus. We did a lot of takes, but he, ah,—oh, I will never forget how humiliated I was when he said, "I just want to hear the guitar on this part here." I wanted to crawl underneath a rock, 'cause I knew I wasn't playing it right. He said, "OK, OK, Larry, don't play this part," he said, "No guitar." I remember I walked out of the

6. Charles Mingus, *Three or Four Shades of Blues*, Atlantic Records, 1977; Charles Mingus, *Me, Myself an Eye*, Atlantic Records, 1979.

session, and you know, I'm so humiliated. That's one thing I liked about him: he didn't mince his words. He didn't beat around the bush, but that was so funny. Yeah, he, gosh, I loved playing with horns, all those horns on that second album, man, this huge orchestra—I loved that—to solo over the horns, that was great.

WE: That brings to mind your work on the JCOA recording organized by Michael Mantler in 1968.[7]

LC: Yeah, Mantler. That was years ahead of its time. I remember that he wanted me to—he said, "Don't do anything until I point to you." 'Cause, like, OK, now we're going to play the arrangement. And they start, and I say to myself, "This is an arrangement?" It sounded like a collision of two radio stations. But I just said, "Oh, God, I can't believe this is happening." Then he would point to me, and then he said, "Go!" And he told me just to freak out! And that's what I did. I said, "What do you want me to play?" He said, "Just freak out, just do your thing."

WE: Were several of the sessions for that record made one after another?

LC: Yes.

WE: So you were among some of the most important musicians in New York at the time. What was that scene like?

LC: It was beautiful. Oh gosh! It was one of the most amazing—it was amazing! 'Cause there you are in New York City doing what you came to New York City to do but never really expecting to do it. All these great players, man. *All* these great players. It was so cool. Big brotherhood. Great, loved that, that's what it's all about.

PR: You made another record with Mantler: *Movies*.[8]

LC: Oh! man, see what I mean, all these—I play so good for other people, really, man. That's why I want to do a lot of studio work, 'cause I can give these people something for only triple scale [laughter]. Hire me and I'll give you the best I can give you. I like to—I like doing it. I've made enough records of my own for a while. I mean, there's plenty of stuff there if people wanna acquaint themselves with what I do. But I have no desire to make a record of my own right now. Next year, you know.

PR: Tell us about that fourth cut on *Movies*, the one that sounds like a gunfight.

LC: Yeah, wasn't that beautiful? It was all overdubbed. I was the only

7. Michael Mantler, *The Jazz Composer's Orchestra*, JCOA Records, 1968.
8. Michael Mantler, *Movies*, JCOA Records, 1978.

musician there. I was playing with Steve Swallow and Tony Williams, but they were only on the tape. They already put their parts down. I did all my work in one day.

WE: How about *Spaces* with John McLaughlin?[9] Don't you think that one of the songs, "Rene's Theme," is reminiscent of Django [Reinhardt]?

LC: John and I had been listening to a Django record that he had a couple of days prior. That's what inspired us to do the release.

Spaces, really, I think, is my most popular album, because John is on there. So that album I am very grateful for, you know, opened up the door for me. What I mean is, apparently *Spaces* is a darn good album.

PR: Do the records you made with Gary Burton, such as *Duster* and the live date at Carnegie Hall, hold up for you?

LC: They hold up for what they are. What they do to me is make me wish that I could do some more work with him, now that I've had some experience under my belt. You know, I really don't believe that we in any way, shape, or form exhausted the possibilities of guitar and vibes. I want to do it again. Now that I've had some experience. But those experiences were great for me.

WE: How long did you play with Sonny Rollins?

LC: Well, we rehearsed. He and I got together for several rehearsals in New York, and then we went out to Berkeley to record the record, and the nice thing about that was that he took his time to make the record.[10] We'd go in there and spend all day to get a sound. Get one song down really good and then go home for the rest of the day. So I liked that. We had a whole day to do our duets, and that was great, absolutely great.

WE: Did you team up only for the studio sessions, or did you go on the road?

LC: No. Just for that. He heard me somewhere. I remember he liked my composition called "The Higher Consciousness" from *Barefoot Boy*.[11] He liked that a lot.

PR: Do you think the "sound" of your generation is an amalgam of rock and jazz?

LC: I see us going back and playing in that acoustic format again. And

9. Larry Coryell and John McLaughlin, *Spaces*, Vanguard Records, recorded 1970, released 1974.

10. Sonny Rollins, *Don't Ask*, Milestone Records, 1979.

11. Larry Coryell, *Barefoot Boy*, RCA Records, 1971.

modernizing it, which is what I think we've done. And I think I did that with Phil Catherine. I think that's what John's doing with Paco de Lucia and Al Di Meola. I think it's great to see acoustic music in the forefront like that.

WE: You didn't play acoustic music for twenty years, then all of a sudden . . .

LC: I made the switch. Big surprise. Very dramatic. I took a left turn.

WE: Was there a galvanizing incident?

LC: I don't remember, I don't remember. I just remembered—it just happened, it just happened. I discovered early on that people loved it 'cause they had been overwhelmed by loudness. And it was so weird, man. I never started making so much money until I switched to acoustic. I never had a wide audience until I switched to acoustic.

PR: We've been talking about all-star bands up in heaven, but what about Jimi Hendrix?

LC: He was the greatest electric guitar player ever to live. Electric blues.

PR: Where do you think he was taking the music?

LC: He was taking it wherever it was supposed to go. He was, what's the word—innovator. He was one of the first supreme artists to use the electric palette to its maximum. And having seen him play at jam sessions in New York when he was a big star—some of my fondest memories. He was like so overwhelming when he was on that you didn't want to play with him. He would ask me to come and play. I said, "Uh uh." And for me, not to want to jump up there, that's not like me. I always wanna sit in, you know. But it wasn't that I was afraid. I just didn't have anything to say. He was saying everything. He created totality. He had sounds—sounds like synthesizers before synthesizers were ever in vogue. Sometimes his guitar would sound like a computer.

PR: Who's picking up where he left off?

LC: Nobody. I'm sure somebody is capable but . . . He is the most imitated of all of the rockers, you know.

WE: Give us your feelings about Charlie Christian.

LC: I now can hear Christian in players like Barney Kessel. Now I can hear it. 'Cause I hadn't heard Charlie Christian before I heard Barney Kessel. But I see now that I was hearing Charlie Christian by hearing Barney Kessel. And Grant Green and people like that—Herb Ellis, Tal Farlow. You know, it's amazing to hear Charlie Christian. I'll hear a phrase, and I say, "Oh, that's where they got it from."

WE: Why don't we listen to some Christian? [12]

LC: Good idea. Oh, what a sound. Damn! What a sound! The attack! Shit! Yeah! Wild! Jesus! Yeah! Wow! Creativity! Yup! Yeah! Hear that? That was *great*, man. What fascinates me about that is his *sound*. Shit! What a sound! The attack—I mean, you feel something in each note. I loved that. I haven't heard that one before. Forty years ago. I can't believe it. Where has the time gone? It's just out the window.

I really don't know if it's possible to sound like that anymore. What got to me when I was listening to it was the attack. His attack was so clear. And I felt it in my gut, every note. And I have been told by cats who saw him play that he was using all downstrokes. So that fascinates me. His time—his rhythm, man, like listening, woo. Those ideas—amazing. I see now what a tremendous contribution he made.

SELECTED DISCOGRAPHY

With Gary Burton. *Duster.* RCA LSP 3835. 1967.
With John McLaughlin. *Spaces.* Vanguard VSD6558. 1970.
Barefoot Boy. RCA AYL1-3961. 1971.
Offering. Vanguard VSD-79319. 1973.
The Eleventh House with Larry Coryell. Vanguard 79342. 1974.
The Restful Mind. Vanguard VSD 79353. 1975.
With Philip Catherine. *Twin House.* Elektra 123. 1976.
With Steve Khan. *Two for the Road.* Arista 4156. 1976.
Standing Ovation. Arista Novus 3024. 1981.
Larry Coryell–Emily Remler: Together. Concord Jazz CCD4289. 1985.
Shining Hour. MCD5360. 1990.

12. "Swing to Bop," on Charlie Christian and Dizzy Gillespie, *The Harlem Jazz Scene— 1941*, Esoteric Records, 1957.

MERCER ELLINGTON

Courtesy Fantasy, Inc.

M ercer Ellington, son of one of the most important figures in jazz, has over a half-century career forged his own identity as a composer, arranger, and bandleader. Born in 1919 in Washington, D.C., Mercer Ellington studied piano and saxophone as a youth, switching to trumpet on the advice of venerated Ellington sideman Cootie Williams. After high school, he attended Columbia University, Juilliard, and New York University.

Mercer played intermittently with the Duke Ellington Orchestra in the late thirties, but he left to form his own short-lived band in 1939. After that band folded, Mercer contributed musical arrangements to the Ellington orchestra. He wrote a variety of jazz compositions, some of which found their way into the Duke's repertoire, including "Blue Serge," "Jumpin' Punkins," and the classic "Things Ain't What They Used to Be." He also worked as a utility trumpet player, handled the Ellington band's finances, and even served as road manager.

Following a tour of duty with the United States Army, Mercer organized a second band of his own, featuring vocalist Carmen McRae. In 1950 he returned to the Duke Ellington Orchestra, playing trumpet and E-flat horn, and also founded Mercer Records, an enterprise that lasted two years. After a brief hiatus from the music business while he worked as a salesman, Mercer again assumed the dual roles of trumpeter and band manager, but this time for Cootie Williams, who had left the senior Ellington to lead his own rhythm-and-blues–tinged ensemble.

Mercer rejoined his father in 1955, and for nine years Duke's orchestra was the home base from which Mercer took occasional leaves to front his own bands. In 1964 Mercer became a full-time member of the Ellington trumpet section. He also resumed his duties as road manager and stayed close to Duke's organization during the last decade of his father's life.

Since Duke Ellington's death in 1974, Mercer has devoted much of his time to perpetuating his father's legacy. He has sustained the Ellington orchestra, uncovered and performed hitherto unknown works by the Duke, and directed the musical tribute to his father, *Sophisticated Ladies*,

from 1981 to 1983. He also has penned his memories and personal esti-
mations of his famous father.[1] The first recording of the Ellington orchestra under Mercer's leadership, *Continuum*, was a critical and popular
success.[2] It included a lineup of Duke Ellington and Billy Strayhorn standards and offered a musical tribute to baritone saxophonist Harry Carney,
a stalwart of the Ellington band for forty-seven years who died six months
after Duke. *Continuum* provided a smooth transition for Ellingtonia fans
worldwide.

Since the mid-seventies the ranks of illustrious Ellington sidemen
have been dramatically thinned by death and illness, and Mercer now
leads a wholly reconstituted road band. A recent release, the Grammy
Award–winning *Digital Duke*, reunited a few of the Duke's men in the
company of a roster of guest soloists.[3] The result is an affectionate romp
through well-trodden Ellington classics in a salute to the Duke and his
peerless contributions to American music.

Recorded 1977
PR: Could you define for us your father's contribution to American
music?
ME: Well, I'll give you a definition in negativity of what his music is.
One thing he said his music was *not* is, it's not jazz. He thought it had a
greater scope. He thought that he belonged to all generations, and he
wanted to have something that was relative to every form of music.

He'd written rock numbers back when—you know, I get accused of
trying to make a transition in the band from time to time with the things
we play. They say, you know, "If your father was here now, he wouldn't
like what you're doin'." I said, "Well, these are his arrangements."

He never wanted to be categorized, so that the music he did for the
church was never named a mass. It's not projected into any *one* religion.
We played it in synagogues and Catholic churches, Episcopalians, and

1. Mercer Ellington with Stanley Dance, *Duke Ellington in Person: An Intimate Memoir* (Boston, 1978).

2. Mercer Ellington and the Duke Ellington Orchestra, *Continuum*, Fantasy Records,
1974–75.

3. Mercer Ellington, conductor, *Digital Duke*, GRP Records, 1987.

Baptist alike, and whatever. He didn't want it held down or to have any boundaries on it. And as a result, if you have any kind of music that you think in terms of, you can find some form of it which has been written by Ellington.

WE: Were there particular, so-called classical composers whose work he enjoyed?

ME: Yeah. There was one English composer—and that's about the only time I've ever heard him absolutely point out something that he liked. And in fact I heard him say this twice: if it was painting it was Monet and most of the artists around the Renaissance period. And [Frederick] Delius was the one person he liked so much in music.

Aside from that, he had been likened to [Arnold] Schoenberg. And finally he said, "Well, you better go off and find out what Schoenberg's doin' so I can check him out" [laughter]. I had to read the book through and come back, and there is a tremendous correlation between the two. And yet there wasn't a [personal] relationship there as was the case with Stravinsky, who used to come by and sit and listen from time to time.

WE: Stravinsky would come by and listen to the band?

ME: Yeah. In the Cotton Club days. They got to know each other pretty well. And Orson Welles used to sit on the bandstand and write his scenarios. He used to like to sit right in the brass section and write while the band was playing [laughter]. Nobody ever knew he was there, you know. He'd just be sittin' there in between the two rows between the trombones and trumpets. And he used to sit there for hours and just write with the band while they played.

PR: Let's turn to the beginnings of big-band jazz. Was Ellington's early band influenced by the achievements of Fletcher Henderson and Don Redman?

ME: Well, he was hoping to arrive at the plateau that Henderson sat on, because, you know, Henderson was so classic in his achievements. He was a great writer. And the guys had to have tremendous ability in order just to be in the band. He got Cootie Williams from Henderson's band because Henderson thought Cootie was a little too slow for him to represent the things he wanted to have done. And they used to write in the most weird keys and at tempos that were blistering, you know. I was lucky to be able to get in the Savoy to hear them, and those few days that I heard them I will well remember.

PR: Did Ellington and Armstrong influence each other?

ME: No. He appreciated Louis. But they were both into their own thing, and they were both like "ground-floor" people. Louis had something that he started, and Ellington represented something else.

When Cootie first came into the band, he adored Louis, and Ellington had to influence him to get him to begin to play like Bubber Miley, his original "growl" trumpet player. And Cootie readily will admit that when he came into the band he just thought it was crazy to be going around doing this stuff. It took him, well, some time before he began to realize that he was in the midst of something that was very constructive. You know, it was a gig to him when he first started off; he didn't think he was gonna be able to stay there too long because it was drivin' him crazy [laughter].

WE: A question about the Cotton Club. We imagine that the pressure on Duke to write so much music probably contributed significantly to his development.

ME: Oh yeah. It contributed because the demand was so great and the amount of arrangements that had to be provided for each show, you know. They changed each production, I'd say on the average of every six months, and new materials had to be gotten, new songs written for it, and eventually he learned that rather than to just trust his own judgment and write the exact number of songs that were necessary, he would do maybe ten extra. And in the last days of the Cotton Club one of the songs he wrote for a show was rejected. That was "I Got It Bad and It Ain't Good" [laughter]. So the show went into the realm of the unremembered, and "I Got It Bad" goes on.

PR: Many jazz writers sum up the early forties as Ellington's "golden period." Do you agree with that?

ME: I don't think that was the greatest era. Composition-wise for him, the greatest era was up to the last day, and he was writing for the doctors and nurses every day, a little short thing for about a half an hour. We had an electric piano there for him, and he'd do that and sing a couple of songs or whatever, and that would be the big deal, you know.

But the thing that we're rehearsing now I consider his greatest work, and that was done somewhere within the last four or five years. It's called *The River*. It was commissioned by the American Ballet Theatre. And we had the good fortune to play it with Alvin Ailey in State Theatre last summer.[4] It was the greatest experience for me to hear a lot of these things, because so many times when he had these special projects I was left on the road with the band. I never had a chance to come in town to know what was happenin'. I had to mind the shop. I always got the dirty work [laughter].

WE: In general, what was the relationship of dance to Duke's music?

ME: Well, he felt that if the arts didn't accompany each other, then there was something missing or something wrong about it. And I think that that was the one thing that led to the demise of bebop—there was no associated art, no dance that went with it, you know.

But for the most part, he loved to write for various occasions. He liked to write background for pictures, and he loved the idea of writing for ballet. In fact, he was very happy to have the commission for *The River* and also for various things that he did for Alvin Ailey from one time to another. And don't forget, he started in the Cotton Club, and that was where he became highly aware of dance.

PR: How much music did Ellington write that hasn't been recorded?

ME: I have absolutely no idea. We keep running into things. For instance, I was listening to some air checks from Sweden, and suddenly I realized that Jimmy Blanton had a duet that he played with the old man that had never been recorded. Evidently it was done on the last concert in Europe, and Jimmy got so sick on the return that they never got around to it. So there are things that you discover by him from time to time.

When we did our first Sacred Concert, we rehearsed most of the music in and around Reno, on the way west to San Francisco. He was flying back and forth, and he had a guy who was a choral director directing the choir in Los Angeles. And he had a copyist working in New York, so we never really heard the first episode until we performed it. Throughout his life he was cryptic, and he never let the right hand know what the left hand was doin', because he always liked the idea of showing surprise. In his words, "the mystery of show business must always be preserved."

We'd sit there by the television, and they'd have these shorts where one camera would pan the other camera and show some of the backstage activity. And he said, "That's terrible," you know, and he just felt that it

4. Ellington is referring to the Alvin Ailey Dance Company.

was a transgression, because the public, in order to have full enjoyment and entertainment, has to have an illusion preserved. And once they begin to see all the other things that make it possible, then it takes some of the joy out of it.

Just like reading a book and then actually seeing the picture, and the book is much more furtive than the picture because it sets your mind to activity. Unless you got a real big person who can enhance the words, the book surpasses that which can be seen, because it sets the imagination into action. This was his belief, which is why there was such a great rapport between he and Billy Strayhorn. They would sit and talk for hours, you know, just way into the early hours of the morning philosophizing and talking about impressions and ways to paint a picture for the listener or the person who was in the audience.

WE: Can you give us some insight into one of Ellington's major works, *Black, Brown and Beige?*

ME: Well, I can never really state it as well as Pop did. But basically *Black, Brown and Beige* was his criticism of his own race. And their prejudices within itself. That there were these different castes: the black, the brown or tan ones, and the ones light enough to pass for white. And yet they wanted, as a whole, the race wanted recognition and equal rights, and yet within themselves they restricted each other.

Also I feel that *Black, Brown and Beige* was the first absolute statement that he made toward the appeal or the influence of the church in his works. Because he does have the work song there, and there's a dirge in some of the slow parts. And of course, the chant, or the work song, is a mixture of the work and a hope for freedom by drowning out your troubles in song. So this was his way of wanting to preserve that which is part of the culture of the race, and also with his subtleties, as was the case with him from time to time, he would come up with a criticism one way or the other, political or racial or whatever.

But he never would want to do it to the point where he would arm the opposition, so he had to be very subtle in it. He thought it was wrong to rant and rave on a soapbox on the five o'clock news because people who were not concerned with the problem would begin to develop a feeling and say, "Oh, well, that's what I've been told to be afraid of." So he didn't want to violate that principle, but yet he wanted to be sure that the next man that met him somewhere in some sort of a situation would know that his name was not George. He was named after another king [laughter].

WE: Duke premiered *Black, Brown and Beige* at Carnegie Hall in 1943.[5] Why didn't he ever present that work in its entirety again?
ME: Well, the only reason he didn't present it in its entirety was that he'd gone on to write other things and he wanted to hear them. He was his own best audience. He loved to hear what he'd written successfully. And I think what he thought was that he took the parts out from the pieces that had the greatest appeal, although "Penthouse Serenade" I thought was a very beautiful work. But for some reason or other, he didn't do it.

Don't forget, he had these soloists, and he had to go through the band. I find it a problem now. And if you give Johnny Hodges everything that's happenin', which if you don't look out in programming you wind up where all the solos are in two places. They're either in the alto chair or the baritone chair. So you've got to be careful not to program one thing too much and too often, and as a result he would have to go to other places. After all, he had Lawrence Brown then and Cat Anderson, Paul Gonsalves, and Jimmy Hamilton on clarinet.
PR: Ellington did record a portion of *Black, Brown and Beige* in 1958 with Mahalia Jackson.
ME: Yeah, that's the "Lord's Prayer" that was done on that. It was very difficult for the two of them to work together, Mahalia and Ellington, though they admired each other desperately. But Mahalia was used to freedom of emotion and so forth. And when the old man wrote—he and Strayhorn used to jump on [Herb] Jeffries for moving the melody maybe a half a beat, because they had somethin' they wanted to happen at that pause, so it made it very difficult.[6] Gradually what he wound up having to do with Mahalia or, say, Paul Gonsalves, 'cause he never knew what he was goin' to do and where he'd move, he just started writing goose eggs, you know. He'd just stay in the background and let 'em go on their own [laughter]. And if they got too free, man, he'd just chop that off and let 'em do what they're gonna do and start back off someplace else where it made sense.
WE: What was the general relationship between improvisation and orchestration in Duke's band?
ME: Well, improvisation added the impact—the first impulse was totally

5. *The Duke Ellington Carnegie Hall Concerts, January, 1943*, Prestige/Fantasy Records, 1977.
6. Jeffries was a vocalist with Ellington's band in the early forties.

free. But once it was done and recorded, then the artist had to remember the exact solo he played. In later years Duke got to a place where he would let them vary, you know, just for his own consumption; that would be like around the Blue Note in Chicago. Then anybody could do anything. When it got changed too much then he'd just rerecord it. And then he would want it to become set again, such as the case with "Crescendo and Diminuendo," which in latter days became known as "27 Choruses."[7] But when he first wrote it he would never of thought about takin' any liberties and openin' it up like that. There were other things that developed by rote, like "Rockin' in Rhythm" and "Caravan." There was never a note written on them, nor "Perdido." These things were totally from the licks and contributions that the guys made themselves from within the band.

I'll tell you about two people that had a tremendous effect on each other. One was Duke Ellington on Dizzy Gillespie, and Dizzy Gillespie on Duke Ellington. Because Duke realized that he was confronted with a different concept of performance, and he had to stop and think about greater liberties for the artist himself. And I think this is when the flexibility began to set in a little.

WE: So Duke composed his pieces pretty rigorously, leaving gaps for the soloists?

ME: Oh sure, sure. Even in some of the extended works he would leave gaps, particularly for somebody like Paul Gonsalves or Ben Webster. Ben had a *nasty* little habit of making a mistake in the part, and the part he played sounded better than what you wrote [laughter]. Ellington used to have to watch that all the time.

PR: You mentioned Dizzy playing with Duke. That moves us to ask about another musician who was professionally close to your father, Charles Mingus.

ME: Mingus worked with all my gigs first, and then he went with Duke Ellington [laughter]. And Mingus and Thelonius [Monk] were around at that particular time, and they were listening very closely to him. And Mingus was interested in wanting to *write* like Duke Ellington, and that was the big influence that he had, but as far as his instrument was concerned, I think it was all Mingus, you know. But many of the things he

7. The "27 Choruses" version of "Diminuendo and Crescendo in Blue" appears on *Ellington at Newport*, Columbia Records, 1956.

put out were likened to a lot of the things the old man had done, like "Tijuana Gift Shop."[8]

PR: Do you know anything about the famous *Money Jungle* session that joined your father with Mingus and Max Roach?[9] Didn't Mingus storm out of that date at one point?

ME: He had an argument with Max Roach, and they vowed never to record again at length, and *didn't* [laughter]. They both had their interpretations of what they thought should be done at the time. In fact, originally, it was a contract for two albums to be dubbed for United Artists, and they only did the one, and they could never get the three of them back together [laughter]. It was very successful, 'cause that was the time when the smaller groups were in great demand.

WE: We hadn't heard that much piano from Duke prior to that album. Had he been reluctant earlier to emphasize his piano playing in public?

ME: The old man? Oh no. I remember one year he won the *Down Beat* piano poll, and he said, "Well, I really fooled 'em that time." He said, "I'm *not* a piano player." But in the earlier days, when he first came out of Washington, he would challenge James P. Johnson and Willie "The Lion" Smith. And they used to stand back, and you know, he'd say, "Get up from there" and "I'm gonna play this." I wasn't there, but I would loved to have been. But I do know this was true to a certain point, and every once in a while, even in later years, he would take serious time out and maybe go and practice on the piano and develop something that he *really* wanted to play.

One of the things that really exhibited well in recent years was the piano solo that he does on "Lotus Blossom."[10] He always did it at the end of concerts as sort of a memorial to Billy Strayhorn. Plus "The Queen's Suite"—he has a thing on there, "Single Petal of a Rose."[11] Those are the two things that he really did to use his technical piano.

But I can tell you this. I think of all times that he was the greatest rhythm-section piano player. He himself alone could either stabilize or move the rhythm section when he wanted to, just with the keys. He used

8. "Tijuana Gift Shop," recorded by Charles Mingus, on *Tijuana Moods*, RCA Records, recorded 1957, released 1962.

9. Duke Ellington, *Money Jungle*, United Artists, 1962; reissued, Blue Note Records, 1987.

10. "Lotus Blossom," recorded by Duke Ellington and His Orchestra, on *And His Mother Called Him Bill*, RCA Records, 1968.

11. "The Queen's Suite," on *The Ellington Suites*, Pablo Records, 1976.

to be able to take that piano, pound on it, double the notes and spread them all over so that [the band] had to hear him, and they had to hear what beat he wanted.

WE: Did his band orchestrations originate from the piano?

ME: I think the thing that was a real tribute to his ability was the fact that he was not a pianistic writer. That was one thing about Ellington's orchestration. You'd think that he played each one of the instruments himself, because he was that much aware of what they should do and what they shouldn't do.

PR: Toward the end of Duke's life, did he know that he was dying of cancer?

ME: I think he knew, but the only way that we might have been able to check on it would have been through our family doctor, Dr. Logan. But unfortunately Dr. Logan died before Duke Ellington did, so when it came [time] to check up on what was wrong and what things had taken place, it was very difficult. And I know that it was only after the autopsy that the doctors really realized that the trouble was in the lymphatic gland, and that's why it spread throughout the blood system and it was so difficult to do anything about it at all.

But he had an awareness—I think it was a sixth sense more than anything else—that he should hurry up and do what he had to do, because that was when he gave up his fear of flying, and he suddenly started takin' the airplane to go anywhere. He and Harry Carney used to race through the nights at 120 miles an hour driving between dates [laughter]. [But toward the end] he'd take private planes and charter flights just to be able to make sure he didn't waste his time in flight and to be someplace where—if he wanted to—he could use a piano. He always had a tape recorder in his pocket, and he had a cryptic notation that he used in order to preserve any thought he had.

But for the most part I think that he was aware of his inability to function as usual for the first time when we did the Sacred Concert at Westminster Abbey. He was never satisfied with the performance, consequently never satisfied with the recordings that we had done. Every shot we had, we'd go back into another studio to brace it up or redo some portion of it.

WE: Let's turn our attention to you, Mercer. Did you want to be a musician from an early age?

ME: Well, I couldn't make up my mind 'til I was about seven years old [laughter]. Stayin' on the road and travelin' with him—there was never any doubt that I wanted to be in show business.

WE: Did you study with your father, or with other teachers?

ME: Well, you know, he was pretty busy. I had the normal run of teachers that you usually have—piano lessons, saxophone lessons—and finally Cootie was the one that said I should turn to trumpet.

But I think the basic and the greatest experience I had in learning music was in 1941. We were in Los Angeles, and Ellington was playing the Casa Manana, and he would leave me with a writing project each night when he went to work. And when he got back he'd just scratch out what he felt was not good, and I'd work on that. I'd hear somethin', and I'd say, "How did you do that?" and he'd just give me the paper and say, "There it is, figure it out."

He never recommended anything. His philosophy in music was much [like] that of life. You could never get a yes or a no from him. Nothing was right, and you didn't have to do anything, and nothing was wrong, and if it was, there must be a place for it [laughter]. We were watching a TV program one night, and he said, "Well, there's the greatest statement of the century." A guy had just said, "The secret of my success was that whatever happened to me, good or bad, I used it" [laughter]. That's pretty much what he did.

WE: When did you write your first piece of music?

ME: I had my first record done when I was fourteen years old. I wrote a thing called "Pigeons and Peppers" [laughter]. That was my big achievement, and I was prouder of that than I think of anything that ever happened afterwards [laughter]. Because my father, one day he said, "You know, you were writing much better before you went to school" [laughter]. And then I had to go through a thorough process of becoming ignorant again in order to feel I was gettin' anywhere.

But he was right. If you write and think in terms of theory while you're doin' it, it inhibits you, and the only thing to do is to catch the natural thought and continue to write what you hear until you run out of what you hear, and then go to work and see where it begins to make sense as far as theorizing or the mechanical process of arranging devices and sound in a section. But as always, the best sound is what sounds good. Strayhorn put it differently: he said, "Never write anything you can't hum back." If you're gonna write somethin' on paper and *you* can't hum it, how do you expect anybody else to retain it?

PR: Tell us something about the band *you* led in the late thirties.

ME: Well, what happened was that we were sittin' in the lunchroom at Juilliard, and we said, "Let's get a band together so we can play some things around." Everybody was writin', and they wanted to hear their stuff. There were some great people around about that time: Calvin Jackson, Luther Henderson, Tony Scott was in that class, and another guy that I don't guess that too many people have heard about, but to my mind he had one of the greatest successes of our gang—a guy by the name of Harry the Horse. He used to take his shoes off and play piano in the basement with his toes [laughter].

But we had a nice bunch of guys, and I think that if we got one job every five months that was a real major accomplishment. But about that same time Dizzy had come up from Philly, and a little later Strayhorn came in from Pittsburgh. Billy was hired originally as a lyricist and a composer. And while he was there I used to get him to do some arrangements for the band we had. But for the most part it was like a conclave of different people who were tryin' to get somewhere. We'd sit around, fool around—I hate to mention it, but we had a lot of fun with ukuleles about that time [laughter]. Now it's guitars. I don't know how the kids get that amount of money, 'cause we had to scuffle gettin' ukes, and they didn't cost anything. And if you were *real* hot you could graduate to a banjo.

PR: Which band was the first one you managed?

ME: Well, actually the first band I managed was Cootie Williams' band. This was when Pearl Bailey was the singer. And then I went off to the army, and I came back, and I managed Cootie again.

The one offer that I had which I will always regret was that Charlie Parker always wanted me to manage him. He was in Cootie's original band. And he wanted me to handle him, and I was always off into somethin' else, concerned about trying to do something musically myself.

WE: Was it difficult to manage Duke's band, since it was loaded with virtuoso musicians who must have had big egos?

ME: It was loaded with a lot of things. It was a very difficult band to handle. The problems of habits and drunkenness and all that were very slight in comparison to one other that I had to face. I had Johnny Hodges, Harry Carney, Cootie Williams, and Lawrence Brown. In the thirties these were the people who used to take me to the beach, hold me by the hand, take me to the movies, buy me lollipops, whatever. And suddenly I was in the position wherein I had to ask them to be onstage at a certain time, get up when they were sleepy, get on the bus when it was time to leave, and so forth. That was the most difficult part of the job, was to go back to these people who you knew loved you and to scream and holler at 'em and jump on 'em and insult them. You know, I could get 'em to do it, but it would call for some very stringent things in order to get 'em to do it. And I had to sacrifice our relationship in order to get a job done. But I weeded out all the bad ones, got the group into good order. We never wound up being late; we never missed a date.

But I had those fights, I had the financial fights with the auditors, I had the road-manager fights with the promoters, I had to fight Ellington, I had to fight the guys in the band, and then in turn I had to fight the office. So you wind up eatin' dinner by yourself a lot of nights—if you've got an appetite, and the money to buy dinner [laughter].

PR: In addition to fronting the Duke Ellington band, haven't you just finished a book with Stanley Dance?

ME: Yeah, that's called *Duke Ellington in Person*. What we tried to do was expose his mind, to uncover the thoughts he had which lay under the veneer that he presented to the public. Like his superstitions. He would never write the finale for a show until the day of the show. He didn't like certain colors, and it was death if anybody brought a newspaper or peanuts into the dressing room or whistled backstage [laughter].

Those are really more the lighter things. In a sense he was a sadomasochist, and I try to point to certain examples of that and where it showed in his works, and so forth.

PR: That's interesting, because we've often wondered about the private side of Ellington.

ME: He could be ranting sometimes backstage, and the minute he crossed the wings the whole complexion and everything else could change. He was the most highly self-disciplined person that I think I've ever been around. He could be in a flaming argument, and two minutes later he'd be completely peaceful, and I'd still be up in the air screamin' and hollerin', and [he'd say], "Whatta you shoutin' about?" [Laughter.]

He always felt that the show must go on. He cited an instance of one guy who saved up for a couple of years in Europe and made his way hitchhiking and walking in order to come hear one concert, and he said, "If that's the concert that you take for granted, then you violate the principle that somewhere there's one man to which that one performance has the greatest meaning of all life, and so therefore every performance must be it. And it must be done to the greatest ability, because you cannot violate that one person who's out there."

In later years he never became unpleasant or acid in his approach to the audience, but there were a couple of times . . . He had this impediment in his right eye, and he usually made a request for people not to pop their flashbulbs, you know, particularly in a low setting that we call for when we're doing something like "Mood Indigo." And one reporter did it to him one night, and he took the glass of pop he had sittin' on the piano and just threw it in his face [laughter]. That's the only time I'd ever seen him react desperately in front of the public. He thought that he was there to entertain. If the audience had trouble, it should be off their minds for at least that brief moment they were there. That was Duke Ellington.

SELECTED DISCOGRAPHY

Steppin' into Swing Society. Coral 57225. 1958.

Colours in Rhythm. Coral 57293. 1959.

With Duke Ellington and His Orchestra. *Far East Suite.* RCA LSP-3782. 1966.

————. *In the Sixties.* RCA PD89565. 1966–67. Formerly called *The Popular Duke Ellington.*

——. *Second Sacred Concert.* Fantasy 8407/8. 1968.

————. *Duke Ellington's 70th Birthday Concert.* Solid State SS19000. 1969.

————. *The Afro-Eurasian Eclipse.* Fantasy F-9498. 1971.

Continuum. Fantasy 9481. 1974–75.

Hot and Bothered (A Re-Creation). Doctor Jazz FW 40029. 1985.

Digital Duke. GRP Records GRD9548. 1987.

BILL EVANS

Courtesy Fantasy, Inc.

B ill Evans, one of the foremost jazz pianists of the postbop era, profoundly influenced three generations of keyboard players. Among contemporary jazz's most popular and accessible artists, he had at least fifty albums as a leader and five Grammy Awards to his credit.

When playing, Evans would sit hunched over the keyboard, head parallel to his large hands, glasses dangling precariously off the bridge of his nose. Combined with the subtly lyric and impressionistic side of his music, his introspective image led to the early criticism that his sense of swing and time were too studied to involve his audiences.

Nowadays it is clear how inaccurate that criticism was. Many of Evans' early recordings as a sideman and a leader exhibit a powerful rhythmic authority, and even his most hushed ballad work rode on a steady inner propulsion. The last half decade of Evans' life saw his music enriched by an even more exuberant drive. This was due in part to changes in his personal life and a deeper confidence in his music but also to the dynamic musical partnerships he formed during that period, particularly with Jack DeJohnette on drums, Eddie Gomez on bass, and the members of his last trio, bassist Marc Johnson and drummer Joe LaBarbera.

Evans' distinctive touch and gorgeous voicings were unmistakable on acoustic or electric piano, inspiring great respect among his contemporaries. Miles Davis reportedly once said, "Bill Evans plays the piano the way it's supposed to be played." Evans drew deeply from the heritage of Western keyboard music, and his expansion of the song form in jazz, wedded to a harmonically rich romanticism, touched pianists as diverse as Keith Jarrett, Chick Corea, Joe Zawinul, George Winston, Herbie Hancock, Marian McPartland, and Paul Bley.

Born in Plainfield, New Jersey, in 1929, Evans began his musical studies at the age of six. After graduating from Southeastern Louisiana College, he worked with a succession of bands, including those fronted by clarinetist Tony Scott, bassist Charles Mingus, and composer George Russell, who first exposed Evans to modal-based jazz.

Evans' debut recording as a leader was *New Jazz Conceptions*, released by Riverside Records in 1958. However, it was not until his association with Miles Davis—he played with the sextet in 1958 and was then rehired in 1959 for the historic *Kind of Blue* recording sessions—that Evans gained international prominence.[1]

In 1959 Evans also established his initial, and many contend his most satisfying, working unit with the late Scott LaFaro on bass and Paul Motian on drums. From its inception, this group displayed an uncanny improvisational rapport and forged the prototype for the "pure" trio in modern jazz. A live recording made at the Village Vanguard in 1961 documents this trio and, in the opinion of some, is Evans' peak accomplishment.[2] Tragically, the glory days of this Evans band were cut short by LaFaro's death in a 1961 car accident. Suffering a profound personal and professional loss, Evans did not record for a year.

In 1962 he returned to the studio with Motian and bassist Chuck Israels, who was a sympathetic improviser in the mold of LaFaro. Evans varied his musical formats to some extent over the next two decades of his life from the occasional large ensemble to a series of duet and solo piano recordings. But until his death in 1980, Evans favored his trios, a setting that enabled him to transcend typical rhythm-section roles and cultivate new levels of interplay among piano, bass, and drums.

Bill Evans' dominance as a pianist has tended to eclipse his achievements as a composer. He left a modest but memorable legacy of jazz tunes, including "Peace Piece," "34 Skidoo," "Show-Type Tune," and perhaps his most inspired melody, the lyrical "Waltz for Debby."

Recorded 1979

WE: Bill, if music can be classified as a language, how does your trio approach this musical language to ensure that your message is reaching an audience?

BE: The language of music is sort of a motivic language. It's a developmental language in a sense, and there is just so many subtle ways that it's used in relationship to the form or the phrase or the period or whatever. I would say that I have worked hardest on my music to develop that kind of language. And I want it to come out of a genuine jazz tradition and to be absolutely a musical language as well, and it is something that I've dealt with personally on a very deep basis as much as I can with the music that we play. And to understand it one would have to listen to it correctly.

1. Miles Davis, *Kind of Blue*, Columbia Records, 1959.
2. Bill Evans, *The Village Vanguard Sessions*, Milestone Records, 1961.

Now some people might listen to our music as just a series of abstract ideas which are related to nothing except themselves. This isn't really enough. In order to really understand our music and the language that we use, one would have to be aware of always where the music is in relationship to the form that is being used in that particular performance or a particular piece. So that might take a little bit of conditioning. However, we do work with popular forms—forms that are felt by people that grow up in this culture—and I don't think it would take too much effort or concentration brought to bear before a person would be able to understand how to listen to our music. And one must really pay attention to it. It can be listened to as music in the background, and one could get an impression that that might be all it is, but really, as I say, in order to appreciate the language, what we're trying to say and the meaning of it, one would have to really know where we are in relationship to the particular thing we're doing.

I mean, I've certainly studied more or less all kinds of approaches to music and opened my mind to them and so on, but I've made the choice for various philosophical and personal reasons to go with the kind of idiomatic and form content that I use. And it can be, as I say, rather abstract if one doesn't tune in to where it's at. But I think the melodic content and harmonic content and even the form content of it all come out of popular music. And the traditional popular forms—not only out of the culture, but I mean really, you know, if we examine classical forms they basically come out of various song forms. Even the symphonic forms are extensions of smaller forms.

So, it's nothing new, but [in] the same way that a person would miss a great deal listening to a symphony if they don't understand the form, they would miss perhaps even more if they don't understand the form with us. But I'm not trying to be hard to understand; that certainly is not my goal as a musician. But of course, having gotten deeper into the music and trying to say more, we have gotten perhaps a little sophisticated. However, we like to feel that if people will make the effort to learn how to listen correctly that they would be rewarded, hopefully.

WE: Could you elaborate on what is meant by the term *song form*?

BE: Well, of course, there are many different kinds of song forms. The most well known would be an *a a b a* form in which there are three identical sections: one repeated at the beginning and then repeated again at the end—*a a*—and then the *b* as a transitional or opposite or different content that occurs. Strictly speaking, they would be like eight measures each; that makes what we call the thirty-two–bar song form. Now there also are, you might say, *a-1* form, which would be sixteen, and sixteen with a slight alteration in the second half; and then there are many different varieties that grow out of this.

Now, most things that I write I find more or less determine their own form out of a conditioning. I have to feel a song form and work some natural changes in it, and I'll be using some extensions and so forth. In fact, I am not even aware of the metric content unless I reexamine what I do. I just really feel the development of it.

So there are many varieties of song form, but when one learns to feel the form, and in listening, to feel the form, as long as it's not a concocted thing, you know, and screwed together somehow, it should be easy to feel. And I just happen to respect forms that come out of history and come out of culture and tradition as something which is substantial and real and which, if one learns to live with them and [they] become part of you, that you can then extend and use these things as organic means to make music.

I respect the American popular song very much and some of the masters that have composed in that form. And it became a means for jazz players to improvise by using a lot of these forms in songs to play off of. And I studied this very hard, analytically and diligently as I was growing, and got deeply enough into it so that I feel it's worthwhile to continue working with it, 'cause there's still explorations that I haven't begun to make yet into handling these things.

PR: As I understand you, you want to make enduring music of classical proportions. But some jazz musicians today seem less bent on classical values than on pursuing sounds and forms that reflect our everyday lives. Are there many current musicians who share your aesthetic?

BE: I think there are quite a few. But I know that there are people that, as you say, work with the everyday. The way I feel about all those things is everybody has to live with themselves, and I think everybody knows inside the reasons for doing what they're doing. "To each his own" is all I can say. I'm just doing a thing that gives me the greatest pleasure. I made my choice for my own reasons, and I'm willing to live with them, and I live with them pretty happily.

But I think that all that controversy about all those things, I don't know whether it really matters that much or not. Certainly *I* want something better than the everyday. When I go to any kind of art I look for something very special. I don't look for the person's bathroom noises or anything else. I don't want something everyday. I want something that they've had to really dedicate their lives to protecting, and nurturing, and cultivating, and searching for and bring me something special, you know, 'cause I could hear the everyday or see the everyday just by going out into the world, and I don't consider that to be art.

PR: As you were growing up, what was your exposure to the heritage of Western culture?

BE: Well, I think one of the primary influences that comes to my mind is the conditioning as children to have a great reverence for art. This is something which happens in certain families today. It doesn't seem to happen as much in the schools as it did then. Like, we were presented even in third and fourth grades and fifth and seventh grades, we would have a listening hour where we'd listen to great music. And whether or not nine out of ten of the kids really tuned in, all of them probably realized that here was something which was being presented with great respect so it must be important even if they didn't tune in. And the ones that did tune in developed that kind of respect.

Also from my family I got it. I think this is basic, in that you respect something which is far out of your sphere; it's not immediately attainable, and placing those artists in the realm of spiritual leaders, great people in history. The trend today is to glorify the mediocre. We'd like to think, it seems like, today that "Gee, if I bought enough electronic equipment and devoted six months of work, I too could be a great musician." But this kind of perspective of really great reverence and respect for something that's considered to be exceptional, then you just naturally devote yourself in a serious way to it. You take it seriously, you won't be satisfied with just superficial things, and I think that has a lot to do with it at bottom, the conditioning that you have towards your goals.

WE: During your formative years, was there a particular person or event that inspired you to become a musician?

BE: I'm sure that happened. The encounters which aren't so glamorous that were important were, for instance, having a wonderful woman as a teacher, my first teacher, who brought me into music and got me to read music, and therefore [I] developed a great ability to explore music through a superior sight-reading ability, without bringing the whip down as far as a type of approach to music like the scales and arpeggios and heavy technical work which would have, with my temperament at that age, turned me against music.

Other than that, there were, of course, many experiences or perhaps a good teacher here and there. Things that I came across, listening experiences, you know. I can remember, for instance, the 78 album of *Petruschka* which I got early on in high school as a Christmas present—a requested Christmas present. And just about wearing it out, learning it. That was the kind of music that at that time I hadn't been exposed to, and it just was a tremendous experience to get into that piece. But there were things like that all along the line.

I remember first hearing some of [Darius] Milhaud's polytonality and actually a piece that he may not think too much of—it was an early piece called *Suite Provençale*—which opened me up to certain things. But there were countless events like that which are all revelations in their own right and inspirational. I don't know, it's such an accumulative thing, you know, the ability to manipulate music in some kind of a comprehensive way. And I've really just kind of dealt with it piece by piece over a long period of time, and it seems that at this point in my idiom I enjoy a certain amount of freedom.

I mean, I've come to the point where I have a great deal of enjoyment playing, whereas for many years it was bringing a *great* deal of concentration to bear—*conscious* concentration of technical things, you know, of having to think a great deal—at the same time trying to leave one part of my mind free to just be the expressive part. Now it's more that I can enjoy almost the total expressive part, and I'm thinking only at less-conscious levels about technical things. So I have arrived at that point, which is very enjoyable, but it's taken a tremendous amount of preparatory years and efforts.

PR: Let's turn for a moment to the first trio you fronted that included bassist Scott LaFaro. How would you estimate LaFaro's contribution to modern bass playing, and what role did he play in the development of that first trio?

BE: In my mind Scott LaFaro was responsible in a lot of ways for the expansion of the bass. I think he is acknowledged, at least within musical circles, as being more or less the father or the wellspring of modern bass players. And when we got together I realized that Scott had the conceptual potential, he had the virtuosity, and he had the experience and the musical responsibility, and so forth, to handle the problem of approaching the bass function in jazz, especially with a trio, which is a very pure kind of setup with more freedom.

I thought I could depend on him to approach this, and we just really accepted a conceptual goal which was more conversational, more a thing where, including the drums, where everybody could contribute. They didn't have to play the roles that were more or less assigned by jazz tradition—that you could only walk at this time, that you could only do this at this time, and you could only do this at this time—but rather leave our minds wide open but with responsibility, so that we weren't just going off into space, that we were using that tradition but allowing ourselves to be a little bit more open within it. And of course, with that trio in a space of about two years we tried to work toward that goal with responsibility . . .

The last night that that trio played together [in July, 1961] before the tragedy of Scott being killed in an automobile accident, I think we had worked toward those goals pretty well. We had reached at least a point of some development in it that meant something. Even on the very first record you could hear that we were already working towards that, but I think it got a much more refined and complete thing by the time we had done the last records.

Musicians, you know, in various countries told us that those particular records seem to have had an impact in that they represented this kind of—wasn't like a kind of a break, an iconoclastic thing, you know, where we just *rebelled* against everything. That wasn't the kind of break it was; it was more like an extension of what had been happening and perhaps more of a completion or something like that.

But anyhow, that was the beginning of it, and that sort of conceptualized the trios that I had after that. I mean, they were more or less modeled on the development that we had made with that trio. And of course, we developed in other ways within those conceptual goals that we had accomplished.

But I might add that—maybe it's a personal thing, you know—I'm also coming into, I think, a new period in the last couple of years or so. But the particular trio I have now with Marc Johnson on bass and Joe LaBarbera on drums is giving me a great deal of pleasure. It has me excited, and [I'm] enjoying myself in a way that—really I can't remember feeling this way *since* that original trio. So it is kind of really a good feeling, and it's also a marvelous thing to feel that a bassist twenty-five years old, Marc Johnson, can come into my trio with all the abilities and aesthetic and love the music and fit right in emotionally and aesthetically, and Joe LaBarbera who is just a little over thirty, because I'm of another generation, and it's encouraging to me that, you know, that they're interested enough in the music in every way to become a real part of it.

PR: Could you elaborate on the musical function of each member in your trio?

BE: This is a rather pure group, in that there's just one person really for each function, and then we cross over the other functions. I mean, the drummer is really controlling timbre and various colors and contributions in the rhythm and, you know, the propulsion and other things, maybe just coloring, or whatever. And then you have the bass function primarily in the bass, and then he becomes a solo voice also, and an accompanying voice. And then, of course, I have most of the time the primary voice in the harmonic content. And of course, we all share all these roles in various degrees as we move around. But I don't really define the roles so much, because at this level it's like we all just approach the music, and I expect them to be responsible to the music and not everybody to be just indulging themselves. And we try to dedicate ourselves to the total musical statement, whatever it might be, and try to shape it according to musical ends and not ego ends.

PR: How do you feel about extended choruses?

BE: I think things get a little lopsided sometimes, when everybody takes seventy choruses. It seems to be justified in certain ways, but to me, it's not just fine in terms of the content or the thing that they're doing—it just stretches it out beyond all dimensions, beyond any kind of emotional shape that's desirable.

If you'll notice, if we play a concert we may do seven, eight, or nine things in the first half. Now, what I try to think of in a set like that is I choose each thing to follow each thing in a way so there's a total pacing to the set. I'm really quite sensitive to that, in that in clubs I won't even predetermine sets, but I have an ability now to pace, let's say, an almost infinite number of combinations of what we do in a way that will generally work out to be a very well-paced set and a very well-shaped set. So that what we're thinking of in terms of individual pieces in effect become almost movements—you might say there will be eight or nine movements in a total work. A set would be like a total work. I'm thinking in terms of the keys and the moods and tempos and all kinds of things, you know— who might be playing a lot on one thing and not much on another. And trying to really shape this thing so that it's an emotional and musical feeling of inevitability in a sense, you know, that one thing moves to another with a sense of purpose.

So I like to feel that we don't work one thing too hard, you know, that before you get feeling like "Gee, they've been on that too long," we move into a change, some sort of a change of mood that is somehow emotionally the next thing that should or could happen that will be satisfying.

WE: Many active pianists have commented on the impact of your conception on their playing. Are you aware of the influence you have had on other players?

BE: No, it's really difficult for me to see or feel those things. I believe it's true, because it's been said so much, you know, and for so long that I suppose there's some truth in it. I don't look for it, and I don't recognize it as much as—once in a while I seem to catch an inkling of it, but of course, I'm not looking for it.

First of all, I never strived for identity. That's something that just has happened automatically as a result, I think, of just putting things together, tearing things apart and putting it together my own way, and somehow I guess the individual comes through eventually. I suppose I could see where I could be an influence, because I think what I've done is I've put something together which is not eccentric; it's a nice kind of eclectic amalgamation of what has gone down maybe before me or something like that. And I think it's something that a student of music who is talented that's coming up can focus on and draw from. Now somebody like Monk or even Erroll Garner who are great are in a sense so stylized, and in the case of Monk even eccentric, that it's sort of very difficult to get into their bag at all or to utilize much of what they've done. You can learn from their spirit more than anything.

So maybe that's one reason why I might have been an influence, and it's something that somebody can pass through also. They can become influenced by it, and they could also just then move through it, because it's not eccentric and it's not so *highly* stylized, I think. At least that's the way I see it, that it might be attractive for that reason.

PR: We're surprised to hear that you never strived for identity. Within four bars your sound is unmistakable!

BE: Well, if there is a striving for identity, it's something that's so much a part of my individuality or personality that it's just automatic. I never said, like, "I want to have an identity," in so many words. What I said was

"I want to approach the musical problems as an individual. I want to build my music from the bottom up, piece by piece, and kind of put it together according to my own way of organizing things. Yet I want it to fit in, but I'm not going to take it *in toto* from any one place," which is what I did, really. I just have a reason that I arrived at myself for every note I play. Now, I think just as a result of that you probably have an identity—just because you are an individual and you see the problem, and so forth, in your own way. But as far as saying, like, "I'm going to project my person-ality" or "I'm going to project an image onto music"—a kind of a per-sonality image onto music, which is kind of the way most people think of identity—that was no part of it whatsoever. And I don't think that can be effective.

I think having one's own sound in a sense is the most fundamental kind of identity in music. But it's a very touchy thing how one arrives at that. It has to be something that comes from inside, and it's a long-term process. It's a product of a total personality. Why one person is going to have it and another person isn't, I don't know why exactly. I think some-times the people I seem to like most as musical artists are people who have had to—they're like late arrivers. Many of them are late arrivers. They've had to work a lot harder in a sense to get facility, to get fluency, and like that. Whereas you see a lot of young talents that have a great deal of fluidity and fluency and facility, and they never really carry it any-place. Because in a way they're not aware enough of what they're doing.

There are certain artists—Miles Davis is a late arriver in a sense. I mean, he arrived early, but you couldn't just hear his development until he *finally* really arrived later. And Tony Bennett is another one that's just always worked and dug and tried to improve, and finally, what he does as a straight singer has a kind of a dimension in it and is able to transport the listener way beyond other singers in his category. Or Thad Jones is another one that I can enjoy listening to play. I enjoy listening to players that think for themselves, especially. I mean, you could line up a hundred players that all more or less sound alike, and they're all good players, and I can even enjoy listening to them. But if just one of them thinks for himself, he stands out like a neon sign. And it's so refreshing to hear someone who thinks for himself.

Now at the same time, the danger of a person grabbing a concept like this is that they think thinking for themselves is being eccentric or being rebellious or being—especially of being "different"—and that's not it.

The idea is to try to be real and right in the core, right in the middle, but still be an individual enough to handle the material in your own way.

PR: So is it fair to say that you consider yourself a late arriver?

BF.: See, I said I was coming into the new period, and it has something to do with this, in that I'm opening up the expressive feeling more. I'm allowing it a little more room, and I think the dimensions are growing, you know, so that the feelings can become a little larger, a little more grand, perhaps, which I don't know makes that much difference. Perhaps those feelings were there all the while, and maybe I'm just going to display them a little bit differently or something.

But yeah, as I say, the early arrivers are always a little suspect to me, although they many times show great facility, and I can enjoy them, but I have generally found that very few of them carry things forward or take things into a new area. Those types of talents generally are very assimilative. They have that ability—some sort of a conglomerate of intuition which just takes and sops up and just sort of comes out, you know, it organizes itself and comes out, but they don't know generally, completely enough, all the constituent things that go into what they do, and therefore, they're not able to really discard and add to in any conscious way, and they're kinda trapped, in a sense, by that facility.

WE: Let's turn to some of our favorite Bill Evans recordings. "My Funny Valentine" from *Undercurrent* is a knockout.[3] Could you give us some insight into that session?

BE: Sure. Alan Douglas was the producer of that album for United Artists. Monty Kay was managing me at the time, and he said, "I've talked to Jim Hall, and if you guys would like to do an album together, it would be nice. Just pick the rhythm section that you want." And it just occurred to me, knowing Jim's ability, the broad ability that he had, that this might be something we could do without [a] rhythm section, that we might do just together, so we proceeded with that conception. And we did it in one night.

However, Alan Douglas asked, as the producer, that we do all low-key, more ballad-type things, totally. So really what happened was that by the time we had done the rest of the record, aside from "Funny Valentine," we were beginning to feel a little frustrated that we hadn't moved into another mood. And we said, "Look, we just gotta do, you know, some-

3. Bill Evans and Jim Hall, *Undercurrent*, United Artists Records, 1962.

thing that moves a little more." And we selected "My Funny Valentine," which we played at a very bright tempo, as you know. And I think one of the reasons that it kind of comes to life is that it was the only thing that we did in that mood.

PR: Another favorite is *Interplay*, with Freddie Hubbard on trumpet.[4] We don't often hear you in the company of horns. Why is that?

BE: I don't know exactly. Of course, I was concentrating a great deal on the trio and its development. But I like that album myself. I love all the musicians on it, and it was just one of those things we did, I think, in one afternoon. The frameworks were rather loose, just enough to give us something to play off of, and these wonderful players, you know, just made a really good-feeling album out of it. And I still enjoy listening to that album.

But I have done some albums more recently with horns. There are two quintet albums that came out recently. One called *Quintessence*, with Ray Brown, Philly Joe Jones, and Harold Land on tenor, and Kenny Burrell on guitar.[5] And then there's another quintet album most recently, called *Cross-Currents*, with Lee Konitz on alto and Warne Marsh on tenor and my trio.[6] And the latest release on Warner Brothers is called *Affinity*, with Toots Thielemans on harmonica featured most prominently, and Larry Schneider plays tenor and soprano on a few tracks.[7] So it does happen—I do try to vary the output—like it'll either be a solo album or perhaps an album with a large orchestra, you know, or a quintet album or trio album. The trio, however, is the fundamental performing group, so that occurs most frequently. But I think there was a stretch where I didn't play with horns for quite a while on record, and I expect I'll make up for that maybe in the future, because I enjoy playing with horns.

WE: Our last question, Bill. A lot of musicians today disavow the term *jazz*. Do you?

BE: No, I don't, because it's just most naturally the term that is associated with our kind of music. Unfortunately, for instance, in the *Book of Lists*—I don't know if you're aware of that book, it just has lists of various things from the five most humorous letters to "Dear Abby" to the seven tallest mountains in the world or whatever—but [of] the seven words in

4. Bill Evans, *Interplay*, Riverside Records, 1962.
5. Bill Evans, *Quintessence*, Fantasy Records, 1976.
6. Bill Evans, *Cross-Currents*, Fantasy Records, recorded 1977, released 1978.
7. Bill Evans, *Affinity*, Warner Brothers Records, 1979.

the English language that elicit the most negative response, one of them is *jazz*.

It was very discouraging to find this in the *Book of Lists*. And I think one of the reasons that some people just adopt a more or less pop-oriented name which is not like the Bill Evans Trio, but you know, we might call ourselves the Light Switch or something and then never use the word *jazz* in association with the music. Surprisingly enough, if you do that you'll probably enjoy a much-greater public acceptance, and it just has a lot to do with the fact that jazz is a categorization that a lot of people do not react positively to. But *I* don't disavow the word.

SELECTED DISCOGRAPHY

Everybody Digs Bill Evans. Riverside VDJ-1517. 1958.
With Scott LaFaro. *The Village Vanguard Sessions*. Milestone 47002. 1961.
The Interplay Sessions. Milestone M-47066. 1962.
With Jim Hall. *Undercurrent*. United Artists 14003. 1962.
Conversations with Myself. Verve 821 984-2. 1963.
The Tokyo Concert. Fantasy F9454. 1973.
With Eddie Gomez. *Intuition*. Fantasy F-9475. 1974.
Alone (Again). Fantasy F-9542. 1975.
Montreux III. Fantasy F-9510. 1975.
The Paris Concert, Edition Two. Elektra Musician E4 60311. 1979.

GIL EVANS

Photograph by Chuck Stewart. Used with permission.

A few years before he died, bandleader-composer-arranger–keyboard wizard Gil Evans met with us in a frigid third-floor New York City loft that served as office space for Artists House Records. The little company, now defunct, had a grand piano in a corner, and Evans had a key to the door.

This true innovator of modern jazz orchestration entertained and educated us. He sat at the piano and played the spine-tingling opening notes of Louis Armstrong's "West End Blues" as he recalled the first time—in 1928—that he had seen the great trumpeter in person.[1] In a flash, Evans slipped from Armstrong to the haunting opening chords of rock guitarist Jimi Hendrix's "The Wind Cries Mary."[2] He pointed out in words and music how he and Miles Davis had incorporated the chords of that tune into Davis' recording of "Filles de Kilimanjaro."[3]

By the time we hopped onto the freight elevator several hours later, we understood what saxophonist Arthur Blythe had told us in a previous interview. "Gil knows everything about jazz, and I mean everything," Blythe had said. "But when you play music with him or talk to him, he's just Gil, a regular guy, funny and smart, and really into the music."

Born Ernest Gilmore Green in Toronto in 1912, Gil Evans (he took the surname of his stepfather) grew up in northern California. Mostly self-taught, Evans worked in radio during the thirties, most notably for Bob Hope's broadcasts, and from 1933 to 1938 he led and wrote for his own bands, first in Stockton and then in Balboa Beach, California. His first major career break came in 1942, when Claude Thornhill hired him to write arrangements for his popular orchestra.

Evans migrated to New York City during the height of the bebop era. There he lived at first in a windowless, one-room basement apartment

1. "West End Blues," on *Louis Armstrong*, vol. 4, *Louis Armstrong and Earl Hines*, Columbia Jazz Masterpieces, recorded 1928, reissued 1989.

2. "The Wind Cries Mary," recorded by Jimi Hendrix, on *Are You Experienced?* Polydor Records, 1967.

3. "Filles de Kilimanjaro," recorded by Miles Davis, on *Filles de Kilimanjaro*, Columbia Records, 1968.

that became a meeting place for several jazz greats, including Charlie "Bird" Parker and an up-and-coming young trumpet player named Miles Davis.

Evans collaborated with Miles Davis between 1948 and 1950, arranging tunes that Miles's nonet recorded during the legendary *Birth of the Cool* sessions.[4] He left the jazz world to work in radio and television during much of the fifties, but he resurfaced with a vengeance when his renewed association with Davis resulted in three of the most memorable albums in all of modern jazz: *Miles Ahead*, *Porgy and Bess*, and *Sketches of Spain*.[5]

Evans released his first album as a leader in 1957.[6] This was followed by dozens of other solid efforts over the next three decades, most of them with various editions of his big band. His release in the early sixties on MCA/Impulse, *Out of the Cool*, remains one of his best—"years ahead of its time," according to one reviewer—with its oddly structured counterrhythms and chromatic bluesy touch.[7] This recording also includes "La Nevada," one of Evans' most unforgettable compositions. A planned project uniting Evans and Jimi Hendrix was thwarted by Hendrix's premature death in 1970. A sense of what this union might have achieved can be found in Evans' 1974 release *Gil Evans Plays the Music of Jimi Hendrix*.[8]

Evans worked sporadically in public throughout most of the eighties, although for several years he appeared on Monday nights with his big band at Sweet Basil, a New York City nightclub that was also the site for several of his last recordings. Seated at the electric keyboard amid a group of fifteen to twenty world-class musicians, this white-haired, craggy-faced veteran would close his eyes and wordlessly introduce one of his tunes with a few carefully placed notes.

Gil Evans' death in 1988 ended one of the most celebrated careers in modern jazz. His legacy places him alongside such figures as Jelly Roll

4. Miles Davis, *Birth of the Cool*, Capitol Records, recorded 1949–50, released, 1957, reissued, 1989.

5. Miles Davis, *Miles Ahead*, Columbia Records, 1957; Miles Davis, *Porgy and Bess*, Columbia Records, 1959; Miles Davis, *Sketches of Spain*, Columbia Records, 1960.

6. *Gil Evans plus Ten*, Prestige Records, 1957.

7. Gil Evans, *Out of the Cool*, MCA/Impulse Records, 1960.

8. *Gil Evans Plays the Music of Jimi Hendrix*, RCA/Bluebird Records, 1974.

Morton, Fletcher Henderson, and Tadd Dameron in the pantheon of enduring jazz writers.

Recorded 1980

PR: Are you a fan of any of today's big bands?

GE: I don't know any other big bands. I mean, I haven't heard any big bands.

PR: How about the Toshiko Akiyoshi–Lew Tabackin Band? They've been getting a lot of press lately.

GE: She writes *good.* Oh yeah, I enjoy her.

PR: Are you impressed with Tabackin's work as a soloist?

GE: I'm not crazy about such long solos, man. I thought he played too long on some of them. I thought he played too long in my opinion, my personal opinion. I'm gettin' kinda down on solos that are too long. It's all right when you're dancin' or somethin', but sittin' and listenin' to them—they better be good. They better be excellent, I mean.

PR: I guess there are very few musicians who . . .

GE: Yeah, that can carry out *that* long. I mean, even Coltrane when he'd go into the second hour would be, you know—the reason Coltrane could do it more than other people is he had an original sound. So my wife and I used to just go there and sit and bathe in that sound. He might play a number that'd last an hour and a half. But with that *sound.* He created a sound that had never been heard before, right? When you got one of those, you got more or less of a free hand. You can do a lot more. You can play a lot more variety of music and longer and get by with it, right?

But if you're playing with a traditional sound and you still have a lot of good music in you, you can't get by too long with arpeggios and things, you know what I mean? For me you can't, anyway. I need better pacing and more space, you know what I mean? You don't have to have a constant sound going like you're squeezing the tube and it's constantly coming out. You never stop it, you know. It has to have pacing.

You know, like Miles Davis, for example, when he plays, a lot of times he needs space. The idea is—if you have a good setting and you like your setting, then you don't mind leaving the space. Let the setting take it along for a while and then you come in—do that kind of thing. But when you play a continual flow for too long a period of time it numbs you out, you know. It can interfere with your attention span, right?

WE: Do the arrangements you're writing now take more advantage of space and pacing than your earlier work?

GE: Well, when you say "my arrangements now"—I haven't written any arrangements for a long time. I've been mostly, I've been domesticating, I guess.

I have a family. I didn't have one before, you know. We have two children; it's an experience for me. I was almost fifty-five when I had the children. 'Cause like I'm pushing seventy now, so they were the first children I ever had. Right now, since I've never had teenagers before and my teenagers have never been teenagers before, we're going through some funny changes, you know. I mean, I didn't really know what to expect. Now they're at the age where they don't want you to run their life and yet they don't want you to *not* run their life.

WE: Are you experiencing the generation gap?

GE: I don't know what "the generation gap" means, really. What does it mean? It might mean that you don't get high the same as your kids, right? Well, I've been smoking grass for forty years, so it's no new thing for me. The drug scene is not a gap between us there, you know. And yet I'm really against it in a sense, even though I drank when I was young; I drank in high school. I have a hard time getting used to the fact that my kids are smokin' grass, you know what I mean? Because it's just a different thing. Anyway, I was kind of shocked about that. I still would appreciate it if they'd confine it to weekends [laughter].

PR: Have you found it tough over the years trying to make a living as a jazz arranger?

GE: I've never really been too money-minded, you know. I was having so much fun at one time writin' the arrangements that I didn't realize that arranging is a loser's game because you don't get paid any royalties. But I had such a juvenile attitude about money up until recently that I used to feel that if I spent the day working that I should find a check in the mailbox the next day. I didn't care who it was from; I had it coming to me, right? It never came.

PE: Did you ever get *any* money for your early arrangements?

GE: No. I've never gotten any royalties for any arrangement I've done. It's a loser's game, but the way that most people make up for it now is that they take a percentage—you know, they get a couple of points in the album. You still can't get any royalties for the arrangements themselves, because whoever writes the melody gets the money, right?

That happened to Stravinsky. He was living in a little French coast town one time writing *Petrushka*. So every day this hurdy-gurdy man would come by, you know, organ grinder come by, playin' this little tune, and so he naturally figured it was public domain, and he put it into *Petrushka*. So he put it in there and found out that it had been written by an Englishman who was still alive, and so he had to pay him 25 percent of the royalties for that thing forever. Of course, that was a big drag for Stravinsky. So I mean, I just thought of that because no matter who wrote the melody, they get the money. No matter what you do with the melody, they still get the money.

PR: That seems strange, since during the heyday of the big bands the arranger was such a powerhouse.

GE: I heard Fletcher Henderson only got fifty dollars apiece for those arrangements. That's what I heard. He was responsible for that band's success—the whole thing.[9] He wrote the original arrangements for that band and set the style for it.

WE: When you were young, did you set out to be an arranger?

GE: I just became—I mean, I never thought about it as a term. That's just what I did.

WE: How did you learn?

GE: I copied records. I copied them. I wrote them down note for note. That's how I learned. I started with Louis Armstrong, as far as getting a feeling for music. I got my feeling for music from Louis Armstrong. I bought every record he ever made from the time I started buying records in 1927.

I learned arranging and the orchestration more from people like Fletcher and Duke and Don Redman and Gene Gifford from the Casa Loma Orchestra. No teacher. I didn't need a teacher for that. But better to have one if you can find a good one. It's better in the sense that it speeds up your education more, you know what I mean? It took me a lot longer to learn than I would've if I'd studied, but at the same time there was no one to study with. At that time, you couldn't find anybody that liked that music who was teaching, you know. Teachers only liked Western European music, classical music.

9. Evans is referring to the Benny Goodman Band.

WE: Where were you living at the time?

GE: I lived in Berkeley, California, when I heard my first jazz. I was goin' to Berkeley High at the time. A friend of mine, his father made a play-room for him and his brother in the basement. He was a very advanced father because he had this idea. He had a whole room for them down there with a set of drums, a piano, and a record player and all that. And this was in 1927, so you know that was somethin'. He took us over to San Francisco, and we heard Duke Ellington for the first time in 1927. He played the Orpheum Theatre there.

PR: We didn't know that Ellington appeared on the West Coast that early in his career.

GE: Yeah, he came out there for that. They played "Mood Indigo" with the original group with Bubber Miley and Joe Nanton and Barney Bi-gard—that was the trio in "Mood Indigo." Sonny Greer was sittin' way up high singin' into a megaphone. The trumpet players were Freddie Jenkins, a left-handed trumpet player who is a showman—trumpets were out in front. And Arthur Wetzel was a beautiful lead player.

PR: Did you hear other bands?

GE: The bands used to broadcast, you know. When I was in Stockton in high school, the bands used to come over from the East Coast, and it was a lot later here, so we got them in the late afternoons sometimes. I used to hear Don Redman, Isham Jones, Casa Loma, Duke, Andy Kirk. Live. Well, there were other big bands then that nobody remembers now— Claude Hopkins. He [still] plays piano, usually around in small groups. He hasn't had a big band for a long time, but he had a good band.

WE: Was anything happening in Los Angeles at that time?

GE: Well, Frank Sebastian's Cotton Club was open then, and there was a band in there called Les Hite. Very good local band, and Lionel [Hampton] was the drummer, right? And Louis Armstrong came out and fronted the band, so to speak. They accompanied him, you know. He made a couple of his best records with Les Hite's band. If you ever get a chance, you oughta hear "Memories of You" and "You're Lucky to Me." Oh man, they're beautiful.

Lionel played, I think he played the first jazz vibes that were ever played. I was playing this record recently of "Memories of You"—it's a ballad, right? And he played an introduction on that ballad that's just as good now as it was in 1930. So one time there was a jazz festival down at the [Carter] White House, a couple of years ago. Lionel was there, and I snuck up to him, and I sang him that introduction, 'cause I remember it [laughter].

One night on the radio they played "Shine." It was a number that Louis used to play, and at the end he plays a high C and ends on a high F, right? Well, this night he played 250 high C's before he hit the high F. The band started counting "one, two, three . . ." And when it got to 50 I was goin' crazy; it got to a hundred, I couldn't believe it; well, finally I stopped, 'cause I didn't know where it was gonna end. Two hundred and fifty high C's before he got to high F!

PR: Did you ever meet Louis Armstrong?

GE: Yeah, I did that here one time at the Astor Hotel when they had those Grammy Awards, and he was up there to get an award for "Hello Dolly!" It's a great big ballroom made into a dining room with tables, and everybody's havin' dinner, and then you go outside and walk a long hall down and back in again to get up on the stage. There was a little table outside—there was some drinks on it—so I was just walkin' along down there, and he was standin' there having a drink. I introduced myself, and we talked for a minute.

PR: Did he know who you were?

GE: Well, yes he did, because he had bought Miles Davis' record that I had made, and I think at that time we had done *Porgy and Bess*. He said that Miles reminded him of Buddy Bolden, which was a funny little side-light, because no one ever heard Buddy Bolden, you know. When I tell some people that, they wonder if Louis Armstrong ever heard Buddy Bolden, and I said, "I don't know, but that's what he said" [laughter].

PR: Did you ever think of making a record with Armstrong?

GE: That night I met him. After we talked for a while and I sang him all these different parts of his records and asked him all these different questions, he said, "Geez, you're"—I said, "I know it. I'm the number one Louis Armstrong expert. I know all about the records." He said, "We should make an album. Why don't you go and see my man, Joe Glaser." So I went and saw Joe Glaser. In the first place, he'd never heard of me. He said, "You have to realize this about Louis Armstrong. He's a very friendly man, and he gets a few drinks in him, and he may have just said something to make you feel good." So we never got to make the album.

WE: Buddy Bolden certainly is a figure shrouded in mystery.

GE: Buddy Bolden was in a mental institution for the last thirty years of his life. I think he lived up until sometime in the late thirties. I don't think he played after around 1910, or somethin' like that, but he lived to be, I think maybe, even to 1940, it was very late that he lived. It was a shame that nobody could get ahold of him and maybe feed him some of the new pills they have, tranquilizers and all that, to maybe straighten him out just to play a little bit longer like they did with Bunk Johnson.

Bunk Johnson came to New York. He had a *ball* here for a while. You know he hadn't played for a long time. But somebody went to a dentist and got him some false teeth, and he played. I was standin' in a bar one night on Fifty-second Street, and he was talkin' there and all, and all of a sudden he said, "I got to go uptown and get me some fuckin'," and away he went, this old man [laughter]. He was seventy-five, something like that. It was funny, you know. He was havin' such a good time.

PR: Did you ever meet Duke Ellington?

GE: Yeah I did. A couple of times. He called me one time and told me that I was his favorite orchestrator. I said, "Well, my, I sure appreciate that." Yeah, he called me on the phone. I found out later that he was a great telephone man anyway. Every time he sat down anywhere he had to telephone people. He did that to me, and I appreciated it.

WE: Let's talk about Claude Thornhill. Do you remember a 1940 recording by Thornhill's band, "Portrait of a Guinea Farm"?[10]

GE: I'm surprised that that tune is not more well known, because it's a masterpiece. A *masterpiece*, that's all. Period. Six notes on that record, right? That's all, just those six notes, man. 'Cause Fazola had a sound, man.[11] He was a New Orleans player with a beautiful sound.

WE: We're curious about the title.

GE: Well, it's a silly name. I'll tell you, the name is trivial compared to the music, in my opinion. Everybody has their own sense of humor, and that's not mine. You know what I mean, it's not that funny to me. I don't think the tune should have had a funny title, 'cause it's a very serious piece. It's a great piece. "Guinea Farm," I mean, that might've been Claude's idea.

PR: What year did you join Thornhill?

GE: Forty-two. But I was only with them a short time. We all got drafted. I was with them maybe a little under a year, I think. Then we all got drafted, and then Claude started the band up again in '46.

10. "Portrait of a Guinea Farm," recorded about 1940, appears on *Best of Big Bands/Claude Thornhill*, Columbia Records, 1990.

11. Irving Fazola was a clarinetist with Thornhill's band.

PR: Was the band performing "Portrait of a Guinea Farm" at that time?
GE: I don't remember whether the band was playin' that. See, because at the time I joined Claude I was so self-centered I wouldn't even ask him to play it. I was too busy writin' the arrangements myself. I mean, I was only interested in my own arrangements for Claude Thornhill. At that time I wouldn't have begged him to play "Portrait of a Guinea Farm."
PR: Were you traveling with the band?
GE: Well, most of the time I lived in Glen Island Casino, and the band was in Glen Island Casino most of the time. And then when they went on the road I'd go somewhere, wherever they were, and rehearse an arrangement and then come home and write another one and go wherever they were again. The only time I traveled with them was at the end when we knew that the band was going to fold. Then I stayed with them on the road for the last tour.
PR: Was it a good band?
GE: It was a great band. It was a shame [it folded], because it was just timed poorly, you know what I mean. Just those four years that Claude was gone the whole music scene changed, and by the time he came back it was too late to be a hit. Bebop and also rhythm and blues—they were in there. They were getting a big come-along about that time. You couldn't really get the prices you used to get, and Claude just couldn't make enough, you know.
WE: Like Bolden, Thornhill also died in obscurity, didn't he?
GE: Yeah, he did. He died the same day my second boy was born. Somebody called me to go to the funeral. I said, "Gee, I can't, I just had a baby, I can't go." He was a great artist, a great piano player. Whew! A beautiful sound. He could've been a great concert piano player if he wanted. A great pianist. And a great orchestrator, too, great arranger.
WE: Did you collaborate with him?
GE: No. There was another arranger that he worked with mostly like that. He would write and sketch out for him. But most of the time he let me work on my own. He liked everything I did until bebop came along. He wasn't too crazy about me doing those.

Bebop came in when I was in the army. I started buyin' Bird's and Dizzy's records, and so by the time I came back I was ready to incorporate that kind of rhythm and harmony. He liked some of it, but he would rather have kept the band playing mostly like his ballad style, you know, which was a very strong style, like "Small Hotel" and "Where or When," that type of thing.

PR: Miles Davis was beginning to attract attention at about that time. How did you first meet him?

GE: I met him on Fifty-second Street. See, I came back to town after I got out of the army. I got off the train, took my bags and went to Fifty-second Street, and checked 'em in a checkroom, and I didn't even have a place to stay. I didn't even care, 'cause I wanted to hear that music. The first person I ran into was Bud Powell. I said, "Bud, you're the greatest." He said, "Yeah? Get me a job" [laughter]. He was unimpressed. He knew he was the greatest. So anyway, that's where I met Miles. He was playin' with Bird.

PR: How long was it before you started working with him?

GE: Well, I had an apartment right near Fifty-second Street. Finally when I got to know everybody, then I just left the door open. It was open twenty-four hours a day, you know. People just came in and out, and I had a record player, and a recorder, and a piano, and that's all you needed. So we'd talk about the music, and that's how it happened.

WE: Were you always in the studio for record dates with Miles? Like, for instance, your first project together, *Birth of the Cool*?

GE: Well, you know, it's a funny thing. Never before or since had I ever written an arrangement where I wasn't at the record date. But everybody was so familiar with that idiom at that time—those players—that I had to go home to California to visit my mother. She wasn't feelin' well or something, so I had to go back to California. And I gave Miles the arrangement of "Boplicity," and they recorded it. And when I heard it, it was perfect. They did it just as though I'd been there. That was the only time I've never been at one.

After that I had to be at every one. Even though everybody was familiar with the music, I still had to be there because it was a larger project, you know. But records like *Miles Ahead*, we did that in three 3-hour sessions with no rehearsal, 'cause that was what you were supposed to do in those days. Everybody was supposed to be able to read and all that. Later when the music changed and the popular music came in, the people were strong on ideas, but it would take them a long time to get the idea under their fingers, you know. So gradually the record companies were allowing more and more time for players who were strong on ideas but needed the time to practice them while making the record. So it got to be up to 100,

150, 200 hours were allowed sometimes to make an album, instead of 9. Nine hours is all we had.

WE: A lot of Miles's music in the seventies has been panned by the critics.

GE: Well, it all depends. You know, some people prefer the acoustic band. And it was a great band, so they just wished he'd always had that. It's always been that way. When anything changes there's always a large segment of the public that doesn't want anything to change because they're feeling very comfortable with what's happening, right?

Every innovator has that problem with sound. Now you know there's a famous story about Prez [Lester Young] when he first came on the scene. They were sayin' "You sound just like an alto. Why don't you have one, why don't you play one?" Because everybody was so used to hearing the tenor sound of Coleman Hawkins, and everybody felt so comfortable with it—and it is beautiful—but nobody wanted it to change. And Prez had a very hard time at first, you know, on account of that. And Coltrane the same. When Coltrane changed the sound of the tenor, people were just beginning to get used to Prez, right? They didn't want to hear that. It's just a question of, you know, you get feeling comfortable, and it's convenient and all that. You know what I mean? Convenience is an addiction in itself.

PR: Did you ever work with Eric Dolphy?

GE: Yeah, I did. I knew Eric, and he was on some of my things. I have nothing where he plays a solo on any of my records, but he plays some parts. I know he's there. Phew!

He could play parts too—not only his solos, but his sound. His sound came more from Ornette [Coleman], you know. Kind of a combination of Ornette and Bird. I had a rehearsal one time with three saxophones just playing unison. I never got to record it. It was Eric Dolphy, Steve Lacy and—who was that Danish saxophone player who died? Well anyway, the Paramount Theatre had a rehearsal place up in the back of the building, and I got to use it one time, and I got them together and had them play all these numbers in unison. Man, you shoulda heard that unison with Eric Dolphy and Steve Lacy. Steve has that perfect pitch, and Dolphy could gliss in and out of the thing, and you never heard such a thing. Those were the days before cassettes, so I never recorded it.

Eric Dolphy died from an overdose of honey, did you know that? Everybody thinks that he died from an overdose of dope, but he was on a health kick. He got instant diabetes. He didn't know he had it, see, so he was on a health kick, and he's eating nuts and eating a couple of these little jars of honey every day. It killed him. He went into a coma and never came out of it.

WE: One of our favorite recordings of yours is the 1973 release *Svengali.*[12] What were the circumstances of that date?

GE: That was a live recording from a church downtown, and it was the best I could get out of it from the balance and all that was there. But it's a pretty good album.

It was a lunch-type thing that they had down there, and people would just come in off the street, and they never knew what was going to be there. They'd just come in and sit in the church, and whatever the program was—and they weren't used to the kind of thing we were doing, because most of that was classical. And while we're still playing and trying to make this live recording, this lady in the wings is saying "All right, you boys, you've got to stop playing now." And you could hear her. We had to finally cut parts of the music out, because you could hear her trying to get rid of us, and the band saying "We'll be through in a minute," you know, that kind of stuff.

It was a funny, informal thing, so I'm glad we got an album out of it. The man who sponsored it was a painter named Ken Noland. He had liked my music, and he said, "This band should make an album." Ken paid the salaries and all that kinda thing. He spent thirty thousand dollars of his own money for that album.

PR: We understand you're about to perform and give a talk at a college in Seattle. Do you enjoy doing clinics?

GE: No, I've never done this before, 'cause I'm not academically inclined, and I never really did like the idea too much to do a thing like this. But the band sounds good, and it started out with the fact that I needed the work, so that was great, but now I'm not so hot about having a band anymore. So I'm going to do this, and if it works out and I like it and the band likes it and all that, then I may do it some more in order to have musical activity and some money, you know.

WE: Have you been playing in other formats?

GE: Lee Konitz and I, we did a duo. I didn't like it. I really wasn't fluent

12. Gil Evans, *Svengali*, Atlantic Records, 1973. *Svengali* is an anagram that jazz baritone saxophonist Gerry Mulligan formed out of Gil Evans' name.

enough, man. It was all right sometimes, but you know, every night I'd go home bloody, and the next night I'd be ready to do it again. I haven't had that kind of experience. So I figured I'd better go home and wood-shed for a year or so before I do it again.

We played ten concerts in Italy in March. In ten days we played ten concerts. The logistics were, of course, a pleasure with just the two of us. I didn't have to worry about a band and nobody complaining about the transportation and the hotels or anything. I did the complaining. So that part was great.

It was so great that I got spoiled. If I do a big-band thing again, I'm going to have myself covered in every department. I'm gonna have road managers, and sound men, and roadies, and the whole thing. I'm gonna have about six nonplayin' people go along with that band.

SELECTED DISCOGRAPHY

Gil Evans plus Ten. Prestige 7120. 1957.
With Cannonball Adderley. *New Bottle Old Wine*. EMI-Manhattan CD7-46855-2. 1958.
With Miles Davis. *Sketches of Spain*. Columbia CS 8271. 1959–60.
Out of the Cool. MCA/Impulse 4. 1960.
Into the Hot. MCA/Impulse 9. 1961.
The Individualism of Gil Evans. Verve 8555. 1963–64.
Blues in Orbit. Ampex 10102. 1969.
Svengali. Atlantic SD-1643. 1973.
Priestess. Antilles J33D 20001. 1977.
Where Flamingos Fly. Artists House AH-14. 1982.

TOMMY FLANAGAN

Courtesy Fantasy, Inc.

D etroit-born pianist Tommy Flanagan has long been considered one of the preeminent accompanists in jazz. Born in 1930, Flanagan sat down at his parents' piano when he was six and tried to imitate the playing of his older brother. Formal lessons followed, and by the time he graduated from high school, Flanagan was jamming with the best jazz players in Detroit.

In 1956 Flanagan and guitarist Kenny Burrell moved to New York from the Motor City. (*Kenny Clarke Meets the Detroit Jazzmen*, recorded in New York City in 1956 and issued on the Savoy label, is a solid, swinging effort that provides a glimpse of the early styles of Flanagan and Burrell.) Both men soon earned their stripes in Big Apple jazz clubs and as sidemen on numerous recording dates.

By the late fifties Flanagan's reputation as a distinguished comping pianist was firmly established. His gifts at melodic invention, his precisely weighted touch and loping swing, and his ability to improvise a memorable chorus in only a few bars made him the ideal sideman but likely overshadowed his potential as a leader in his own right.

His brilliance as an accompanist earned him a place on a host of important dates during this period. In 1959 he backed John Coltrane on *Giant Steps*, universally touted as one of the essential recordings in modern jazz.[1] He was an integral part of a 1960 Wes Montgomery date that became an instant classic.[2] He was a regular member of Coleman Hawkins' rhythm section in the early sixties, recording several acclaimed albums with the "Bean," and he was part of the 1964 Sonny Rollins ensemble that recorded the undisputed masterpiece "Blue Seven" for the *Saxophone Colossus* album.[3]

Flanagan worked as Ella Fitzgerald's accompanist for two months in 1956 and also from 1963 to 1965. Fitzgerald rehired him in 1968 for a demanding decade-long stint that provided Flanagan with international exposure. Accompanying a vocalist, even one with Ella's superb musicianship, however, proved to be somewhat limiting for Flanagan. His stretch

1. John Coltrane, *Giant Steps*, Atlantic Records, 1959.
2. *The Incredible Jazz Guitar of Wes Montgomery*, Riverside Records, 1960.
3. Sonny Rollins, *Saxophone Colossus*, Prestige Records, 1964.

with Ella ended with his heart attack in 1978. Following a recovery period, he decided against further gigs with vocalists (he also had backed
Tony Bennett for a year) and went on the road as a single.

Flanagan made some fine recordings in the mid-seventies with trios
assembled in the studio.[4] It wasn't until the eighties, though, that he began to take the limelight as a leader. Flanagan recorded duets with pianists Hank Jones and Kenny Barron and also with saxophonist J. R. Mon-
terose, but he seemed most comfortable in a solo or trio format.

Thelonica, a tribute by the Tommy Flanagan Trio to the late Thelonious Monk and jazz patron the Baroness Pannonica de Koenigswarter,
won awards in several European and Japanese jazz journals as Record
of the Year in 1982.[5] Other highly regarded releases, such as *Jazz Poet*,
have also sold well in Europe and Japan, leading to numerous overseas
tours.[6] Although widespread popularity in the United States has been
elusive, Tommy Flanagan today has emerged to take his place as a major
voice in contemporary acoustic jazz piano. He finished second only to
Cecil Taylor in the acoustic piano category in *Down Beat* magazine's 1991
critics' poll.

Recorded 1976

PR: Tommy, how did you get started on the piano?

TF: I played by ear for about four years. I was about six years old at this
time when I first started foolin' around. I guess I got good enough; I
started taking lessons when I was about ten—ten or eleven—and I stayed
with the same teacher for about six or seven years, up until I finished high
school and figured I'd learned enough from her and I was getting into
jazz. I didn't need her anymore. So I was, like, taking gigs. I met a lot of
good musicians around Detroit about that time, '45, '46, '47, up until
the time I went into the army. The guys are well known now, you know,
like Kenny Burrell and Thad Jones, Elvin [Jones], Billy Mitchell, Yusef
Lateef. I mean, the line goes on.

PR: Did you all play together regularly?

TF: We used to practice a lot together, you know, jam together a lot. It

4. Two examples are *The Tommy Flanagan Tokyo Recital*, Pablo Records, 1975, and Tommy
Flanagan, *Eclypso*, Inner City Records, 1977.

5. Tommy Flanagan, *Thelonica*, Enja Records, 1982.

6. Tommy Flanagan, *Jazz Poet*, Timeless Records, 1989.

was a big thing around Detroit; there was always a place to play. Parents were away at work. Like we'd have the house to ourselves. There would be two or three good bass players, you know, Paul Chambers, Doug Watkins, Ernie Farrow. We'd usually be at Hugh Lawson's house, you know. It just happened his parents both worked; like we had the house for about three to four hours that we could play. Frank Foster was around at that time. He was a good influence on young Detroiters. He wrote a lot of original music. We thought at the time—well, we didn't know about Coltrane that much then, but later on, you know, we kinda equated him with like a Coltrane at that time. It was a good experience for us.

WE: How did you first get into jazz?

TF: Just from listenin' to my brother's records. Fats Waller's probably the first jazz pianist I heard. Fats Waller and Teddy Wilson, with that old Billie Holiday series, you know. From there it was Art Tatum and Bud Powell and Hank Jones. That was enough for me to, like, get my basics from. I just took it from there.

WF: Did you ever meet Tatum?

TF: I met him when I was just a teenager, almost out of high school. There was an after-hours place in Detroit. He used to go there after his jobs, and I was working at the same time, and I used to hear about "Art Tatum's gonna be at this after-hours place." So I would make it a point, like, to go see this man play, you know, like in person. He was just incredible, an amazing pianist. Like on a terrible, upright little spinet he made it sound just like his recordings, you know; it sounded like a Steinway [laughter]. I couldn't believe it. The fella that played before him was influenced a lot by Art. His name was Willie Hawkins, but he couldn't get that same sound out of the piano that Art did. It was like two different pianos [laughter]. It was incredible.

WE: Was your piano conception influenced by Tatum?

TF: I loved Tatum's playing. But I think I was really influenced by Charlie Parker, you know, as a horn-style kinda playing on the piano, like the phrasing. I mean, really, he just overwhelmed me, his style of playing. Bud Powell helped that too, because he played in that same vein, you know. Tatum was a little bit too much for a youngster to really grasp all of that, you know. A little too much piano. So I kinda economize; like, I try to play Charlie Parker piano, you might say.

PR: Was jazz a popular music when you were growing up?

TF: Jazz was very popular at that time. We had a Paradise Theatre where all your name groups came to. We were crazy about Charlie Parker and Dizzy at that time. They came to Detroit quite a bit, you know. It was like we religiously went to see them, like at dances and at the theaters.

PR: So were Parker and Gillespie your role models, rather than, say, an established figure like Ellington?

TF: I think so, 'cause they really encouraged us. We always had a lot of respect and we were in kinda awe of Ellington. We couldn't get that close to him. Really, his name almost kept you away from him, you know, "The Duke" [laughter]. But you could get closer to Dizzy. Plus his sidemen—he had a few musicians from Detroit—Milt Jackson—like that kinda meant that we had a chance to join somebody of that caliber. Here's somebody right from our ranks, you know, that went in. I had worked with Milt Jackson around Detroit.

WE: Earlier you mentioned Kenny Burrell. Didn't you go to New York with Burrell?

TF: Yeah. We left Detroit together. Like early '56. We just kinda got fed up with Detroit. There was only the same jobs repeating themselves; we made all the cycles. We felt it was time for us to go to New York, to see if Detroit jazz could stand up in New York, you know. And it did. We kinda knew it would if we just had a chance to play.

WE: Did you think that Detroit jazz sounded different than what was coming out of New York?

TF: I kinda thought so. I thought New York musicians were almost too much into Bud and Charlie Parker. I mean, we loved them, but we thought that there was somethin' else that we had; what it was I don't know. I think it was a little more lyrical with still the same drive, you know. I think it had a little more technique with the taste. It's just my opinion; I may be wrong.

PR: You work primarily as an accompanist. Is that role satisfying for you?

TF: Yeah, I like to do it, 'cause I don't really consider myself as being, like, a solo pianist, but I think I'm a good accompanist. And I work at it, you know. There are a few people that I like that accompany, and they influence me—like a John Lewis or a Jimmy Jones. And Hank [Jones], I think, is a great solo pianist, but he's also a great accompanist.

Like, being a sideman is a lot easier, you know, walkin' in a date. Although in the fifties when I did a lot of recordings it wasn't that easy, 'cause you almost had to arrange everything in your head, you know, the intros and the endings and think about your solo. So it was a good period for me, just to play. A lot of playing with top musicians, but it took a lot of my hair out [laughter].

PR: You mean that back in the fifties there wouldn't be arrangements set up and rehearsals prior to the studio date?

TF: Hardly any rehearsal at all. It's all done right at the date, and there were usually just, you know, one session. Not like they do now, like they could go on for a month or two for one album, or longer than that. I've heard of some groups taking almost a year to do an album so it's perfect. We thought we were doin' it perfect right there in one afternoon [laughter].

PR: Is that the way musicians preferred to record in those days? Or was it more a matter of finances?

TF: Low finances, and we knew we wouldn't have another chance [laughter]. Plus they didn't make that many demands about how perfect the sounds were supposed to be, you know, how perfect a solo was supposed to be. They edit out things they don't like now, you know, but back then you heard everything—mistakes and all. And I liked it better then.

WE: When you worked with Sonny Rollins on the classic *Saxophone Colossus* session, was there an air of excitement in the studio?

TF: I don't remember the songs being that exciting. I was just excited being on a date with Sonny Rollins. I'd say, outside of Coleman Hawkins, I thought he was my favorite saxophonist, at that time.

WE: How about the acclaim "Blue Seven" received and Rollins' subsequent retirement from public performance. Did all that floor you?

TF: No, that didn't floor me. I know Sonny as a kind of a—he's almost a shy person, I mean *away* from his music, I mean *away* from the bandstand. I think it'd be hard for somebody to really approach him to get him into an interview. I mean, he almost has a kind of a peekaboo style about him when he's approaching the bandstand. He doesn't wanna be that close to people that much. I mean, he's just such a marvelous musician, I'm sure all the acclaim about "Blue Seven" didn't mean that much to him [laughter]. I've heard him play much better than that.

PR: You had the opportunity to work with Wes Montgomery on one of his earliest records.[7] Could you tell us something about him?

TF: Well, we had heard a lot about Wes, you know, like he was a legend even before he started to record. We heard a lot about this guitar player

7. *The Incredible Jazz Guitar of Wes Montgomery.*

that played with his thumb, you know, no pick. I mean, he'd chord just chorus after chorus and not repeat himself, and sure enough here he is on this date. He was that incredible. He did everything I'd heard, and he was very shy about it, like he didn't want any praise about "Wow, let's hear that back again" or "Wow! did you really do that?" He didn't want you to talk about it, you know.

He was funny, because he thought he wasn't a very good musician because he didn't read. But that happens to a lot of musicians; they're marvelous, and they think they're not really up to it because they don't read, you know, like Erroll Garner is one. They're, like, the top of the field, 'cause they're not inhibited by, you know, like all the academics that most musicians go through.

WE: Let's turn to Coleman Hawkins. How did you meet him?

TF: I don't know. It's kind of a mystery how I met Coleman. I can't remember when; it seems like, after I got to know him, it seems like I'd known him forever. He was kinda hard to meet at first, but once he, like, took you in, it was like you're part of his family. Probably the best musician I'd ever heard, the most knowledgeable musician that I've known.

One record date I'm on, the *No Strings* album?[8] It was another one of those dates where nothing's prepared. They give you some sheet music, and Coleman, he transposed everything from the bass clef of the piano to his horn. He played it and made arrangements out of it. Sounds like it was written out for a quartet. It was just amazing how he could do that. You know, he'd say, "I'll take this bottom line, you play the melody, you play the intro." And we'd do it like that. And a lot of times, like when we'd play club dates, if a recording was out people would ask for it. But you know, like he'd only play it once; he'd play it in the studio and forget it [laughter]. It's sorta like Miles Davis, in a way. He did a lot of things in the studio that he never played again.

WE: Do you get offers to do solo albums?

TF: Yeah. I've been approached a lot to do a solo album or do more trios, you know, do more albums under my name. But I haven't been active in writing, and if I play somethin' like a trio date, I like to prepare it. You know, [to] be prepared to do something, I'd like to listen to myself, and I haven't had time to do that. I haven't given a lot of time to it, working with Ella.

8. Coleman Hawkins, *The Jazz Version "No Strings,"* Moodsville, 1962.

PR: You've been with Ella Fitzgerald pretty much since 1968. Are there things you can't do accompanying her that you could do behind a horn player?

TF: Yeah, you have to be a little more subtle and a little more straight, too. Even though she can do things like an instrument with her voice, you know, her harmonic knowledge is not as great as a musician playing a horn. You can almost do anything with a horn player. So you have to be careful not to overplay. Of course, it's not good taste anyway to overplay. I mean, to give a singer something that's out of *her* context. That's what you have to think about when you accompany.

Ella does a lot of scatting, so sometimes I can do a little more, but when she's doing a ballad or somethin', you know, I can't go into a lot of alternate changes like you would with a horn. They can play anything that they hear. When you're stickin' to a lyric and a melody line, you have to stick pretty close to the pattern of a song.

PR: So what's your life like, being a sideman for Ella?

TF: I spend a lot of time on the road.

PR: Do you enjoy it?

TF: Well, I'm doin' mostly now—I'm trying to—well, what should I say?—keep Ella from going through another scene with another pianist, I've been with her for so long [laughter]. But it's a good living. You know, a lot of traveling. I don't like so much the one-night stands. But if I can sit down for a while on the job I don't mind it so much.

I'm not satisfied with it, but it's better than, you know, tryin' to keep a trio working just by myself. I mean, that's pretty hard. I mean, I've seen it happen to a lot of good trios. If you don't have a real strong agent and some good, you know, promo, you're not goin' anywhere. I mean, it's just maybe to satisfy your ego, that's all.

WE: Do you yearn for more commercial success?

TF: No. I've heard that I have six thousand people in the country that'll buy anything I make. I got six thousand [laughter]. Norman Granz told me this. I mean, he's not wild about not having any more sales. I mean, that's just in the United States. I have a bigger appeal in Europe and Japan. So it ends up being pretty good for a jazz album; I may get maybe twenty, twenty-five thousand sales, and that's pretty good.

WE: Are you happy with Granz's operation at Pablo?

TF: I like what he's doing, because he does what he wants to do. Nobody gets in his way, [and] he encourages his people. I mean, he does have like a stable of his own. I always appreciated him for having recorded so much Art Tatum and Charlie Parker. He's always had the good taste—I don't know if it's good taste, but he's been lucky enough to have the better musicians.

PR: As a jazz pianist, do you consider yourself to be more of a fine artist or a folk artist?

TF: I'm somewhere in between a folk and a fine artist. Somewhere in between there. Probably closer to a folk [laughter].

PR: Do you think that jazz stands comparison with classical music?

TF: Music like Duke Ellington's music I'd stand up against anybody's classical music. But there's not enough people, black artists, that are writing music that is really that identifiable. It's getting too European-like. Nobody has the raw talent that Ellington had. I don't see it coming.

PR: Could you enlarge on that?

TF: Well, what I mean is that Duke Ellington from his very beginning, I mean everybody knows that's Duke Ellington. It's Ellingtonia, you know, it's very *black* music, that's about as close as I can get to it. That's really black music, and it's classical black music. What I mean by *European* is like all the techniques that've come in; like people have been studying over in Europe, you know, like Quincy Jones with Madame Boulanger, and Oliver Nelson was a very skilled musician, but you know, using those European harmonics, like it's almost from the French school. I mean, it's beautiful, but it's not really black to me like Ellington is.

Even before that, like Fats Waller and James P. Johnson, and Scott Joplin's thing he wrote years ago—he wrote an opera. I haven't heard it lately. I'm sure black music is out there somewhere from people we don't hear that much about. I mean, we hear a lot about Quincy, and since Oliver's died we hear a lot of his music. I think Benny Golson wrote some, like it's more Western, but it's black too. I think Tom McIntosh really gets kinda close to—it's really Americana. He's got a lot of knowledge in his writing, but it's got black roots. He's got the knowledge, but the black roots still come out. He wrote a thing called "Great Day" for James Moody. I think it almost sounds like a very hip spiritual [laughter]. And Thad Jones, I think, is like a follow-up of Duke Ellington. I think Thad's writing is very deep-rooted. It's got his stamp on it, and well, you don't hear it anywhere else. You get a lot of imitators, like they tried to imitate Ellington. Nobody can, you know, it's not honest. That's what it is; it's really honest music.

WE: Is it possible for you to be a bit more specific in your definition of *black music*?

TF: It's hard to define, 'cause it goes beyond the sound. I mean, the sound has gotta be there. Benny Carter, now there's another person. I don't think he had all that much training. His music is a little more polished, but that's black music. Maybe a little higher level, not as raw as Duke, but it's really good. He's a marvelous musician.

PR: When you speak of Ellington, are you referring to the full range of his output?

TF: Yeah, even his piano playing is very black. I mean, just the man's whole musical character. It's obvious it's indescribable. Indescribably black [laughter].

PR: How about the jazz superstars? In your estimation are they creating black music?

TF: No, I don't think they're coming close to it. I just think it's more important to them right now to further themselves, you know, monetarily. I think their talent's gonna fail if they keep that up, you know. They're gonna lose some of what they've had. I mean, I've seen a lot of groups lately just splinter off because somebody thought they could make a little more money doin' it this way. They keep their same names, you know, but there's two factions, going two different ways with the same names. I mean, how can you have—it's almost like those groups the Ink Spots. There's about twelve of them, you know. None of 'em are original.

But it's the same thing happenin' now in jazz. People are saying this is this and when it isn't. You're not gettin' the original. Somebody's exploiting the name because it had a lot of integrity to begin with. They have a top-twenty jazz list too, you know. And it's sad to hear some of the jazz stations just play like a certain label because that's all they're striving for is that market.

You know, that's one thing about the Pablo label. They're doin' the old things like they used to be. No striving for a hit. It's just making sure that the older musicians are being heard the way they always were. You know, like a Benny Carter, Roy Eldridge, Dizzy.

WE: Are there more hopeful signs in the music of younger jazz musicians?

TF: I think that they seem like they're trying to get away from their roots. It's gettin' too slick now. There's not enough of the basics that still come through. A lot of surface music goin' on now. No roots.

WE: Are there some younger players whose work you enjoy?

TF: Yeah. A lot of them. Soloists are still playing, but I'm talkin' about the writing is not coming through. The soloists are still playing for you. You can hear that all the time. Not so much for the young ones, though. That seems to be a little on the surface.

WE: Do younger players come to you to learn?

TF: I have a few, but not enough. Not enough black players, young black players. It's like they're afraid. I mean, it's hard to find a good young black player, like under twenty-five. It's almost like they've been told it's somethin' not to do.

I think they think it's a little easier to make money quicker if they get in a rhythm, a heavy-rhythm thing, you know, a rock thing. It doesn't take as much time. I mean playin' jazz, it takes a lot of time to cultivate. That might be the difference, I mean because the economy is really, it's put on young people today. You know, you gotta make the money. They know if you go to school, there's nothing for you after you finish. So they're gettin' it while they can.

WE: Chick Corea and Keith Jarrett have growing reputations.

TF: Yeah, but they're not really black. we're talking about black musicians. And there's just not that many that I know of except McCoy Tyner. When Herbie Hancock stops commercializing [laughter], he can have the roots; I think he can revert back to them. He's gone somewhere else now, but I think he may return. It's just a little departure I think he had to do just to see if he could do it. And since he's done it, I think he'll be—well, he knows he can make money, right? So he'll go back to maybe writing some good music.

PR: Do you feel that nonblack musicians can play authentic jazz?

TF: There are exceptions. It's mostly in piano and on the saxophone and bass, which is new, you know. In the last ten years—well, that's the European influence too—there's an awful lot of good jazz bass players comin' from Europe. But they're all using that European technique. But you know, it's understandable the way music is changing; you have to play more—music's gettin' more demanding. People are writing more intricate things, you know.

PR: You're saying that if a nonblack musician is going to contribute to jazz it will be most likely on piano, bass, or sax?

TF: That seems to me.

PR: Why?

TF: I think they're easy to get to; I mean, it's easier to produce on them. I think trumpet is very hard. I mean, I haven't heard like a white trumpet player or any brass player that could ever fool me by saying that they were black. But saxophones, they can fool me anytime, even singers too. All those cats from England [laughter].

PR: Could you be fooled by, say, the playing of Eric Dolphy?

TF: Eric Dolphy. I know he's a fine musician. He's a little scary in his approach. He changed kinda drastically after Ornette Coleman hit the scene. He was playing more like Charlie Parker, I thought, before that. I'm saying he was a little scary because he came by my house once when my son was just a baby, and he was playing and scared the kid to death [laughter].

WE: Is there a connection between black music as you describe it and rhythm and blues, like James Brown, for instance?

TF: Please [laughter]. I don't think that's anything. I don't know what you would call that.

WE: Has rhythm and blues influenced your playing at all?

TF: No. Only when I was playin' locally around Detroit, where if you didn't play certain things you wouldn't have a gig. I mean, it's required for the piano player to play "After Hours" on Saturday night, you know, as maybe the closing tune or something [laughter]. I enjoyed it, 'cause you had to play it with spirit or it won't mean nothin'. That's all right, but that's not like rhythm and blues; that's like a blues piano classic, you know. Like required, you know. Especially in Detroit on Saturday night [laughter].

PR: You said earlier you don't have the time to compose. Do you plan to take the time eventually to write some original music?

TF: Yeah, I do. I did in the past, you know. But I didn't do that much. Some of the songs I think I could play again; I like 'em enough to play again. I'd like to advance more. I haven't done anything really in about fifteen or twenty years in original music. I like to arrange music, you know, like the album *Tokyo Recital*. It's like framework kinda things; some of 'em I really thought about and worked out. You know, sorta like Art Tatum never wrote a lot of original music, but he sure could arrange everybody else's music, very individual and memorable kind of things.

WE: Perhaps you'll write black music as you want to hear it?

TF: Oh, that's a funny thing. I guess I came up within a funny time. But I always had it in my head, like, the European music myself. Close as I can get to black music is, I don't know, maybe through the blues, and I think the blues has been worn out. Not too much you can do with it. I mean, it's just your own individual experience, you know. You can't write anymore on it. All you can do is express it through some solo voice.

My way of thinkin' about writing is I just want to write somethin' that would be good enough to be played by somebody else, not just me. I mean, if it turns out black-sounding, I'll be happy about it. I'm not makin' an effort to make it sound Ellington or anything like that. Just to be an individual, which is gonna take time, 'cause I'm startin' late [laughter].

SELECTED DISCOGRAPHY

Jazz at the Santa Monica Civic Center '72. Pablo 2625–701. 1972.
The Tommy Flanagan Tokyo Recital. Pablo 2310724. 1975.
Confirmation. Enja 4014. 1977.
Montreux '77. Pablo 2308–202. 1977.
With Hank Jones. *Our Delights.* Galaxy 513. 1978.
Something Borrowed, Something Blue. Galaxy 5110. 1980.
A Little Pleasure. Reservoir 109. 1981.
Thelonica. Enja R2–79615. 1982.
With Red Mitchell. *You're Me.* Phontastic CD-7528. 1988.
Jazz Poet. Timeless 30. 1989.

DIZZY GILLESPIE

Courtesy Fantasy, Inc.

John Birks "Dizzy" Gillespie is a giant among jazz musicians. In a career spanning more than five decades, he has been acclaimed as a jazz innovator, an incomparable trumpet virtuoso, and a high-spirited showman who ranks among the premier ambassadors of jazz.

Gillespie's rise to fame was inseparable from the advent of bop. Founded in the early forties by Gillespie and his friend and coconspirator altoist Charlie Parker, bop was a radical departure—harmonically, melodically, and especially rhythmically—from the music of the swing era that preceded it. Gillespie blazed trails during bop's heyday. Decked out in goatee, horn-rimmed glasses, and beret, his ebullience as a performer and his high jinks on stage made him an international figure and excited widespread interest in jazz.

Born on October 21, 1917, in Cheraw, South Carolina, Gillespie started on trombone at fourteen, switching to trumpet less than a year later. Although his formal training was minimal, his natural ability won him a scholarship to study theory and harmony at North Carolina's Laurinburg Institute, a boarding school for black students.

In 1935 the Gillespie family moved to Philadelphia. Modeling his playing after Roy Eldridge, a star trumpet player of the day, Dizzy left for New York and joined the Teddy Hill Band in 1937. After that band folded two years later, Gillespie began touring with the Cab Calloway Orchestra.

Gillespie's association with Calloway ended abruptly in 1941, after Gillespie had a well-publicized backstage brawl with the leader; according to lore, Calloway was cut on his backside and required ten stitches. Nonetheless, Gillespie's stint with Calloway was memorable for more than fisticuffs. He made important strides as a soloist, and his talents as a composer and an arranger began to emerge. Most significant, Gillespie met Charlie Parker on a road trip through Kansas City.

In 1942 Gillespie and Parker renewed their acquaintance as members of Earl Hines's orchestra, which became a virtual hotbed of bop. That band also included trombonist Bennie Green, drummer Shadow Wilson, and Billy Eckstine on vocals. Hines's group, though, was not the only environment for bop experiments. During this period, Gillespie and

Parker joined pianist-composer Thelonious Monk and drummer Kenny Clarke at after-hours clubs in Harlem, including Minton's Playhouse and Clark Monroe's Uptown House, to jam. Eventually they laid the foundation for modern jazz.

In 1943, Billy Eckstine left Hines to form a big band that became one of the most celebrated ensembles in jazz history. Its lineup included Gillespie, Parker, and vocalist Sarah Vaughan, all of whom had defected from Hines's band to join Eckstine. Art Blakey propelled the band from his drum chair. Unfortunately, a union ban on recording was in effect from 1942 to 1944, so the Hines and the Eckstine bands from that period live on only in memory.

In 1945, Gillespie and Parker finally did a studio session together, collaborating on the Guild-Musicraft recordings that include celebrated versions of "Groovin' High," "Salt Peanuts," and "Hot House."[1] The next five years marked a watershed in the public's acceptance of bop. Gillespie's popularity soared, enabling him to maintain big bands from 1946 to 1950. During this period, Dizzy and Cuban drummer Chano Pozo introduced Afro-Cuban rhythms into big-band charts, pioneering what became known as Latin jazz.

Economics forced Dizzy to break up his band in 1950 (he did not front a working big band again until assembling one for the first State Department tour overseas, which lasted from 1956 to 1958). Since that time, his incomparable artistry and magisterial technique have been showcased mainly in small-group studio dates, although in 1991 he formed his critically embraced fifteen-piece United Nation Orchestra.

Today Dizzy Gillespie is the premier elder statesman of jazz. His crackling, brassy style has inspired a lineage of superb trumpet players, including Fats Navarro, Clifford Brown, Woody Shaw, Jon Faddis, and Wynton Marsalis. Gillespie's association with the Pablo label during the eighties saw the expressive, blues-drenched values of his playing deepen and his popular appeal rejuvenated.

Recorded 1976

WE: Dizzy, describe for us the way you were as a child.

DG: I was pretty weird. I used to get into things a lot. I was what you

---

1. The Guild-Musicraft recordings have been reissued on Dizzy Gillespie, *In the Beginning*, Prestige Records, 1973.

would call a "daredevil." As a matter of fact, the guys used to call me Devil. Because I was—I would say precocious. I was never doing the things the other kids did, I don't think. Oh, I played a little baseball, football when I was in high school. But I think I was interested in music all my life, so it sort of took up my time.

WE: Were you interested in music at a pretty early age?

DG: About two and a half, there about. I used to play "Coon-shine Lady" on the piano.

You see, my father was a musician, and he had all these instruments in the house, and I'm the youngest of nine, and he died when I was goin' on ten. And he didn't know I was going to be a musician, but he tried to beat it into the rest of my older brothers and sisters, and they wouldn't go for it. But I used to fool around—I remember I could pick out something on the piano before I could reach the keyboard. So that's a long time ago.

WE: Did you study someplace?

DG: No. I just had good ears, I guess.

WE: Did you attend a church where gospel music was played?

DG: I was a Methodist. They didn't shout or anything like that. But the Sanctified Church was right down the street from me, so I heard that every Sunday, you know. I used to go down there.

PR: When did you begin playing professionally?

DG: I played professionally all through high school. And then I moved to Philadelphia in 1935.

PR: Weren't you listening to Roy Eldridge?

DG: Yes, from down south. He used to have a program that came up every Saturday or something like that from the Savoy Ballroom. And I said, "I want to play with that band." And that's the first job I got when I got to New York.

PR: That was with the Teddy Hill Band, wasn't it? Wasn't Eldridge playing with Teddy Hill?

DG: Yup.

PR: Did you take his place?

DG: No, I took Frankie Newton's place. Frankie Newton took Roy's place. Roy went with Fletcher Henderson. And Frankie Newton wanted to stay in New York. He didn't want to go to Europe. That was in '37. And I was only nineteen.

Well, it was pretty weird the way I went to New York, too. I was playing in a band in Philadelphia—called Frankie Fairfax with Charlie

Shavers. You probably don't remember him. And another boy named Carl Warwick—we called him Bama. They left and went with Tiny Bradshaw. They tried to get me to go over to Baltimore with Tiny Bradshaw, and I wouldn't leave home. I was sort of scared. And then they came through again with Lucky Millinder, and they cruised me out this time to New York. To go with Lucky Millinder. I was supposed to take Harry Edison's place. Well, Lucky said yes first, and then when I got to New York he decided not to. So I was stranded—no, I wasn't exactly stranded in New York. My brother was there, and I was stayin' with my brother. But Teddy Hill needed a trumpet player just at that moment.

Most show business, man, you be at the right place at the right moment. You know how I got the job? I was used to going to Savoy and jam. You know, I played with Chick Webb, he took a liking to me. I was a young dude, and maybe he saw something. So I used to sit in Chick's band, read the parts. Willie Bryant, Teddy, the Savoy Sultans, Claude Hopkins—anybody up there, I used to go up there, and then we would go to other jam sessions, you know, in clubs. We'd spend all night doing that and 'til the next day. And so Teddy just happened to ask me, he say, "You know where I can find a trumpet player? I'm going to Europe." Before he could get it out of his mouth, I said, "Hey, you got one."

WE: When did you first meet Charlie Parker?

DG: Around 1940. I was with Cab Calloway in Kansas City when I ran into him. Well, I didn't exactly run into him. This trumpet player, Buddy Anderson, he was a trumpet player with Jay McShann, and I knew him, and he invited me up to the hotel room, and he said, "I want you to hear this saxophone player." I wasn't too enthused, because I had played with all the guys. You know, I had played with Chu Berry, Coleman Hawkins, Lester Young, Don Byas—those were the *leading* saxophone players. I had played with them, so I said I had heard all this music. But he said, "You gotta hear this boy." And boy! When I first hear him I couldn't believe it.

PR: Have you read *Bird Lives*, by Ross Russell?[2]

DG: I read about one chapter, and I put it down. Because it wasn't exactly—it wasn't his life. It was a figment of the imagination of the author. There was a little truth in a lot of the things that he said, but he blew it up so big that you couldn't even detect the truth.

2. Ross Russell, *Bird Lives: The High Life and Hard Times of Charlie "Yardbird" Parker* (New York, 1973).

PR: One of the most striking parts of the book reported on Parker's feelings while incarcerated in Camarillo.[3] Parker felt he invented the music, and there he was locked up while you were out making money playing it.

DG: That's not true. There was never any resentment or jealousy or anything as far as we two were concerned. Because we knew the contribution of each. You see, the followers always do that. They do that all the time, you know, the followers, in religion, for an instance. The followers of Jesus wouldn't go along with the message from Muhammad, which was on the same level with the message of Jesus. Ah, but it's the followers. Muhammad made a statement one time in the Koran where he said, "I am Christ." You know, because he had the same holy spirit that Christ had, so they got to be even. And all the prophets, they—I speak this way because I belong to the Baha'i faith, and they teach us that religion is one and these great teachers come for different intervals in our spiritual development that raises mankind to unprecedented heights. So our music, the followers of Charlie Parker say "Aw, Dizzy," and the ones that think that I did it say "Aw, Charlie Parker is good, but Dizzy's the main contributor." But each one of us know what we contributed, so there was no animosity or anything.

I was blessed that I got married early and had a good wife. That sort of kept me straight. Probably I would have been like Charlie Parker, you know, involved in drugs or alcohol or something like that if I hadn't had this stability. But one time, boy, it really touched me, one time he told me, say, "Why don't you save me?" He told me this, oh, just before he died. But you know, I didn't know what to do. I said, "What do you want me to do to save you?" He said, you know, he was despondent and felt rejected. But I imagine one of the things that he wanted to do was come to play. But I already had my group, and he was on an equal level with me, so he could have got his—if he was takin' care of business. He just didn't take care of business. He didn't have anybody to help him. He needed help.

WE: You mentioned that you both knew what your contributions were. Define them for us.

DG: My contribution was mostly rhythm and harmonic. I figured out all the chord changes to all the things and, you know, the substitute chords

---

3. Parker, suffering a breakdown caused by alcohol and drug abuse, recuperated for seven months in 1946 at Camarillo State Hospital in southern California.

and all that—I figured all that out. And I taught a lot of the piano players and the drummers and the rhythm. Because we were doing things in the forties that—close to a bigger intellectual degree [than] they're doin' now, such as the bass line. When we came along the bass was goin' [hums a regularly accented bass line]. Now what we had [hums the irregularly accented bass line of "A Night in Tunisia"]. We were doing that in 1947. And the contribution of Charlie Parker was mostly in the, let's see, how do you explain that, explain the major contribution of an artist? Let's see, in the way that we play, you know, the phrasing of Charlie Parker.

PR: Bop has been described as a revolution.

DG: They should have taken one of the letters off that.

PR: Make it evolution?

DG: Yes.

WE: I think LeRoi Jones stated in one of his books, *Black Music*, perhaps, that bop was a response to white "swing" music.[4]

DG: There was no such thing as "white" in our music, because most of the contributors, most of the "boss" instrumentalists, the "boss" creators were black, so we weren't bothered by that. Because we knew that the white guy was only copying what he'd heard the black guys do. The way that we played—that's what they copied. And the way that we—our harmony, our rhythm, our figures and everything—they copied everything. A good example of that is Woody Herman's band. There's a record of Woody's called "Apple Honey." Everybody just *knew* that I had arranged that for Woody Herman. I said, "No, I didn't do it." It was just the followers, you know.

I never did go along with the picture of quote "white-black." I was always, even before I became a Baha'i, I was always aware of the fact that we were all from the same source. And it's just a matter of environment that makes me act one way and makes a white guy act another way who comes from another ethnic background. I was not too much interested in black-white anything. It never actually crossed . . . unless somebody, you know, call you a nigger.

One time we were on Fifty-second Street—we were playing the Onyx Club—and Jimmy Dorsey came in. He couldn't believe what we were doing down there. It was brand new then, and Max Roach, Oscar Pettiford, George Wallington, Don Byas, we were gettin' it, and he got drunk.

4. LeRoi Jones, *Black Music* (New York, 1967).

The next night he came in, he stayed sober all night. And then he invited me to a party afterwards—of course he was working out of the New Yorker Hotel—and he had his arms around me, and we were walking down the street, and he said, "Boy," he said, "I'd love to have you in my band, but you're *so* dark." And he said, "If you were sort of white." I said, "You know any white guys who play like me?" He said no. I said, "Well, I play what I am."

PR: What was it like in Minton's at that time?

DG: There was a lot of excitement in Minton's. Not only Minton's but the Uptown House, Clark Monroe's Uptown House. That was an after-hour joint in Harlem, that we used to go and play *after hours.* That was a great ground for improvisation and for creativity. Right now, I don't know which one played the best part—the most important part—Monroe's or Minton's. Sort of six of one and half a dozen of the other.

PR: What role did Thelonious Monk play in the evolution of bop?

DG: Well, Monk and I used to get together on harmonic things. My contribution—my harmonic structure—was strictly European. You know, goin' in fifths, from the C, F, B-flat, E-flat, A-flat, D-flat, G-flat, C-flat. But Monk sometime would go another way. But I always sort of followed that pretty closely, the harmonic structure of the . . . fundamental harmony. Even now, if you notice, that upper part might not sound, but if you listen to the bass while it's going [hums], you know, those circle of fifths.

PR: Is there any truth behind the anecdote that you and Monk would get together in the afternoons and put together as complex a situation as you could so you could blow the other guys off the bandstand during the evening jam sessions?

DG: The way that Monk wrote tunes, man, if you didn't know what you were doing you were out of it. We'd be playing one of Monk's tunes—boy, you won't find many guys playing it. Because Monk was so unorthodox. He was very, very unorthodox. Notice that not many people copy Monk. They don't try to play like Monk, because Monk is out there by himself. Charlie Parker and I are more together than either Monk and me or Monk and Charlie.

WE: Chroniclers of jazz in the forties often portray you and Charlie Parker as not conforming to the image of a passive black musician when playing the South.

DG: We weren't of the cut of the older musicians. The older musicians, remember, they did what they had to do. But in the age that we came up in we didn't have to do those things, you know? Tommin' and things like that or, say, condescending. We just figured, we felt like we were liberated people, and we *acted* like liberated people.

WE: So it was your generation?

DG: Yes, the whole generation was like that.

WE: Did you have some rough times in the South?

DG: Almost got my head knocked off down one time in Pine Bluffs, Arkansas, for nothin'.

WE: What happened?

DG: At a dance hall, I was playing the piano at intermission, and some guy threw a penny up on the stage and said, "Play something," and I did like that with my foot, and nothing happened, so later on at night after everybody had gone, I decided to go to the men's room. It was a white dance, and I thought everybody had gone. Apparently everybody hadn't gone—this guy was *there*. When I stepped out of the men's room, he hit me in the head with a bottle. Seven stitches. Charlie Parker walked up to him and said "You took advantage of my friend, you cur." He called him a cur [laughter].

PR: Dizzy, you had three big bands from 1946 to 1950. Were those bands a realization of a lot of dreams?

DG: All musicians say that if anybody should be a big-band leader it should be me because—they seem to think that I do in front of a band what's supposed to be done. In all of its aspects. But as far as personal preference, I'd be just as happy playing with a harmonica if the guy is good. Of course, I did that in London once. You know Larry Adler? I did a whole television show with a harmonica, trumpet and harmonica. It was delightful; it was just beautiful, and both of us had deep respect for the other one, and it was just great.

But it doesn't matter to me, because we play at all kinds of situations now. I play with symphony orchestras, with high school bands and college bands. Sometimes Newport Jazz Festival jam sessions with my personal group. Sometimes I get a big band together to do something, like when I went to Canada, I went to England, I took my music, and it's nice, well, you know, it's like, if I were *that* way, like being in the company of an African lady, and then you go to South America and be in the company with, you know—it's just a matter of broadening your outlook. I played with the sambas school in Brazil. It was beautiful. I expect to go to Cuba too, sometime. Of course they've got some good music comin' out of Cuba.

PR: Is that a Cuban cigar you're smoking?

DG: Cuban tobacco. We're not allowed to smoke Cuban cigars in the United States [laughter]. We're so highly sophisticated, and then we are so petty at the same time.

WE: You just referred to the musics of Cuba and Brazil. Since the forties you've been incorporating Afro-Cuban and Brazilian rhythms into your music. Do you consider yourself a pioneer for doing this?

DG: I introduced most of those. See, I was always a Cubaphile. Heh, heh, it's a good word, right? Yeah, I always was interested in Cuban music, even like in 1938, 1937.

WE: How did you first hear Cuban music?

DG: Well, I played with a Spanish band. I played trumpet and maracas with a guy named Alberto Socarras, flautist. Hmm, hmm, could he play! I played with him in the Savoy.

WE: Did you play in New York with Machito?

DG: Mario, the leader of the Machito band, was like my godfather. He's the one who got me the job with Cab Calloway. And he was the first trumpet player was with Chick Webb, when Chick used to let me sit in. So I used to ask him, "Man, I brought that music for you alls." You know, I said, "I want to learn about it." So he got me records for me to listen to.

PR: How do you feel about the bossa nova craze that occurred in the sixties?

DG: It's nice, but I was in South America, and the real music is the samba. That's like the blues and pop music.

PR: Chano Pozo is a figure from that era who is shrouded in mystery. Can you tell us something about him?

DG: Chano—I brought him into jazz. We were the first ones to incorporate Afro-Cuban rhythm. You see, Chano Pozo's the cause of my playing the conga.

Well, all of it is the same, you know, the rhythm. We Americans during slavery time, the slave owners forbade the slaves for using the drums. Now that was our main means of expression. Why, they had to devise another means, and when they came up with the gospel and the blues and ragtime and all this stuff, they were mostly monorhythm. Africans were polyrhythm. So that's why our music is different. But they're bringing it back now through rock and roll. The rock-and-roll guys have combined our rock beat with the Afro-Cuban. Come up with somethin' nice, didn't they? You see that's multirhythm, when all the guys doing something different. And it makes it nice. I'm glad to see it.

WE: Gil Fuller was an important contributor to those bands, wasn't he?

DG: He was my chief arranger, yes.

WE: Where is he now?

DG: He's making films, television films. We're getting ready to make TV cassettes—lessons about our music. 'Cause it's lost, man; nobody knows exactly what happened. I'm the only one that can tell them.

WE: Where are you going to distribute these cassettes?

DG: Going to distribute them to the schools—whoever wants them—in all the foreign countries and explain in their language.

WE: Is this project being funded by a grant or private party?

DG: No, it's being funded by us [laughter].

PR: Speaking of big bands, we talked to Art Blakey not long ago, and he was flabbergasted still by the Billy Eckstine Band that he played with in the middle forties. He said everybody was a soloist; everybody was that great. Do you have memories of that band?

DG: That was a good band. I was the musical director of that band.

PR: What did you do?

DG: I rehearsed the band, conducted it, everything. Billy didn't do anything but sing. It was nice.

PR: Was Eckstine the main attraction?

DG: Billy Eckstine was a big "jelly-jelly," "Stormy Monday" bluesman, so they thought they'd get him a band. That was the idea, for a vocalist to have a band. [The crowds] came in to hear Billy Eckstine—they'd start screamin' where they hear "jelly, jelly, jelly." But for "A Night in Tunisia" and "Salt Peanuts" and things like that, they didn't. It was a good band, though. It was the first bop big band.

WE: You went overseas with your own band in about '48?

DG: Yeah.

WE: How was the reception there?

DG: Fantastic! We got stranded in Sweden. This crook ran away with the money. We were stranded, and our manager, who was Billy Eckstine's manager too [Billy Shaw], came over to extricate us from this dilemma. We went to Paris. We went straight to Paris from Sweden, and our music didn't get there. We were late. We were two hours and a half late and still

didn't have no music. We played without music, and that record is out now. It was one of the best records. The guys didn't have—not one note.
WE: That record wasn't available in the States until about 1970.[5]
DG: Yeah, "an historical concert," they call it. People still remember that. After almost thirty years they still remember that concert. I have people tell me now when I go to Paris, they say, "That concert at Salle Pleyel." You see, our music was the first to get over there; they never heard nothin' like that before.
PR: Since you've done a number of State Department tours, do you have views about jazz being used for purposes of international politics?
DG: It was definitely used [that way] with us. If it hadn't been for us—it was a big success with "little" people. A lot of things I did over there, man, that was really on a very high level, a noble level, I'd say. Because like in Karachi, Pakistan, the local promoters were charging them so much to come in that there weren't many people at the first show. Because they didn't have the money. So I looked out there and didn't see nobody, and I say what was that, and they say, "Well, the people don't have the money." I said, "The State Department is sponsoring it with the money so why—we come over to play for these people." I said, "Give me some free tickets." I took about two hundred tickets, man, and gave 'em out, and we had a full house. And I played with a snake. That was a fun experience. I had one snake wrapped around my head.
PR: What kind of a snake?
DG: *Big one!* I don't know what kind it was, but boy, it was a *big* bugger! Whoo! It was about this big around, man, and the girl vocalist was holding the tail. And she missed the show that night. She was so terrified that she got drunk and missed the show.

And then this cobra—they ain't to be trusted. I was sitting there with this other snake around my head, sitting next to the cobra guy that plays the little flute. So we're standing there, and he says, "OK, now, when I say, you take your horn. When I bring him out, he'll go from side to side. You take your horn and start playin' and put your horn right where mine is, and you just move your horn from side to side, and he'll follow it." I say, "Yeah? OK." So I started playing in a mute. Apparently I got too close to him, and he [lunges] at my horn. Well, at that moment I made a world-record back-jump [laughter]. I jumped—I must have jumped two

5. *The Dizzy Gillespie Orchestra at Salle Pleyel, Paris, France*, Prestige Records, 1970.

hundred feet back. And then later I read in the newspaper where this snake was supposed to have been defanged. But I read in the paper where there was a cobra that was supposed to have been defanged that wasn't, and he bit the guy, and the guy died.

WE: What's it like to perform night after night in a club atmosphere?

DG: Well, you strive for inspiration and just hope that you get inspired enough to really do something worthwhile. That's all there is to it, and it's another job, aside from that.

WE: Do you challenge yourself when playing?

DG: All the time—that horn challenges you every time you pick it up [laughter]. It's a monster.

WE: Would it be correct to say that jazz is a young man's art?

DG: Any physical thing that you do is a young man's business, 'cause you need strength to perform. When you get old and all, your bones hurt; every time you touch somethin' it hurts. It blights your creativity, because your—you know that what you know and what you can do are two different things. Oh, when I can no longer do what I know, I'm gonna quit.

PR: What is your stature with younger musicians?

DG: I am held with extreme reverence because I always help young musicians. I wasn't like the older guys; the older guys didn't help young musicians at all. Very seldom you find an old guy who'd help. I went into Duke Ellington's band once, played in Duke Ellington's band for four weeks in a theater. And Duke go from—his music is not straight down from the left-hand corner all the way down, and the reeds go down so far, and then he'd jump to letter E, and he'd jump back to letter A, and all this. Nobody'd tell you nothin'. You'd be playin', man, and you'd wonder what—and not only *that*, but they played differently, and it doesn't sound like what's on the music. But I had a good time playing; it's a great experience playing with Duke Ellington.

PR: How does a musician get to play with you?

DG: Through other musicians.

PR: Have there been times when someone has asked to audition?

DG: Well, once in Milano, the concert was over with, and I was in the bathroom, and the bathroom door busted open, and I was sitting down, and this guy walked in and said, "Me play guitar." It was Elek Bacsik.[6]

6. Elek Bacsik appears on *Dizzy on the French Riviera*, Philips Records, 1962.

And he brought his guitar in the bathroom and played for me while I was sitting there. It was nice. It was a nice concert. I was very comfortable.

SELECTED DISCOGRAPHY

The Development of an American Artist. Smithsonian Collection R-004. 1940–46. (Includes Gillespie with the bands of Cab Calloway, Les Hite, Lucky Millinder, and Billy Eckstine.)

In the Beginning. Prestige P24030. 1945–50.

With Chano Pozo. *The Dizzy Gillespie Orchestra at Salle Pleyel, Paris, France.* Prestige PR 7818. Recorded 1948, released 1970.

With Charlie Parker, Bud Powell, Max Roach, and Charles Mingus. *Jazz at Massey Hall.* Prestige PR 24024. 1953.

A Jazz Portrait of Duke Ellington. Verve 817 102-2. 1960.

With Bud Powell. *Dizzy Gillespie and the Double Six of Paris.* Verve 830 224-2. 1963.

With Mary Lou Williams. *Giants.* Perception PLP19. 1971.

With Machito. *Afro-Cuban Jazz Moods.* Pablo 2310-771. 1975.

With Max Roach. *Dizzy and Max.* A&M 6404. 1989.

With United Nation Orchestra. *Live at the Royal Festival Hall.* Enja R2 79658. 1991.

CHICO HAMILTON

Photograph by David D. Spitzer.   Used with permission.

Virtuoso drummer Foreststorn "Chico" Hamilton is one of the most inventive percussionists in modern jazz. He innovated bottomless heads for his drum kit and is known for his understated but fiercely swinging style, using mallets, brushes, and sticks to generate a complex interweaving of rhythms, textures, and timbres. An accomplished composer, Hamilton has also been an influential bandleader since his contributions to so-called West Coast jazz in the mid-fifties.

Born in 1921, Hamilton took up the drums at age ten and began playing them professionally as a teenager in his native Los Angeles. While still in high school, he organized a band with his classmates, who included future jazz stars Dexter Gordon, Ernie Royal, Buddy Collette, Illinois Jacquet, and Charles Mingus. Between 1940 and 1941 Hamilton occupied the drum chair in swing-era groups led by Floyd Ray, Lionel Hampton, and Lester Young. Afterward he spent four years in the army, where he came under the tutelage of masterful Count Basie drummer Jo Jones.

Discharged from the army, Hamilton worked as a house drummer in Billy Berg's Swing Club in Hollywood, site of the celebrated Parker-Gillespie performances in 1945, and then in 1948 he joined singer Lena Horne, beginning a musical relationship that lasted on and off for seven years. Also during this period Hamilton was a founding member of Gerry Mulligan's celebrated pianoless quartet (with trumpeter Chet Baker), which made its debut in 1952 at the Haig, a Los Angeles cocktail lounge.

Hamilton left the Mulligan ensemble in 1954 and the next year resumed touring with Lena Horne. In 1955 he formed the Chico Hamilton Quintet, the first in a string of successful small combos under his leadership. The unusual instrumentation of this band, with Buddy Collette on flute and Fred Katz on cello, earned it national attention as one of the hottest new groups in jazz. Hamilton's fame widened when he and his band were featured in the 1957 hit movie *The Sweet Smell of Success.* Along with Mulligan's unit and the Dave Brubek Quartet, Hamilton's quintet helped set the tone for what the critics dubbed "West Coast" or "chamber" jazz.

Like his drumming contemporary Art Blakey, Hamilton built his career as a bandleader on his astute choices of sidemen. His various bands through the mid-sixties introduced a succession of later-famous musicians, including reed players Arthur Blythe, Charles Lloyd, Paul Horn, and Eric Dolphy, guitarists Jim Hall, Gábor Szabó, and Larry Coryell, and bassist Ron Carter.

Hamilton's visibility as a jazz musician diminished after 1966, when he moved to New York City and formed his own production company. He specialized in writing and playing soundtracks for radio, television, and movies and composing catchy tunes for the advertising industry. Throughout much of the seventies Hamilton wrote and produced up to five jingles a week. Hamilton performed with his own groups infrequently during this period, but he did give free concerts and lectures in schools and community centers in disadvantaged neighborhoods.

Hamilton returned to the road in the early eighties. Since that time he has led a series of eclectic new bands that play the gamut—everything from straightahead swing and bebop to Latin, blues and rock. He is recording regularly again, primarily with his working quartet, Euphoria, and he continues to score and record music for films and commercials. At age seventy, Chico Hamilton is also considering his achievements in retrospect: in 1991, sessions reuniting the original members of his 1955 quintet were released on the Soul Note label, and he is currently completing his autobiography, "The Skin You Love to Touch." [1]

Recorded 1981
PR: In the mid-fifties you led a quintet with the unusual instrumentation of flute, guitar, cello and drums. How did that group come about?
CH: Well, that came about through self-defense, because if you recall, everybody was goin', at that time, by the way of all flesh. You know, the rock thing had just begun, and rhythm and blues, et cetera, et cetera, which there was nothing wrong with that, but by the same token the producers and people who were involved in the record business started to put unbelievable demands on musicians. They were making saxophone players put gloves on when they played, you know, things like that. And a lot of bad music was on the scene. Just out of self-defense, man, just in order for me to play the way that I wanted to play, I had to form my own group.

1. *The Original Chico Hamilton Quintet—Reunion*, Soul Note Records, 1991.

WE: You're not currently signed with a recording company. Are you anxious to record?

CH: I'm lookin' forward to recording, more so than ever. What I'm doing now musically, I feel very strong about it. You know, I'm doing it all—by *me*, I mean the group—we're covering all exits, man, we're playing all kinds of music. And it's good. It's really good music, and I think it's very important right now to have good music again on the scene. But here again good music don't stand a chance, because the goddamn media is doin' a number on us. I mean, you know, it's totally impossible.

There's some stations in New York, man, the one station in particular, where they claim to be a jazz station, and they have all these promos going—Miles Davis! John Coltrane! all that kinda thing, right? Man, they haven't played a Miles Davis record in years. They haven't played a Coltrane record in years. And I don't know, it's not fair, but what *is* fair, you know, as far as the day's thing is concerned?

WE: How do you feel about the current state of the jazz world?

CH: Well, I really don't know. I've been lucky. I just started back into it within the last three years or so, very seriously, trying to get myself reoriented, you know, and trying to get popular again so that people will buy, or at least the promoters or the people who control this thing, will start buying me again, you know.

But jazz itself, the music itself, is constantly improving because of the combination of a whole lot of things in regards to the fact that the different, let's say the input of rock music, the input of pop music, the input of, I guess the rhythm and blues, if you want to call it, the input of soul, whatever you want to call it, plus the fact of the introduction of electronic instruments, you know. However, that can leave you cold, too.

But I think the combination of everything, of all of these elements, will eventually, we will have some super music again. Because there's no new music. We're still playing the twelve-tone system, you know, the European school of music, and ain't nobody's going to top Beethoven—*nobody*. And nobody's going to top Duke Ellington.

WE: What do you say to people who are against incorporating all those elements into jazz and who want to see the music remain pure?

CH: What is *pure jazz*?

WE: Some people would say that pure jazz is acoustic and follows, for instance, the Armstrong to Parker to Coltrane lineage.

CH: No, that's not so. That doesn't make it pure because it's acoustic.

That doesn't make it pure because it came from Louis Armstrong or it came from Bird, Charlie Parker, or if it came from 'Trane. That doesn't make it pure. I mean *music* is *music*, you know. How pure is someone's soul? That's what we're dealing in. So who knows what's pure? Who is to say that some young dude that wrote a pop tune, that he's not pure. As far as I'm concerned, man, it's an open thing. Music is *Godness*, and you know, God's will will be done. It's part of it, part of the world, part of life. So who in the hell . . . that bugs me, I guess [laughter].

PR: You've always been able to recruit good younger players into your groups. Have you been a mentorlike figure for many of them?

CH: Well, I consider this as one of my rewards. I haven't made an exceedingly large amount of money makin' music or playin' music—playin' the kind of music that I do play. But however, to compensate for that my phone constantly rings, and I constantly get calls, and I'm constantly introduced to young talented players, guys who want to play with me. And man, this is flattering as hell, you know. They want to play with "The Cheeks" because, hey, number one, they know they'll get a chance to play. They'll get a chance to develop, you know.

As well as develop musically, I try to, you know, help them along other lines just as far as being a professional musician. Young guys haven't changed; they were the same ten years ago, they were the same twenty years ago. It was just like, hey, I got help when I came up. I was fortunate enough to be helped. I was helped by some of the best. People like Lester Young, Charlie Parker, people like that, you know. Duke Ellington, Billy Strayhorn, people like this helped me considerably, and all I'm doing is just trying to repay, you know, give something back. Music has been awfully good to me, so I'm just trying to give something back to it.

WE: But it seems that, more than just helping out, you have created contexts in which younger musicians flourish, sometimes playing the best music of their careers. Does your role as a drummer have anything to do with this?

CH: Art Blakey, Max Roach, Gene Krupa, Buddy Rich, Chick Webb— every drummer that you've heard of or know of that had a band had the best band around. The band hits completely, the precision; it's a well-organized sound as far as the musical content is concerned. And that just doesn't happen; it comes about because of the fact that I think that drummers, all drummers, have the patience of Job, man, that's what it is.

You gotta realize that a horn player, or any other player other than a drummer, he can sort of get his own kicks, because he plays an instrument that's melodic and everything, so if he's involved in the melody he can get carried away, things like that. It's a real ego thing for the average player. And what you don't realize, man, is that the drummer has got to sit there and wade through all them bad notes and keep some time and still try to get inspired, when you know, man, this ain't happenin' [laughter]. But anyway, I think this is one way you learn a lot of patience.

And drummers are very astute in regards to rehearsing. They're sticklers for rehearsal. They know that sloppy playin' won't allow—it throws the rhythm off; it throws everything off. So I guess, here again I'm just sorta speaking technically, maybe in regards to practicing the craft. But that would be my reason of saying, hey, that's why most drummers have good bands.

PR: Could you comment on some of the better-known players that have passed through your bands, starting with Eric Dolphy?

CH: You know, Eric was introduced to me by my brother; him and Eric went to school together. He's an actor. I don't know whether—you ever see "Starsky and Hutch"? You know the guy who plays Captain Dolby? That's my brother [laughter]. Anyway, Bernie and Eric went to school together in L.A., and I think it was when Paul Horn left the band I put the word out. And so my brother, Bernie, says, "Hey, man, there's a friend of mine you oughta take a listen to." And it turned out to be Eric. At that time he was playing with Gerald Wilson's big band when Gerald had a workshop there in L.A. So naturally Eric said yeah, that kinda thing, and that was his first opportunity not only to go on the road, but with me. And when he was with my band he got into the bass clarinet.

Eric Dolphy, I tell you, was perhaps one of the most dedicated musicians I have ever known in my whole entire life. Music was his total life. And there was some difficult times with us for the simple reason that the public in general wasn't ready for Eric when he was on my band. As a matter of fact, people used to say, "Man, you oughta get rid of him." And I said, "Hey, are you kiddin'." But they weren't quite ready for Eric at that time, because he was such a completely different kind of player than Paul Horn, needless to say. After Paul Horn played the melody, that was it. Whereas Eric, the word is *improvisation* [laughter].

Eric was such an original type of player. He had a legitimate background in music to the extent of the classics, and he studied with [William] Kincaid. He did everything correct. He was total music. The form of music which was known as jazz, I guess, just happened to be an incidental. It was a coincidence that he got off into that.

WE: Wasn't Ron Carter's first professional engagement in your band?

CH: That was it. Right after he graduated from Eastman he came on the band. At the time it was Ron and Eric; I had both of them in the band at the same time [laughter]. Oh man, we had a helluva band. I've had some bands that've been super. The band that I put together with Charles [Lloyd] and Gábor [Szabó] and Albert Stinson—that was a super band. That was a band that started people thinking differently about small-group concepts, you know.

PR: How about Arthur Blythe?

CH: Arthur! He's a player, man. Arthur played with me for about two or three years. Things are beginning to happen for him, and he's very deserving of them. He realized that he had to get away from the West Coast. He had just reached a point that nothing was happening for him out there. To play is one thing, but to play and be sort of compensated for it, if nothing else than to be recognized. That's some kinda compensation. Man, he just packed up bag and baggage, his wife and two kids, and man, he took his chance, and fortunately for me he took that chance [laughter], because we have a very good relationship.

WE: You were a big success on the West Coast, musically at least. What reasons motivated your move to New York in the middle sixties?

CH: I had just come from London, where I had finished the film *Repulsion* with Roman Polanski, and on my way back to California I stopped in New York, and I did a commercial. I made so much money with that one commercial that it just didn't make sense. I never made that much money before in my life makin' music or playin' music, so I decided, "Well, let me go back to New York" [laughter].

And I went back and formed my company, and it's strange as hell, because it never occurred to, I guess, all the guys back in New York—they were busy doing all the recording on all the dates, but, I guess it never occurred to them, "Hey, well why not have a company like everybody else." So I went back and formed my company and became very successful, needless to say, and that's what I did for damn near ten years. Until I got really uptight, started gettin' bored and stuff, boozin' and things like that and becomin' a bad guy. So I had a coat-puller, you know, a little message from the Man Upstairs. I survived, and I just turned my life around again. I started doin'—let me do what I do and that's play; I'm a player. I'm back out here again.

WE: So you got back on the road by choice, not because you had to?

CH: No. I came back out here because I wanted to, not because I had to. Well, I *had* to in a sense to get my head together again too. Also, the only way you are goin' to find out what in the hell is goin' on, man, is by being out here. You can't judge it by the media anymore. Some of the best music that was ever on television, man, was commercial music at one time, but even that has gone by the way. But if you recall the commercial music in the late sixties or early seventies, it was dynamite, really super, 'cause primarily all the jazz musicians were making commercials.

WE: One more question about your move to the East Coast. Since your bands were so strong in the sixties, didn't you regret leaving those accomplishments behind?

CH: Well, the key to any situation is realizing when you've sort of peaked. I guess this is one of my voodooisms or somethin'. There's somethin' that always comes about to let me know that I've sorta peaked this particular style or this particular group or this particular kind of thing. I never fired people, but when it gets to a point, it plays itself out as far as I'm concerned.

It's nice to have guys be together for years, but on the other hand it's not good, because familiarity breeds contempt. That's what it amounts to. That's the same thing that's involved with one's emotions. When you know everything a guy's going to play before he plays it—you know, a guy hits a chord, or he'll hit a note, man, and you know what direction he's gonna go in—it takes all the excitement out of it, for *me*, I don't know about anyone else, but for me. Plus the fact, new guys, that's new energy, new ideas, new thoughts—different thoughts, let's put it like that.

PR: Let's switch the emphasis to your early years. Dexter Gordon and you grew up in Los Angeles at about the same time. Did you know each other as kids?

CH: Listen, we went to school together. Dexter and I grew up together, and we were in the same class. He and I and another musician, his name was James Robinson, a trombone player, in our senior year, or somethin' like that—it was in high school—we all three were in the same class. It was a fact, an established fact, that the hardest teacher in the whole system was an English teacher, I forget her name, but she was a stickler. Dexter, myself, and James Robinson were the only three students out of that whole graduating class who got A's in her class, in English. I tell you, man, this was a fact. And if you ever see Dexter again, ask him about it. I can't recall her name—matter of fact the last time I saw Dex, we talked about that. But Dexter Gordon, Buddy Collette, Charlie Mingus, Ernie Royal, Jack Kelso—we all grew up together.

PR: We know that Dexter left L.A. in Lionel Hampton's band . . .

CH: Well, I was with Lionel's first band too. I was with the band before Dexter was on the band. As a matter of fact, I got fired out of that band. That's the only band I've ever been fired out of, and I think that was the best thing that ever happened to me.

PR: Do you want to talk about the circumstances?

CH: The bottom line was I wasn't ready. Hamp took me out of school, took me right out of Jefferson High School, and because, I think, previous to that, I had played with Duke Ellington when I was sixteen years old, you know [laughter]. Hamp took me out of school, and man, I was a kid, you know. It was just over my head at that time. It was his first band; it was a swing band, and he was just with Benny Goodman and came back—he was from L.A. too. So I built up a good reputation around town that I was a good drummer, being able to sweep, use good brushes, keep good time—that's all drummers had to do during that time.

WE: How did you get to play with Duke Ellington?

CH: The only reason why I figured that I got the job is because they couldn't find anybody else [laughter]. I was out with my wife, who at that time was my date. I'm still married to the same lady—ain't that somethin'? Anyway, Sonny Greer had become ill. Duke's band was in Culver City playing at the ballroom out there, and they needed a drummer. I don't know how it came about, but anyway, I ended up bein' on the bandstand, and I played the entire engagement. I evidently did so well that Sonny just decided to take it easy for a while [laughter].

So while they were on the West Coast I stayed with the band. It wasn't a long period, but at least it was an unbelievable experience. As a matter of fact, that band, when I got there to the ballroom we came in through the backstage, and that band was cookin' so *hard* that I swore up and down that there was a drummer playin'. And when I went through the curtain backstage and looked up there, the band was just hittin', just hittin' beautifully.

WE: About what year was this?

CH: Well, Jimmy Blanton was alive, was on the band. Tricky Sam [Nanton], you remember the trombone player, was on the band. Freddy Guy was on the band. I think Ben Webster was on the band, and naturally Johnny Hodges and Cootie Williams, Harry Carney, Rex Stewart was on the band. That was the classic band. It was, whew, man, it was somethin'.

PR: Before we close, we have some questions about your style of playing. First, you haven't featured many pianists in your group. Has that been a matter of choice or circumstance?

CH: Both. I've thought about it from time to time. And all the piano players that I've personally dug had their own thing goin'. So they weren't goin' to give up what they had goin' to play with me, you know, that kind of thing.

I've stayed away from piano for the simple reason that there's not that many piano players know how to play with groups. Piano locks you in, it really locks you in, and you don't have the freedom, the looseness that you do with the guitar. Because when I play, I'm playing piano in my group, more or less, the way I play my instrument—drums. I do all the trills, you know, ordinarily where the piano would, the way maybe I would like for a piano player to play, to accompany, you know. Plus the fact it really improves the hearing and the, well, you have to really develop an ear to play without piano, that kind of thing. I mean, you don't have to use it as a crutch. 'Cause most players use—when a piano's in a group they use it as a crutch. They wait for the piano player to hit the chord, and they go from there, you know, as opposed to them leading the piano player.

WE: Drums are usually thought of as rhythmic instruments, but you call your drumming style "melodic." Could you tell us why?

CH: Well, first of all, I don't consider myself a drummer; I really consider myself more of a percussionist than a drummer. The foremost thing that I'm interested in is a sound. I'm fortunate, because like that old saying, "All God's children," you know, so I got rhythm [laughter]. I don't have to worry about that. But I'm more interested in creating a sound, getting a sound to facilitate whatever the implements are, whether it's the brushes or the sticks or mallets.

I did very little playing with my hands, because I have very tender hands. To get callouses would only help destroy my touch that I have for brushes, or sticks, or mallets. So that's the reason I don't fool around with my hands tryin' to play congas and things like that. I leave those to the conga players.

But in order to get this sound, it requires a touch, and subsequently I'm also involved in the harmonic structure and the interval aspect and the melodic aspect of a melody or an arrangement, et cetera, et cetera. I just try to blend as closely as I possibly can with what I do, whether I'm playing on a cymbal or a snare drum or tom-tom or whatever. I'm more interested in having a sound. That's the reason my bands get the sound that they do and the feeling that they do is because of me. It's the way that I play. In other words, even when the cello was there, the cello isn't the gimmick. I'm the gimmick [laughter].

WE: Do you have your drumsticks custom-made, or do you use what is commercially marketed?

CH: Well, I use what's commercially marketed. When I go to pick out a pair of sticks, I'll just go through the crop until I find what feels good to me. I know what size—they have measurements—and I know what particular type of stick that I like, and you just do that until you get the feel. And if it feels right, then that's what it's all about.

The same thing with cymbals. You know, drums are very personal. Picking out cymbals is like picking out a wife. It all depends on what you hear. What you hear is what kind of sound you have. Everyone has their sound, musician or not; every human being has his own sound. When you hear that sound and you know it's your sound, hey, the vibes are there. You say, "Hey, I like that, that's it." You know what I mean? You don't have to know whether it's an A or a B or a C; it could be a Z. It doesn't matter. That's your sound, and that's the truth of the matter as far as I'm concerned. I could become very technical and give you a lot of B.S. which doesn't mean anything, but that's what the bottom line is—whenever your sound comes around, that's it.

SELECTED DISCOGRAPHY

The Chico Hamilton / Buddy Collette Quintet. Pacific Jazz PJ 1209. 1955.
The Chico Hamilton Quintet. Pacific Jazz 1225. 1956.
The Sweet Smell of Success. Decca 8641. 1957.
With Eric Dolphy. *Gongs East.* Warner Brothers 1271. 1958.
With Charles Lloyd. *The Chico Hamilton Special.* Columbia CL 1619.
    1960.

El Exigente. Flying Dutchman FDS-135. 1970.

Peregrinations. Blue Note LA 520G. 1975.

Tanganyika. VSP-20. 1984.

Euphoria. Swallow CHEM 7 (English label). 1989.

Arroyo. Soul Note 121241. 1991.

LEE KONITZ

Photograph by Jimmy Katz / Giant Steps.   Used with permission.

Alto saxophonist Lee Konitz has been called one of the most original voices on his instrument in modern jazz. Since the early fifties his plush, vibratoless sound has represented one of the true alternatives to the prevailing style of Charlie Parker. Konitz is the ultimate no-frills jazz player. Paring a tune down to its essentials, he typically improvises with a composer's sense of form, constructing solos that are keenly proportioned, elliptical, and leavened with a surprising emotional bite.

Born and reared in Chicago, Konitz took up the clarinet after hearing Benny Goodman on the radio. By his sixteenth birthday he was adept enough to play alto sax with a Chicago-based touring band. He stayed in the Midwest until a gig with Claude Thornhill's big band at the age of nineteen deposited him in the jazz mecca of New York City.

There Konitz resumed his tutelage under fabled blind pianist Lennie Tristano, from whom he had taken lessons for a time in Chicago. From the mid-forties through the early fifties Tristano was widely acknowledged as the leader of a new, so-called cool style of playing that was in stark contrast to the emotionally molten conception of bop.

Tristano and his small band of disciples, including Konitz, tenor saxophonist Warne Marsh, and guitarist Billy Bauer, played intricate compositions and finely chiseled, brainy solos that must have sounded comparatively bloodless at the time. In 1949 Konitz played on the groundbreaking Tristano album *Crosscurrents*, and the same year he was one of the key soloists on Miles Davis' historic *Birth of the Cool* recordings.[1]

In the early fifties Konitz broke with Tristano. After a tour of Scandinavia, this die-hard modernist surprised almost everyone by joining the Stan Kenton Orchestra, then a throwback to dance bands of the forties. Konitz worked with Kenton from 1952 to 1953, then returned to New York City. For the remainder of the decade, Konitz led his own groups and taught privately. Occasionally he rejoined Tristano; in 1955 they

---

1. Lennie Tristano, *Crosscurrents*, Capitol Records, 1949; Miles Davis, *Birth of the Cool*, Capitol Records, recorded 1949–50, released 1957, reissued 1989.

recorded a session live from the Sing Song Room of the Confucius Restaurant.[2]

Public interest in cool jazz ebbed by 1960. His style no longer fashionable, Konitz moved to California, did odd jobs, and effectively retired from the music scene. He returned in 1965, lured by an offer from Lennie Tristano to play Carnegie Hall. A contract with Milestone Records and other labels followed, and between 1967 and 1980 he recorded a remarkable series of albums, using a variety of formats and combinations of musicians (including kindred spirit Warne Marsh) that put him back in the limelight with a new generation of jazz fans. In the late seventies he also formed his own critically acclaimed nonet, inspired by the Davis prototype.

Now in his mid-sixties, Konitz is a popular figure at clubs and festivals internationally; he won Denmark's Jazzpar Prize in 1991. He also occupies a perhaps unanticipated role as a musical model for younger musicians. The quiet man from Chicago, who for so long avoided publicity, has forged an enduring place in jazz history.

Recorded 1980

WE: Lee, is it true that you are attracted to the period called the "prerenaissance," when there was not a premium placed on individual achievement?

LK: Yeah, of course. I think that the age of anonymity was a very healthy time, and I think this music especially has suffered a great deal. The music itself has suffered a great deal from the so-called cult of personalities.

I think that there are thousands and thousands of saxophone players around the planet who I'm sure can play better than me—well, you know, hundreds, maybe. I mean, they're very capable players, and for some combination of reasons I got some notoriety in the process. And I'm using it certainly in this day to earn my living and things like that, and it's a great way for me to earn my rent money.

But I can certainly see working on a farm and playing the instrument for the joy of it in the evenings or whatever. Well, you'd have to invite some fellow farmers over sometime—once a week—to either play for them or with them to make it a complete communication cycle.

2. *Lennie Tristano*, Atlantic Records, 1955.

VE: In what ways has that "cult of personalities" been damaging to jazz?
LK: Well, all you have to do is reflect on the number of musicians in jazz that have preceded us and their troubled life-styles, if you will, and the way they chose to cope with those problems with drugs and things like that. That's certainly one flagrant indication of being in a position of power that they were unable to handle.

I mean, this could all be handled, you know, if you have the proper information. But it's a tough position to be in, because people begin to— I just had a brief interview across the street here with a guy, and he was talking about interviewing Gerry Mulligan, and this guy, a lovely guy, asked Gerry something about playing—whether he was playing any other instruments besides the baritone—and Gerry got very indignant that he didn't know he was playing soprano also. And I thought, "Gee, he must really think he's extra special" [laughter]. Well, he *is*, you know, but sometimes it's hard to handle it. I mean, we're all extra special, but being a performer is some kind of weird relief to the rest of [the] people, somehow, and whew! It's a very, very precarious balance to tread.

PR: Somewhere we read that you're after a "timeless" music.
LK: There's no concern in doing these processes in the timeless aspect of the music. That certainly is a great reward if we can look back twenty-five years later and it still sounds valid in some way and not dated. But the idea is still for me that I'm doing precisely the same thing, I think, that I did philosophically, if you will, when I was eleven years old and picked up the instrument, and the so-called avant-garde people are doing that same thing too. That's the way one starts, with some materials. You feel them, and you make different designs and make funny sounds, and you have a good time with it; and then, if you have really such a good time, you learn something about it, and you can do it more formally and within all of the beautiful tradition we've inherited.

I am very fortunate to have been part of some recordings in the late forties that sound to me really quite OK today, and that's a great reward to me. And certainly in the front of my mind that occurs to me if I do everything right that should happen, but initially that wasn't what I was setting out to do. That was all after the fact.

PR: You mentioned that, in general, everyone picks up the instrument and starts with the same materials. But do you see any differences in the way some of the younger musicians today, like Arthur Blythe

and Henry Threadgill, have approached their instruments and their art?
LK: Yes, I think there are different elements now that come into the total music that are not really, directly, traditionally inherited. They're lookin' around for new things to add to the whole vocabulary.

I heard Arthur Blythe recently at Newport Festival, and he was surprisingly—because the first time I heard him was in the Village Vanguard. I was working there, and they were playing Lester Young and Nat Cole records during the intermission, and it was really a nice thing to be in the room with that music happening. And one intermission I heard this very strident alto player, and I was talking to someone, and it kept attracting my attention, and I finally started to walk over to the bar to tell the bartender to please turn it lower or something 'cause it was really, whew! rough . . .

But at the concert—at Avery Fisher Hall—he was getting a beautiful sound out of the instrument, and he was playing some nice music, all original music and a good rhythm section, and it was OK, you know. And then he played for the next selection "Misty," and I thought he was putting us on—which I'm sure he wasn't. Obviously he indicated where he was on the traditional part of the music.
PR: Interestingly, his group is called In the Tradition.
LK: Whatever I heard of that record was extremely like a caricature to me.
PR: Like "Misty" was a caricature?
LK: Well, it was embarrassing, you know. It was while I was sitting with Martial Solal. So [he said] "What's happening?" you know, in French [laughter].

Anyway, I think that [Blythe] and the others are working for other kinds of things—a very expressive thing, a very, very energetic thing, certainly—and sometimes the balance gets a little out of kilter to me, and it doesn't end up sounding like a total fine art music to me.
WE: What do you mean when you say that Blythe's music is "energetic"?
LK: I'm saying that it becomes a distortion of energy. Their emphasis is too strongly on energy and endurance and physical aspects of the music, maybe. And so it doesn't end up being a balanced art form, a fine art, I would say.
WE: Do you think that some of the so-called avant-garde black jazz mu-

sicians purposely sacrificed a classic balance in their music in order to express their feelings about social and political matters that affected them personally?

LK: Oh yes, very extramusical factors involved in all that music, I think. And in that way extremely dramatic and, I mean, that group from Chicago, what are they called, the Art Ensemble of Chicago, they're doing the whole theater, a piece of theater, and that's beautiful. Although they blew me out of the Keystone Corner one night, I swear. 'Cause, in addition to all the costumes and everything, they are setting up a very strong wave of vibrations up there, and they wouldn't stop. Jesus, they just kept going, just volume-wise, density-wise, intensity-wise, *every-wise*. It was just the height of bad taste to me.

WE: It's a small club, too.

LK: Yeah, for a few moments it's a very dramatic touch in their whole thing as I perceive what they're doing. But they get into it, and it's like a cathartic of some kind for them. When you're doing that kind of thing you really can work up a sweat, and it feels great, but if you're not participating it can be a total bore.

WE: Don't you think that all those extramusical factors can have a strong impact on the audience?

LK: Well, it certainly can. I'm thinking of Max Roach, for example, like one period when he came walking out on the stage during a Miles Davis concert with a big sign and started making some political points on the stage. It was a height of bad taste, I think, from one aspect. Another aspect, I remember Max, in the early days when he was just interested in playing and gettin' stoned and those kinda things, you know. And so I can certainly admire him for broadening his spectrum, his viewpoint, and taking a stand politically and all that. But I do think that it is using a space unethically.

WE: You're saying to keep the music separate from the politics?

LK: I think so. And all the music that he did that I know about—I haven't heard all of it with Abbey Lincoln and all that—that doesn't compare to me now years later at all to the way he sounded when he played with Charlie Parker. 'Cause he was masterful in those choruses he played along with Charlie, and these other things are trying to do things, and I don't think they'll be preserved as well, somehow.

And please understand that whatever these people are doing I know it's coming from some strong motivation, and I have no desire to really criticize what they're doing. I'm trying to put things into perspective, and I think that's what you're trying to do too, and so sometimes, though, people take a little bit out of context, and I've had reviews where the last line of the review sounded like "Yes, but I don't dig the avant-garde" or something like that, which is not the way it is at all.

I have been invited to avant-garde concerts, so to speak, as kind of the daddy, so to speak, 'cause I really am part of the group that made the first free-form record in 1949. I mean, I've chosen since then to stay with the tradition. That's my choice because it offered that many challenges to me, and I'm more concerned with mastering that more to my satisfaction than looking around for a lot of different approaches.

PR: Anthony Braxton might be called an avant-garde player, or at least a nontraditional player. Were you aware of his two-record solo album, *For Alto*, prior to making your own solo record?[3]

LK: I was aware of it. I hadn't actually heard it. But it occurred to me, I'm certain, that that was really an interesting thing that was inevitable, but I didn't really realize it was time for that to happen—where a single-note instrument could play a solo concert or make a record. And well, I thought that Anthony had a lot of chutzpah, as they say, to make a double set, and Phil Woods thought even stronger about that, as I remember. He really put that whole approach down pretty strongly. You know, Anthony was involved with making sounds other than just playing lines in a traditional way, so there was a bigger palette for him to use for that.

When I decided to do that, it was after having made a record with Red Mitchell for Steeplechase, and I said, "If you're interested, if you can give me an hour's studio time, I'd like to do what I do at home and see if anybody is interested. You could call it 'warming up a riff' or 'before and after' or whatever. Maybe sell it as a music-minus-three record" [laughter].

And I did forty minutes of "The Song Is You" and twenty minutes of "Cherokee." And he wrote me back a couple of weeks later. Neils Winter, the director of the company, wanted to put out the forty minutes of "The Song Is You." I said, "As long as they gotta turn the record over, why don't we change the key and get a different progression at least." So anyway, I was pleased that there was that interest in it.

3. Anthony Braxton, *For Alto*, Delmark Records, 1968; Lee Konitz, *Lone-Lee*, Steeplechase Records, 1974.

PR: We've noticed that on some of your albums certain standards re-appear and, also, that on other tunes the changes sound very similar.

LK: You say, first of all, the changes, the tunes were similar? I don't know what you mean by that.

PR: The chord changes.

LK: I know what you mean by chord changes, but what tunes I wonder did you have in mind?

PR: "I'll Remember April." There are other songs that sound like that one. One may even be called "April," but on a different record.

LK: Oh, they're all "I Remember April" but with different titles. Oh, I see what you mean. Well, that's simply a result of, I mean that's basically my repertoire, that few dozen tunes. And if I'm not setting up a special set of material for a record, I will choose those songs I like best and try 'em again, without the melody, say, just using the structure of the song.

WE: So you prefer having a limited body of material to play?

LK: If we have a little short confessional here [laughter], I keep thinking that it doesn't matter what tunes you play. The process is the same, and if it works then it's like a new piece, you know. And it is a fact that the better you know the song the more chances you might dare take. And so that's why Bird played a dozen tunes all his life, basically, and most of the people that were improvising—Tristano played the same dozen tunes all his life. And you know, it's amazing what depth he got. He wouldn't have gotten that otherwise, I don't think, in that particular way.

I think it's something similar to Monet painting the lily pond at all times of the day, catching the reflection of the light. I just feel with each situation I'm in, different rhythm sections or whatever, that "I'll Re-member April" becomes just something else. And it is a very preferable point—that's the main thing. Everybody who knows that material knows that material pretty well—the listeners and the musicians. So they know, you can just nakedly reveal if anything's happening or not; there's no subterfuge. And that aspect of it is appealing to me, I think.

PR: Let's get into a little bit of your history before we get much farther along.

LK: I was born at a very early age [laughter].

PR: And then what happened?

LK: And then I was trying to figure out what happened [laughter]. I am still trying to figure that out.

WE: We know you were born in Chicago. As you grew up, were you aware of the Chicago school of musicians?

LK: Well, I just was aware of Benny Goodman, actually, from having listened to the radio a lot and heard the remotes that they had in those days of the dance bands from different hotels and ballrooms around the country. He really got to me, but I didn't know quite why yet, you know. I didn't have any impetus in my family, immediate family, and it wasn't 'til I got out and started playing around a little bit that I realized that there really was an awful lot happening, and fortunately at about the age of fifteen or so I met Tristano, and he kind of clued me in to the fact that this was a serious art form.

WE: How did you meet him?

LK: I was working a job across the street in a ballroom and went across to a bar where a piano player friend of mine was working to hear him. And he said, "Listen to this guy." He was playing with a rumba band, a Spanish rumba band, playing with locked hands kinds of things on the rumbas—whew! And so we started to talk, and pretty soon I asked him if he could help me to learn this music, and I started to study with him.

PR: In the jazz history books, Tristano is cited as an alternative to bop. Does that make any sense to you?

LK: Yeah, it does in a way. But they missed the point, really, because he's just used all of those materials and tried to make the rhythms different and the harmonies in a different fashion, and it's right out of there, you know.

PR: After 1964 you don't hear much about him.

LK: He dropped out in '64.

PR: Allegedly, Tristano had conflicts with luminaries like Thelonious Monk and Charles Mingus. Is there any substance to these stories? Was he a volatile personality?

LK: He was that, and he was blind and chose to live as the king of his castle, so to speak, and not go out. When he had his first attempt, he was surrounded by students—me, and Warne Marsh, and the rhythm section that he chose and all studied with him—and he was willing to go out 'cause he was well guarded, so to speak, and represented. They even referred to us as "six blind mice" once.

But when we learned that that wasn't going to work, he chose just to stay home and teach and put things into perspective in a way by discriminating in terms of differentiating between one thing and another. It ended up, I mean, at the age of fifty-five he was doing a radio interview, and he was still putting Monk down as a pianist. I thought that a little peculiar. I mean, I don't think it takes much experience to know that Monk wasn't a helluva pianist, but it also doesn't take much to know that no one else sounded like him. I wonder why he just wouldn't acknowledge that.

There was a resentment and a bitterness, I think, as part of not being recognized more or some damn thing. I mean, he certainly got a lot of recognition. He was a goddamn legend during his life. And he was a very brilliant man in many respects, you know. He had his great problems too, and he finally succumbed to them. But he certainly is a direct development, or "white" development, if you will. And I think there's a basis of different environmental experience to make that distinction. That he used all of those materials that were basically brought to their full fruition by black men and he did it from his experiences in Italian-American.

WE: Could you give us some insights into Tristano's teaching methods?

LK: I can't remember too much of what I learned material-wise, for example, but there was [an] extraordinary impetus to be very dedicated to this premise, this subject, and that's probably the biggest thing. Any of the students over these few generations seem to have a common, I *think*, viewpoint about that. They're all fanatically devoted to playing "I'll Remember April" [laughter] or whatever, you know? And playing the goddamn best chorus they can play, you know, and not going out and doing it in public, most of them.

The whole group of Tristanoites that are carrying on the tradition—well, they come out every once in a while, and when they do, all the rest of the students in that circle crowd and flock into—the first time Warne Marsh worked at the Village Vanguard the club filled up with these little kiddies, and they're sitting at the tables with the Coke in front of them and singing along with the choruses, and Max is looking around with a cigar in his mouth—what?[4] In fact, a friend of mine walked in, and he said he heard the music, and he saw all these kids sitting with their eyes closed, and he looked around, and Max was sleeping in the back [laughter].

4. Max Gordon owned the Village Vanguard in New York City.

PR: In the late forties you played with Claude Thornhill and made your first records. What did you think of his band?

LK: It was a beautiful ballad band, that's what it was. A dance band. And they played gorgeous ballads with two french horns and a tuba, clarinets. Whew! Just gorgeous! And with Gil [Evans] writing it was a thrill to play ballads with the band. And then Gil tried to teach—he literally taught the band how to phrase the bop lines, 'cause a lot of guys in the band were older musicians, and that's as close as it came to playing jazz. Although they played—they had some lovely Gerry Mulligan arrangements. He wrote some beautiful things for that band.

PR: Was Thornhill a jazz player?

LK: Well, he played, you know, out of Teddy Wilson, I would guess [laughter]. He was a real character. I never really got to know him too well, 'cause I wasn't much of a drinkin' buddy, and they were hittin' it pretty hard usually.

PR: Was that a road band?

LK: Yeah.

PR: Travel the country?

LK: Yeah. I left Chicago with that band with the intentions of getting to New York where Tristano was in '47. And it took me ten months to get to New York. I could have gotten there faster on a covered wagon [laughter].

WE: You were a member of Miles Davis' *Birth of the Cool* nonet back in 1948. We recently found a record called *Pre-Birth of the Cool*, from a live date at the Royal Roost prior to the famous studio sessions.[5] The difference in the way the band plays on these two records is, to our ears, pretty dramatic.

LK: Yeah. First of all I have that bootleg record, and my first recollection is that one side of it ends in the middle of my solo on "Israel." Well, this didn't help me by cutting off in the middle of my solo as far as getting gigs, and anyway, that's just an aside.

I remember the music as being very kinda loose in the club but pretty sloppy, and we had some people sitting in, I think, that hadn't rehearsed with the band too much. And the band hadn't rehearsed enough all to-

---

5. *Miles Davis and His Tuba Band: Pre-Birth of the Cool.* Cicala Records (Italian label), recorded 1948, released *ca.* 1974.

gether, so that the studio date is even sloppy, as you must have noticed. But because there is such substance to the music and the musicians, it still was a, certainly a, what turned out to be a significant record. Did that answer all the aspects of your question?

WE: Well, it seemed that the band was much more demure in the studio.

LK: I think that was inevitable for a studio. I didn't quite realize that fully 'til I was reminded again, having heard a Miles Davis concert. Gil Evans gave me a tape of a '59 concert in Amsterdam with Coltrane, and Paul Chambers, and Wynton Kelly. Whew! They never got that on a record, and it's really different. And Miles's band with Wayne Shorter and them in some of those concerts—it's different. As good as they could get on the record, it's different in person.

PR: Were you going to say something about your nonet?

LK: I was going to say that that music of Miles's nonet has become another reality to me now, because Martin Williams, who's at the Smithsonian Institution, heard the records of my nonet and asked me if I would play a concert there this coming January, and I said, "Certainly." And he said, "How would you feel about playing some of the Miles Davis things, since it's a similar instrumentation and you were with the band, et cetera." I said, "I'd love to. I've been looking for that music," and I called Miles.

And then, you know, I found out that that music didn't seem to be available. So he said, "Would you want to transcribe some of it?" And I said, "I've been wanting to do that for twenty-five years," but I chickened out every time 'cause I couldn't really hear it all. And apparently no one else can, 'cause I don't know anybody else that's really done that. Those arrangements, which are little classics—every one of them—have not been extant all these years.

So I accepted the proposal, and I think it took me six months or more to get to it, 'cause I was really intimidated by it. I just couldn't hear some of the inner voices. And something happened to my brain every time I listened to it. I finally got the more obvious parts down on the six arrangements that he asked me to do.

And then I said, "Wait a minute, the important thing is that this music appear for the Smithsonian in as accurate a form as possible." So I called John Lewis, and I called Gerry Mulligan, and I called Johnny Carisi, and I went to Gerry Mulligan's house in Connecticut. I showed him what I had done, and he said, "I think it would be easier for me to just do it over again."

He said he went to Miles's house, and he looked through Miles's music, and he couldn't find the scores. Miles didn't know where they were. For four hours Gerry stood at his table and went back to the record and wrote—rewrote [George] Wallington's "Godchild," one of the tunes, and *he* couldn't hear the voicings he wrote either. I was very pleased to learn that [laughter].

So he wrote them, you know, as logically as he could, so we might have even a better version of that arrangement now, but it's probably pretty close. And John Lewis gave me a sketch of a "Move" that he did, and I took the parts off the sketch, and so that's now in existence. And I got a score of "Israel," Johnny Carisi's score of "Israel." And so the music is gradually being recomposed.

PR: A nonet's a strange type of group. It's not your big band, and it's not a small group. It's both at the same time.

LK: Yeah, that's one of the reasons I like it, 'cause it has the weight of a big band and it has the potential of a small-band looseness.

PR: It seems like you're trying to re-create a classic form in your band, getting the old arrangements out . . .

LK: I just find that there's a written phenomenon which all my playing life has been devoted mostly to just winging it, as they say, and suddenly there's an opportunity to kinda get really a stock of the best materials, whatever they are in jazz, and I'm just able to confine it to the jazz tradition as I understand it, and it's a nice project in that sense.

WE: Some jazz critics have grouped you and Art Pepper together as an alternative to Charlie Parker's music. Does that make any sense to you?

LK: Well, of course, I can't speak for Pepper, but I finally realized when people were talking about me during the early fifties or late forties as an alternative to Parker. But I was very involved in Tristano's school at that time, and it was a very potent thing in my life—in all of our lives, you know—and so I found myself, at those times, even denying myself the pleasure of Charlie Parker's music for fear that I would have the strong influence that everyone else seemed to be having. And so that was partly by default.

I finally, when I got a perspective on—a better perspective—someone interviewed me one time, and my answer at that point was that that music was just, well, in a different context, anyway, my answer was that it was just too *hard*. And not stretching out to include the influence was absolutely necessary, if you really listen to Charlie Parker, because it's the perfect music, and you can't hear it without wanting to reproduce it in some way. So it took a few years for me to get around to that.

PR: In the fifties you were with Atlantic and Verve. But in the sixties there's a paucity of records by you. What happened during most of that decade? Was your music different than the dominant mode of the time?

LK: Well, I'm afraid it has always been *that*, for better or worse. But it just seemed like, since I wasn't really one to really take care of business, as they say in the idiom, that I wasn't hustling enough work for myself, and they weren't tearing down the lines to get me to work, so I just figured it wasn't my time to work now, and I did my teaching and my practicing. It's a fact, I didn't work very much during those years.

PR: Then in the seventies you sprung up on small labels all over the place.

LK: Right.

PR: Was that just the times, or did you start hustling work?

LK: No, it was just the times. It seemed to start when I started working steadily at a couple of clubs in New York City, and during that two- or three-year period my name was always in a magazine, appearing in the *New Yorker* or something, and somehow that made me a viable product, I think. 'Cause I was getting all kinds of opportunities to work as a result of that, I think.

It's just like getting out of the house and, you know, someone knowing that you exist. I just chose to live quietly and had no PR at all. I still haven't had any. Whatever I've gotten has been not my initiation somehow. And I'm not bragging—a little bit bragging, I guess. But you need to have that to take care of business properly, you know, and I don't have that yet. I mean, I'm going to be fifty-three in a couple of months, and so that's rather stupid, I think [laughter]. In that sense.

WE: You were on Norman Granz's old label, Verve. Has he approached you for a recording date on his new label, Pablo?

LK: No. I even asked his lady friday, and I never got an answer. I liked working for Norman very much. I worked for him for five years at Verve, and he was great, and he didn't even like the way I played. So the guys that he liked he really took care of pretty good [laughter].

PR: Recently we heard you on an album with the French pianist Martial Solal.[6] Tell us something about him.

---

6. Lee Konitz and Martial Solal, *Duplicity*, Horo Records (Italian label), 1977.

LK: Well, he's considered the master over there, but he's never really fully scored, somehow, for a number of reasons that are valid, I think, [that] I won't get into now. But we have a nice opposing influence on each other. We're quite different from each other, and it sometimes becomes quite an unusual music as a result of it. So a deep, intuitive thing there, and it works sometimes like magic.

But for him personally, well, I just heard him at Carnegie Hall during the Newport thing, and at the end of the concert, Dick Katz, a fine piano player, was walking downstairs just goggle-eyed, and he said, "How come more people don't know that he's one of the great piano players in the world?" He just couldn't believe it. He's an extraordinary—as close to what you might imagine Art Tatum possibly being in 1980. He has that kind of breadth of virtuosity, certainly, and musicianship.

WE: Lee, one last question. How do you pronounce your last name?

LK: I pronounce it "Ko-nitz." Some people say "Kan-itz." If they spell it correctly on the check, I say fine [laughter].

SELECTED DISCOGRAPHY

With Lennie Tristano. *Crosscurrents*. Capitol M-11060. 1949.
Ezz-Thetic. Prestige 7827. 1951.
With Gerry Mulligan. *Konitz Meets Mulligan*. Pacific Jazz / Capitol
    CDP7-46847-2. 1953.
The Real Lee Konitz. Atlantic 1273. 1957.
The Lee Konitz Duets. Milestone MSP9013. 1967.
Spirits. Milestone 9038. 1971.
Lone-Lee. Steeplechase 1035. 1974.
With Martial Solal. *Duplicity*. Horo HDP17-18. 1977.
Lee Konitz Nonet Live at Laren. Soul Note SN1069CD. 1979.
Round and Round. Musicmasters C1JD 60167M. 1989.

CHARLES MINGUS

Photograph by Grover Sales.   Courtesy Fantasy, Inc.

C harles Mingus, one of the most celebrated figures in all of modern jazz, was a composer-arranger of the first rank, a bandleader of enduring influence, and a bassist of extraordinary power.

Born in 1922 in Nogales, Arizona, Mingus grew up in Los Angeles. As a youth, he steeped himself in an assortment of music, including the sanctified settings of the Pentecostal and Holiness churches, big-band jazz, and the works of nineteenth-century European composers. Trombone was his first instrument, and he played cello in his high school band. Mingus had ambitions to play classical cello, but he switched to bass after he learned that black cellists had no future in symphony orchestras.

Mingus' professional career began in the early forties, when he played in the New Orleans–style swing bands of Louis Armstrong and Kid Ory. Later he was a sideman for vibists Lionel Hampton and Red Norvo, among others. By the early fifties he had founded Debut Records, among the first of such efforts by a jazz musician. Perhaps this label's most important release, *Jazz at Massey Hall*, demonstrated Mingus' authority in the company of bop greats Charlie Parker, Dizzy Gillespie, Bud Powell, and Max Roach.[1]

From influential small-group recordings collected under the title *Pithecanthropus Erectus* in the midfifties to extended orchestral works of the seventies, Mingus' achievements as a composer-arranger place him alongside Thelonious Monk as second only to Duke Ellington in the jazz idiom.[2] He developed his often-complex compositions with a succession of ensembles, each called the Charles Mingus Jazz Workshop. Mingus founded his first workshop in 1954 and continued to explore this format until his death in January, 1979.

Mingus' workshops were prime incubators for young, prodigiously talented musicians, many of whom did the best work of their careers under his direction. The musicians who passed under Mingus' influence included Eric Dolphy, Rahsaan Roland Kirk, Clifford Jordan, Jackie

1. The original concert was recorded in Toronto's Massey Hall in 1953. A recent reissue is *Debut Records Presents the Quintet at Massey Hall*, Debut Jazz Classics, 1989.

2. Charles Mingus, *Pithecanthropus Erectus*, Atlantic Records, 1956–61; reissued on Charles Mingus, *Passions of a Man*, Atlantic Records, 1973–77.

McLean, Booker Ervin, George Adams, Dannie Richmond, Hamiet
Bluiett, Yusef Lateef, John Handy, Ricky Ford, and Don Pullen.

Dubbed "the university of Mingus" by his sidemen, the workshop
provided an intense and exacting training ground, characterized by long
hours of rehearsal and punctuated by the frequent eruptions of Mingus'
volcanic personality. As a bandleader, Mingus was notoriously short-
tempered with sloppy or superficial playing. During rehearsals, and even
onstage, he was known to stop a number in midstream to chastise a band
member; he commonly warned, "Respect the melody" and "Play in
tune." Sometimes in concert he would order his musicians to start a piece
all over again.

During the sixties the audience for jazz dwindled. Mingus, arguably at
the height of his powers, fell into obscurity and did not record from 1966
to 1970. During those years he was a recluse, haunting the streets of New
York City and occasionally showing up at a nightclub but playing no music publicly.

Early in 1970, however, Mingus formed a new band and released several memorable large- and small-group records. But it was the 1977 release of *Three or Four Shades of Blues* that fully revived Mingus' career.[3]
That recording, using three electric guitarists, including Larry Coryell,
sold over fifty thousand copies. It was the best-selling record Mingus
ever made.

Mingus was diagnosed as having amyotrophic lateral sclerosis (Lou
Gehrig's disease) shortly after completing *Three or Four Shades of Blues*.
By 1978 he was unable to play the bass, but he continued to compose,
and from a wheelchair he led large ensembles in several dates, including
the *Me, Myself an Eye* sessions. These recordings were released after Mingus' death.[4] Since that time the Mingus Dynasty Band, consisting predominantly of Mingus alumni, has kept Mingus' repertory alive with a
fidelity to the original spirit of the master's conception.

Mingus' stature as a composer and bandleader has somewhat overshadowed his accomplishments as a bassist. A founding father of modern
bass playing, Mingus significantly extended the range of the instrument
from the Walter Page–Jimmy Blanton–Oscar Pettiford lineage into the
present era. Blessed with remarkable prowess, he long has been acknowledged by jazz musicians and critics as a premier soloist.

3. Charles Mingus, *Three or Four Shades of Blues*, Atlantic Records, 1977.
4. Charles Mingus, *Me, Myself an Eye*, Atlantic Records, 1979.

The breadth of Mingus' work and influence can only be suggested here. A fuller account of his life can be found in his autobiography, *Beneath the Underdog*, originally published in 1971.[5] Not for the faint of heart, this book is at once a stunning indictment of racial discrimination, a detailed description of Mingus' initiations into sex, music, and love, and an almost surreal evocation of Duke Ellington and trumpeter Fats Navarro, who, according to Mingus, prompted him to play modern jazz.

Recorded 1977

WE: Charles, what does *tradition* in music mean to you?

CM: Well, in classical music, tradition means that a boy or a girl who wants to play music, they go to school, they study with all the past composers. What you have to do to get out of school, you supposed to learn and duplicate just what they did and forget about yourself. You supposed to learn Beethoven, Bach, Brahms, Stravinsky, everybody, you know. Even the string quartets, people who wrote for string quartets only. And then the teacher says, "Go and write something, now that you heard all these good musicians." And most of the kids give up. They just end up being copies.

But in jazz, the kids who come in today don't think they need any background. Ornette Coleman said he was an elevator operator where he used to look across the street at the theater from where he worked, and there was all the pretty girls and all the guys dressed in suits and uniforms. And they looked good to him, and he saw their horns. So he went and bought a horn and started playing it. He wanted to be famous, and he never asked anybody how to play. He didn't say whether he studied from anybody or not. And he came up with a style that is not too much different than a guy in New York who used to come to Minton's and try and sit in. They called him the Demon. You couldn't understand anything he was doing.

The reason that I know about this was that Eddie "Lockjaw" Davis, who used to play with Count Basie way back—he used to be the one you used to audition for—told me. To play at Minton's you couldn't just walk in and grab a bass. They made you go in a back room or a kitchen and call a few tunes. They did it to me too. They said, "Can you play 'Perdido'? Can you play 'Body and Soul'?"

5. Charles Mingus, *Beneath the Underdog*, ed. Nel King (1971; rpr. New York, 1991).

But the Demon is said to have been farther out than Ornette Coleman. Ornette is not really too far out if you've been to the Caribbean. Ornette's style of music is very calypso, very much like West Indian. In St. Martin's, I heard a kid who played like him.

Now if [Ornette] had studied with someone like Lloyd Reese or Buddy Collette . . . Ben Webster, Harry Carney, both of whom played with Duke Ellington's band, whenever they came to L.A. they studied with Lloyd Reese. For instance, I was told that Lloyd Reese taught Harry Carney the complete techniques of the bass clarinet. He wasn't playing bass clarinet at first; Lloyd taught him. Lloyd's structure was tradition, because he defies you to say that you can play without any history of the history of jazz—and he's right.

But it gets pretty bad when, for instance, George Wein of the Newport Jazz Festival has many times told me that he would like to have Ornette on the jam session. That means that different guys—Ornette, myself, Sonny Rollins, Dizzy Gillespie, Snooky Young—musicians who have never played together otherwise, get together and jam. So ya get together and call Ornette, and they did call him once, and they called "Perdido." He said, "What?" He didn't even know what "Perdido" was. Well, let's play the blues. He didn't even know what the blues was. Basically he played in the key of C.

I haven't listened to him that much, but when he first came I listened to him. I went to hear him twice, once with Monk. It was very funny. I walked in with Monk. I said, "It's a new guy, better than Bird." Monk walks in, spun around, says, "Hell, I did that twenty-five years ago, but I didn't do it on every tune," and he walked out.

Someone like Monk, who is a creative genius, can play stride piano, can play like Fats Waller, can play like Duke; he can play like Basie. Everyone was saying that, oh, he's just jealous of the guy getting famous and not playing like him. Well, it's hard to say, man. If your kid picks up a stethoscope and scalpel and tells you he's gonna cut out your appendix, Daddy, you don't have to go to the hospital, you'd be a lot more hesitant than you would in music. In music, you see, you can fool people, but doctors can't fool people. They get cadavers to practice on.

Tradition, to me, is the only way a person is gonna do anything good. That's to answer your question. You just can't come in by yourself. If you're in sports, football, you got to know what guys have done, from Knute Rockne on back.

PR: Could you tell us about your early musical training and why you chose the bass?

CM: First thing I got was a trombone in a box from Sears-Roebuck. My sister, who studied classical piano—that's all you could study, I guess, in those days—had a guy around—great protégé. He grew his hair down. He was a black guy; I don't know how he had hair grow down like that, but he used to shake his hair like he was Tchaikovsky or somebody. Anyway, this teacher who taught my sister and the choir conductor at the church, he played trombone, so my parents asked him if he would give me lessons.

So he came and gave me my first lesson. He said to learn the lines and spaces. He didn't write them out for me. He said, "Ask your sister. She plays piano." So he gave me a week to learn the lines and spaces. He came back and said, "You're stupid, you don't know one line from another, you'll never make a musician," and I didn't know what to say. It took me years to find out that I wasn't really stupid, and that he was the one who was stupid, 'cause he was the choir conductor, and the choir is usually written—other than the bass sections—in the treble clef. And why didn't he recognize that I was reading off the treble-clef scale and say, "Well, you have to learn the bass clef"?

So I always hated him so much for wasting my time, 'cause I probably would have been a much better musician if I had started earlier in my studies. And I think my sister finally did show me the bass clef, and the next thing, I told him that I wanted to turn the trombone in because I didn't want to play it. Then they decided I should play cello, because one sister played violin and we should have a little trio to play in church.

So they got a cello, and they got a white teacher, who, I don't know if it's a fallacy or not, but I've heard it said that black people have real good ears, natural ears for music. I don't know if it's true or not, but this guy took advantage that I happened to have ears. He'd put my finger on the right note, and I'd find the rest. He never taught me any fingering. He taught me how to tune the cello, a few notes and positions, and I knew what the melody was when I looked at the position, and I knew what the melody was when I looked at the paper, in my head. So if I missed a fingering, he'd say, "That's the second fingering."

I'd always sound good. My parents wanted me to sound good. So he found a way to teach the black kids. When they were playing for their parents they'd be able to play a little tune, but they weren't learning any music. And I didn't learn that until I got into the Junior Philharmonic Orchestra, with thousands of other kids who really played—who knew what reading was. They could play in any key. So by the time I got to high school everybody was waiting for this cello player to come, the only cello player that they had at the high school. Oh, there was another girl who played cello in a lower grade in the grammar school I went to; her name was Barbara. So they said they've got two cellos, and they put me up there in the section, and I'd just look at the music, 'cause I couldn't play it. And I didn't feel embarrassed. I'd been through that.

So I had already chose the music class, or at least they chose me before I got there, because they had heard that I had played in the Junior Philharmonic Orchestra. Hiding behind all the cello players so I wouldn't go to rehearsals, I would just stay in the musicians' band room and play with all the instruments. I got so I could play the tuba; I got so I could play the trumpet. Lloyd Reese used to let me play in the rehearsal band on Sundays.

Then I led a band called the Hep-Cats. Schoolteacher decided to call it the Hep-Cat Band. They still didn't give me a chance on bass. On that, they got another guy who couldn't play or read as good. I was so unpredictable, but I knew I could play something. So they had a parade, and they had a tuba, so I took a tuba out and played by ear those parade songs.

Finally I met Buddy Collette, and he said, "You should play bass anyway, because a black cello player is not going to get anywhere in music." So I was shining shoes around Watts and different places, and this guy I'd seen in the senior orchestra asked me to shine his shoes. I shined his shoes, and he had a lot of money. I asked him how he got so much money, and he said he had a little band, the Stars of Swing or something. They might have called it Buddy Collette and His Orchestra, or something. He said, "You change from cello, you got a job in my band. You get a bass, I'll teach you how to read."

So I told my father, and he turned my cello in, because I never played it. So he trusted me once more and turned the cello in and went to Sherman's Music Company, talked to the man in the department, who gave him a price and gave him a pretty good bass. So I called Buddy and said, "I've got a bass." So they fired the tuba player. He was very angry, and he was a doctor's son, I remember, and he said, "Well, I can stay in the band too." It would have been nice; they should have kept him, but they couldn't afford it, so he got nasty with me. I told him, "You can't slap a tuba." 'Cause in those days it was very prominent.

Ya remember when Bobby Haggart was playing "Big Noise from Winnetka"? I learned that right away, because there was a bass player in town who finally went with King Cole's trio; his name was Joe Comfort. His whole family was musicians—father, mother, sisters, everybody. Joe Comfort could play any instrument. If you made a new one, he would have played it in five minutes. I asked Joe if he could give me some lessons. He said, "Just tune the bass up, play the notes, turn on the radio, and start playing."

I didn't know he wasn't a great reader either. He just had perfect ears; he had perfect pitch. Bass parts in those days were very simple, so I tuned it up, and the way he told me to tune it was backwards. He told me E-A-D-G, which is violin tuning, and I tuned it from the top. The bass violin in fourths is backwards from the violin, at G-D-A-E. I started playing from the radio and got pretty good, and I started carrying my bass to school with me. I met Joe on the street one time, and he asked to see my bass. He slipped the cover off, man, and he started playing. He said, "You've got it tuned wrong; you got it backwards." So he opened it up, and he tuned it, and I couldn't play a note then, 'cause it was in fourths. "So you mean I got to start again?" He said yeah. He started playing. He could slap; he could do everything.

Then I went and sat down by the radio again. My parents never thought about getting a good teacher, you know, and I got so I went over to play with Buddy's band, and what I couldn't play he would take time to show me. Then a band came to town; this is around the forties now, '39, '40. There was a record called "Jack the Bear." Jimmy Blanton came to town, and I knew he wasn't no Joe Comfort, 'cause he was playing very complicated things. I couldn't afford to go hear him play, but I heard him on the radio a couple of times. Next thing I know, Joe Comfort comes by my house. [Mingus hums a tune.] I say, "How can you play that, man? You can't even read." He says, "I can hear." So he taught it to me. He had learned Jimmy Blanton's solo. He learned it before anyone in California, I think. He also could play like Slam Stewart; he could do anything any of the great bass players did. So people came and heard him play. They didn't care whether he could read or not. If he played one chord, he'd watch the little finger on the piano and play somewhere near the tonic or the fifth.

WE: What prompted you to start composing?

CM: Well, I always wrote. There was a piano in the house, and I always played the piano. Nobody showed me what to do, so I did what I wanted to do at the piano. They might show me "Mother, Mother, May I Go?" but by the next time I'd have ten notes in the chords.

Buddy Collette suggested that I go to Lloyd Reese and play the piano, which would also help cover the bass. I couldn't afford to go to both Lloyd Reese and Red Callender—that's who taught me the beginnings of jazz on bass—so I quit. Red and I went to Lloyd Reese for a while. Then he suggested, "You play a good bass. Why don't you get a symphonic teacher to teach you?"

So he got this guy named Hermann Rheinschagen. He used to be the principal bassist for the New York Philharmonic, and he helped rewrite the *Simandls*.[6] So I studied with him. He was one that always said Negroes can't read and all that. So I finally read to him in Latin. I took Jimmy Blanton to my lesson one day; he said he wanted to meet Rheinschagen. He says, "Why did you bring him along?" I said, "He's a good bass player. He's with Duke Ellington." He says, "Can he read?" a little sarcastic. Jimmy says, "I can read. What do you got?" Mr. Rheinschagen says, "Well, I've got some things I wrote myself." Jimmy says, "Let me see those." He ran right through them, and Rheinschagen wouldn't even pick the bass up.

What had happened was that they had a movie, and the camera was trained on the bass section for a while, and they thought it would be a good idea to show a black in the section, and Rheinschagen told me they had heard of Slam Stewart, and they sent for him, and he didn't know any of the bowings, that his bow was all going the wrong way. He said that he couldn't even read. So Rheinschagen assumed that no black man could read. Blanton straightened him out on that subject. Another good bass player named Bill Hadnott went to him, and he straightened him out too.

When I began to write, I started to write bass solos. I took one of my solos to Rheinschagen, and he said, "Who wrote this?" I said that I wrote

---

6. *Simandls* is a two-volume work of methods and études for the bass, written by Franz Simandl in the late nineteenth century.

it, and I wanted him to show me how to play it. "Show me the right bowing and fingerings, 'cause I don't play it right." He says "You can play this?" I said, "Yeah, you know I can play it, I wrote it. But I don't play it like you would play it. I play it wrong." But he wouldn't try and play it; he was afraid. He said, "You leave it for a couple of days, and I'll transcribe it, 'cause your handwriting is nervous, and I can't read some of the notes."

He never came up with it. I'd go to my lesson each week. I'd be on the train—he lived way out in Hollywood—and there was Bill Hadnott, who went an hour earlier than me. I was early, and we were on the same train, and he said, "Man, you sure write hard. You know, Rheinschagen gave me your piece." And I said, "Well, he hasn't given it to me yet, and I'm the one who wrote it." He say, "Well, that's one of the most complicated things for bass I've ever seen."

So that got me into writing for people like Dinah Washington, T-Bone Walker, Joe Turner, Jimmy Witherspoon. We were in a car going to a record date, and Dinah Washington says, "I don't have any music. I've got the blues in F, but I don't have any music." So I write it in the car. I wrote the arrangements in the car. This is all due to Lloyd Reese, you know. He taught me all the voicings. It's very simple to take simple scales and write music. But you can fool people using chromatics, you know, because it happens so quickly that you can have four wrong notes for one right one.

And so I always had a few jobs with singers, and it was hard to do both, because I'd always rather write. But when Charlie Parker came along, I gave up wanting to be a composer-arranger, and I wanted to play—to play with someone like him who composed on his horn, because that's what good jazz is—spontaneous composition. I wrote some things now and then, but I really got down with the bass and started trying to solo myself, and I used to blow a lot. They were all jam groups. You never knew who you were going to be playing with.

Miles Davis was on the same set with me, and they were playing "Body and Soul," and he said, "Man, put that bow down. This ain't no symphony. This is jazz, man." So I put it down for good, and the next thing I know, four or five years later, he hires a bass player named Paul Chambers who did nothing but bow. I would have been far advanced in jazz bow. I was playing most of the classical solos when I was with Rheinschagen. But jazz bowing, if you just include the classical bowings, you get a much better swing than if you just play up and down like some guys do.

PR: Let's turn to one of your favorite subjects, Duke Ellington.

CM: While I was at Berkeley, there was a tribute to Ellington. We all were supposed to give speeches about Ellington and give tribute to him. I refused to speak, other than to play some of his music.

Duke had told me he was gonna play one of my tunes with his big band—"The Clown." And he said he wanted me to help him rehearse it. So I went up to his house, and he said, "Ya all have been doing some writing, and it's different from what the older fellows in the band have been doing." He said, "I don't know what to do. I can't get them to play it." So I said, "Well, why don't you play it yourself on the piano?" And to my surprise he did "The Clown" at the concert that night, as much as he could do it. He asked me to come onstage with him. He asked me to conduct the musicians, and I refused, 'cause I didn't know how he could have gotten along with some of the guys in the band. They were so evil.

I think Duke's one of the first people who started writing in two keys at once, and I don't know why any critic has never said that. And he had a third key, what his melodic structure was on. So he was actually able to use chromatics in all his compositions. I got a feeling that maybe he studied that from somebody; I know that [Billy] Strayhorn wrote similar, but a lot less complicated.

I can't tell you why, but people are born to like certain things. When I was a kid in my teens I was listening on my father's earphones, crystal set. I heard this thing, "St. Louis Toodle-oo"—no audience, just me—and I almost flipped, because I knew I couldn't play it again. I hardly even knew what a record was. And that inspired me when we got our first radio. I found out how to connect earphones up to it, and I found out how to connect a turntable to it.

We had a RCA. We always got the big ones, the best. A big RCA radio which had a very good sound, and I sold magazines, and I bought Ellington records. And that doesn't say why either, 'cause I heard a very simple song called "Black Narcissus," or maybe just "Narcissus"; I was in school, about four or five years old. I was walking past a music class, and I got glued to the door, and they came and slapped me around. Said, "You're supposed to be in class," and that music stayed with me.

I knew that I was in love with music. I fell in love so early. And I guess that your styles come out of other composers that you've heard, rather than what goes on today. Today musicians listen to see who makes the most money on a style, and then they set to copying him. And they don't copy the ones that are beautiful, creative, and good. The difference is, a musician who is going to exalt the music that he loves, and that when he writes, he will write music that other people will love. Not everybody, not the millions of records that are sold to rock audiences or to electronic fans.

Electronic music is really a waste of time, because you could take a full symphony orchestra and write twice, even an eighth note behind the melody, and get the echo effect of an electronic machine. It doesn't have to be done with electronics. It'll sound pure, it'll sound more beautiful, and it'll certainly be more enjoyable than when you have to push a button to get an effect. That's no pleasure, pushing your buttons and turning your wa-wa foot pedal on. I wouldn't quit; first I'd just go underground and write before I would use that kind of electronics. Yeah, I would quit. I'd get a day job.

WE: Have you attempted to re-create the Ellington sound?

CM: "Don't Be Afraid, the Clown's Afraid Too."[7] That was written for Harry Carney on baritone, but every time I would offer Harry Carney a recording date—and this goes back to the forties—he [Ellington] knew that Harry was the key to his band. He knew that if I invited Harry Carney to play my music, people would know we were very close, 'cause that baritone stood out, and I knew it. I knew it just wasn't Johnny Hodges; it was the bottom note. And so he would just toy me along, playing in a sophisticated club in New York, and Harry would say, "I'll make it to the next practice. A thousand dollars is OK." Then a couple of days later I'd get a call, "The band is leaving for Dayton, Ohio," so I had to get somebody else.

I had one case, I said, "I'm gonna get Harry." I had two baritones, a bass clarinet, and a bassoon, also a contrabass clarinet. I had them all playing the same part, and that's the closest I ever got to getting the sound of Ellington in the reed section. If Duke had written for symphony orchestra, I don't think anyone could have said—other than jazz folks— whether the man was black or white.

7. "Don't Be Afraid, the Clown's Afraid Too," recorded by Charles Mingus, on *Let My Children Hear Music*, Columbia Records, 1977.

PR: Earlier you said that electronic music is a waste of time. Is it difficult to find young musicians to work for you who aren't involved with electronics?

CM: Well, there are quite a few of them coming up now in New York. I don't know where he came from, but there's George Coleman, and quite a few musicians over there who are continuing on the bebop era and advance it from there. There's some guys that are carrying the tradition on. A young guy who is very capable of doing that is this tenor player who has his own loft in New York, and I hear he is doing some good things, Sam Rivers. I know it's gotta be good, because he played in my band, and he's very knowledgeable. He acknowledges the past—he did then. He was able to play my music, to play anybody else's music, and he had a style of his own. I hear that he's ventured out into atonality. I don't know if it's proper atonality. I don't know if he studied it.

This world can be fooled so easy. I know when I was in Red Norvo's trio there was a Spanish composer. Anyway, these people invited Red, myself, and Tal Farlow, the guitar player, to dinner. They said they wanted to hear some quarter-tone music, was his name Varèse? Anyway, they put this record on, and I didn't say nothing for a couple of hours. They kept playing this quarter-tone music. So in the middle of the tune I went over to the piano and played B-natural, C-natural, E-natural, G-natural, B-natural, and A-flat in the bass, and they said, "How did you do that?" I said, "That's quarter-tone music. It's diatonics, chromatics." They thought I was a genius; they wanted me to keep on doin' it. I said, "I'm not gonna show you how I did that." Well, it just so happened that he came to a part that I was familiar with. It was nothing but quarter tones. Quarter tones just mean playing in between the fingering on the violin. You can only use stringed instruments on quarter-tone or sixteenth-tone music. And nobody's cut Bach yet. Bach is the most complicated, and he's strictly diatonic.

[Our time ran out, but Mingus made one final plea for jazz.] I want to thank you for doing what you're doing, 'cause you'll straighten out some of those kids that have been brainwashed with electronic music. They should know that there's another kind of music besides just wa-wa foot pedals and trumpet players that just play up and down the chromatic scale with no melodic thought. And if they hear somebody talk, they might give jazz a chance.

SELECTED DISCOGRAPHY

Charles Mingus/Passions of a Man. (An anthology of his Atlantic record-
   ings, Atlantic SD3-600. 1980. 1956–61, 1973–77.)
New York Sketchbook. Affinity CD Charly 19. 1986. (Reissue of *East
   Coasting*, with Bill Evans, 1957.)
Tijuana Moods. RCA LSP 2533. 1957.
Better Git It in Your Soul. Columbia CG-30628. 1974. (Reissue of *Mingus-
   Ah-Um* and *Mingus Dynasty*, 1959.)
With Eric Dolphy. *Charles Mingus Presents Charles Mingus.* Candid
   9005. 1960.
Charles Mingus: The Impulse Years. Impulse AS-9234-2. 1973. (Reissue of
   the *Black Saint and the Sinner Lady* and *Mingus, Mingus, Mingus, Mingus,
   Mingus*, 1963.)
Mingus Plays Piano. Impulse A-60. 1963.
The Great Concert of Charles Mingus. Prestige PR-34001. 1964.
Cumbia and Jazz Fusion. Atlantic SD8801. 1976–77.
Three or Four Shades of Blues. Atlantic 1700-2. 1977.

JOE PASS

Photograph by Phil Bray.   Courtesy Fantasy, Inc.

J oseph Anthony Jacobi Passalaqua, more commonly known as Joe
Pass, is one of the most brilliant heirs to the jazz guitar lineage established by Django Reinhardt, Charlie Christian, and Wes Montgomery. Pass possesses a sonorous tone and impeccable technique, with a
rhythmic and harmonic conception that is deeply rooted in the bop tradition. Although the vicissitudes of his profession, combined with personal crises, made Pass's ascendancy painfully slow, he has enjoyed international acclaim since the mid-seventies.

Born in 1929, Pass began performing for dances and weddings at the
age of fourteen in his hometown of Johnstown, Pennsylvania. His exposure to bop in the late forties helped shape his musical direction, but Pass
also became addicted to heroin along the way. That addiction consumed
him for more than a decade, until he committed himself in 1960 to Synanon, a well-known drug rehabilitation facility based in Los Angeles. Pass
spent three years at Synanon, emerging with renewed commitment to his
music and a vision about a life free from drugs. In 1962 Dick Bock, owner
of World Pacific Records and one of Synanon's sponsors, heard the little-
known Pass play in a band composed of Synanon residents. He quickly
arranged a recording for the group and launched Pass's career.[1]

Over the next year Pass did studio work accompanying World Pacific
stablemates Gerald Wilson, Richard "Groove" Holmes, and Les McCann
on a series of recordings. He stayed away from drugs during this critical
period, erasing questions about his professional reliability, and he established credentials as a first-rate jazz soloist.

Pass's growing reputation within the inner circle of jazz was confirmed
in the spring of 1963 when he won a *Down Beat* magazine poll as the best
new voice on his instrument. On the heels of that award, World Pacific
Records released *Catch Me!*, Pass's much-praised first album as a leader.[2]

During the next decade Pass played on numerous recording sessions;
he also did television work and toured with George Shearing. In 1974 his
fortunes rose dramatically, when jazz impresario Norman Granz signed

---

1. *Sounds of Synanon*, World Pacific Jazz Records, 1962.
2. Joe Pass, *Catch Me!* World Pacific Jazz Records, 1964.

Pass to his newly formed label, Pablo. Pass's first recording for Pablo, *Virtuoso*, was a stunning solo *tour de force* that proved how satisfying an unaccompanied single-line instrumental performance could be.[3] That recording earned him accolades from listeners and critics alike.

Since the unprecedented success of *Virtuoso* and the quality of its successors (*Virtuoso II-IV*), Pass has been a prolific and consistently inspired recording artist.[4] He is in demand worldwide as a solo act and in the company of other jazz luminaries, such as vocalist Ella Fitzgerald, trombonist J. J. Johnson, and pianist Oscar Peterson. Joe Pass today is one of the giants of the jazz guitar.

Recorded 1980

PR: How did you get started in music, Joe?

JP: All I remember is that I was nine years old, and I asked for a guitar for my birthday, and I got one, an old Harmony guitar. I started playing for neighbors, Italian friends of my father's, and I learned the chords from them. My introduction to the guitar, was, I think, I heard Gene Autry once in the movies. As a matter of fact, I saw the movie was advertised in the local papers to play tonight. It's called *Ride, Tenderfoot, Ride*. But no one in my family played any music, so I just asked for a guitar and got it. I learned what the local neighborhood players played, and then I studied with a friend of my father's for about a year. He played violin and saxophone, but he taught me to read music. Not really hard music, but just Nick Lucas books—simple guitar chords—and the rest is just playing.

PR: When did you start playing professionally?

JP: I started playing gigs when I was about thirteen or fourteen. I played weekends at local clubs and parties. My father had some friends that were in the music business. They were barbers by day and musicians by night [laughter]. I played with their group. It was called the Gentlemen of Rhythm. It was two guitars, a bass, a violin, and it was modeled after Django Reinhardt's Hot Club of France. Somehow I learned how to play melodies quick, so I played lead. I played all the pop tunes, "Stardust," all the tunes, and it was always a swing kind of group, and I played with this group around Johnstown, Pennsylvania. And I played with a group

3. Joe Pass, *Virtuoso*, Pablo Records, 1974.

4. Joe Pass, *Virtuoso II*, *Virtuoso III*, and *Virtuoso IV*, Pablo Records, 1977, 1978, and 1983.

called Mason and His Madcaps, which was a blues-swing group. Then when I was about fourteen or fifteen I got involved with Tony Pastor's Orchestra, and I went on a tour of theaters with him. At that time they had theaters where they had a movie and a stage show on weekends. Bands toured all over the western part of Pennsylvania and in Ohio and Maryland and Jersey. I couldn't work any clubs, or if they went to the Hotel Pennsylvania in New York, I couldn't do that—I was too young.

Then I played with Johnny Long's Orchestra in the same fashion— sort of in a package. I would come out and play a few solos with the band, and that was that. And then most of the time I just played with a lot of jazz groups.

WE: There must have been quite a jazz scene back then in Pennsylvania?

JP: In Johnstown, there were a great many older musicians that played in big bands. Ray McKinley's band and Artie Shaw's band—and there were many musicians, maybe ten or fifteen guys, saxophone players, piano players. One piano player, Johnny Betoker, played with the Dorsey Band when it was at the height of its popularity. So there was a great deal of interest in jazz in Johnstown, and the gigs I played were like jam-session gigs. We listened very much to Jazz at the Philharmonic, which was very popular then. I played with this group—the violin player played like Stephane Grappelli, and that's who we listened to. So right from the word go I was playing swing or jazz music—"Night and Day," "Lady Be Good"—and it just started like that. There's a tendency for players that are interested in jazz music to kind of get together, and Johnstown being a town that's not too big, we made sure that we got together on all the gigs. Every time musicians or bands would come through town—there was a great deal of bands going through town every week—Mel Hallett, Bob Chester, and bands you probably wouldn't have known about. Tony Pastor, Johnny Long, Duke Ellington, Count Basie—there'd be jam sessions, and that's where I really got my feet wet learning to play.

WE: At what point did you move away from Pennsylvania?

JP: I went to New York and played with Brew Moore, around 1948 or 1949. I played with a lot of jazz groups, but most of the time there wasn't a lot of work. Most of the time I was just sort of goofing around, just being around listening to everybody play on Fifty-Second Street— Charlie Parker and those. I would go out on the road and tour with different little trios and quartets when I needed the money. Then I'd come back to the city and hang around. Then I went to New Orleans and did some playing there. There are lots of jazz players that have never made a national name for themselves, but they're known with the musicians. There was a long period of time where I didn't play. I got involved in personal problems, and I didn't really function as a working musician, fully. I spent so much time trying to get everything straightened out. It took me many years, about twelve years. So that would take me up to about 1960. Oh, I worked in Las Vegas for a while, and I played with various kinds of show groups; that was just working. But I always played jazz, always played gigs somewhere where I could play.

PR: Did you pay close attention to well-known guitarists as you were growing up and breaking into the business?

JP: The first guitarist I heard was Django Reinhardt. It was acoustic guitar. Charlie Christian played acoustic guitar. There was a little different concept there, I mean as far as an approach to rhythmic things. I would say that Django was more guitaristic, and Charlie Christian played more like a horn player, but I don't think there was any great deal of difference. The music was much the same. One played more notes than the other.

Then there were a lot of other guitarists during that time. There was Chuck Wayne, and Tal Farlow, and Jimmy Raney, but you see, I didn't listen to a lot of guitar players. I listened a little bit to Django and some to Charlie. I didn't have a record player, and you couldn't even get all the records in Johnstown. The stores wouldn't bring any of these records in. They brought in Perry Como [laughter]. Not that there's anything wrong with Perry Como, but we had a hard time getting a jazz record. But I heard some Charlie Parker records about 1950—maybe a little earlier. That's what really excited me, and that's the music I started to copy. I would copy horn players.

The first jazz record I heard, I would say, was Coleman Hawkins' "Body and Soul." That was the first thing that I really flipped over. I used to hang around a music store, and one of the clerks was really interested in jazz, so he would sneak in some of the orders—one or two copies—and we'd sit around and listen. There would always be a new record every week—Dizzy Gillespie; I remember Al Haig and Stan Getz. They were young players then.

My influence in my guitar playing came mainly from horn and piano players. In fact, I made a point of avoiding any guitaristic playing. There are certain things that are peculiar to the guitar that a lot of guitar players use—certain bending of notes, certain interval sounds, and rhythmic ways of playing that you could trace right through the history of electric jazz guitar—and I didn't do any of them. I played straight lines and horn-like lines, and I didn't play rhythm 4/4; I comped like a piano way back, so it has been only the last ten years that I started to listen to guitar players more. I don't listen to very many guitar players now. I still listen to horns or orchestras, but my influences were mainly from bebop players or swing—Lester Young, Don Byas, those kinds of players. I remember Barney Kessel a little bit on some records. One in particular was "Swedish Pastry," with a clarinet player. I used to listen to Artie Shaw and copy his things off of his big band—only his solos and things like that.

PR: What about the blues players? Did you check them out too?

JP: I never made a special point of listening to any blues guitar players. I knew about B. B. King a long time ago and some of the old blues players. I'll tell you one thing: we read about the great influences in music, and all these names mentioned have been known worldwide, but I think when you are first starting out as a musician you may hear some players like Charlie Parker or Django Reinhardt, but I think the big influences come from your immediate surroundings—the guys that you play with, who are never heard of. But they somehow have that feeling for playing, and you, as a new player, naturally join the local groups that are playing. And that's where your training ground and your musical thing starts to happen. Whatever town you are in. There were guitar players around—the Cashaw brothers, you never heard of them. One was a bass player, and one a guitar player. They played blues as good as any blues player around. I played with them. So I guess I can say the Cashaw brothers were instrumental in the blues for me.

WE: Joe, it's well known that you were addicted to heroin from about 1949 to 1960. Could you speak a bit about that time in your life?

JP: Well, offhand I'd say it was a waste of time. Many times I had opportunities to play. Johnny Smith, the guitar player, called me in New York and said to be in a certain place about a certain job. And of course, I was so busy doing the other thing that I never went. There were many opportunities I had that I missed because of not being responsible and being hung up. I don't think it did any good for my music. I found that the best music and the better things happened when I was sober, when I played clear-headed with all my faculties. If anything, drugs just set you back. I mean, it's an illusion. You think you are really doing a lot, but if you want to find out, you make a record under, and then listen to something when you're not, when you're straight, and listen to the difference.

WE: Dick Bock of World Pacific Records was kind of your savior in a musical sense, wasn't he?

JP: Well, Dick Bock came to Synanon and was sort of a sponsor of it and heard me play there. I played on Saturday nights for the guests—we had open house—and he said he would like me to make a record. We had a little group at that time playing, so we made a record. That was my introduction to records. I had made some records before; I made one with Tony Pastor and one with Dick Contino. But I never heard of them or saw them. I don't know where they are. Bock made the first record I was on in '62 or '63.[5]

My first record [after leaving Synanon], *Catch Me!* was my album. I had played several gigs with Clare Fischer and Ralph Peña, so when Dick Bock asked me who I would like to get—I mean, I only knew two guys [laughter]—so I said, "Clare Fischer and Ralph Peña." That's the way it works. Sometimes a record company will suggest to me, "I have a couple of players that are really good. Would you like to do a record with them?" Like they put me with Groove Holmes or Les McCann, or Gerald Wilson's big band.

WE: Even on those early records you have a distinctive identity, a distinctive sound.

JP: I think there's an identity to my playing that you could hear. Lots of guys, guitarists especially, would know. I can identify certain guitarists; certain others, I can't. I can confuse them with other players, but there are certain ones that I can tell you exactly who they are as soon as I hear them because it's their character, their identity, and I think I had that a long time ago.

It's just the way I play, my musical ideas or whatever, and I notice since I've been playing solo that there has been a certain style or a certain approach to the playing that has developed just from the sheer fact that I'd have to get out there and play. I was out there playing, and this was all going on subconsciously, like what do I do next to get from here to there.

None of it is worked out or practiced. I don't sit at home and say,

5. *Sounds of Synanon.*

"OK, I'm going to play this run or this chord, and then I'm going to do that." But actually, I do it by going out on the gig and doing it. And from that I've developed a kind of approach. I think what happens is when you play alone and you don't work things out, you're forced to develop some kind of style or approach just on the gig. Once you start that and you're doing it live, in person, for real, that stays with you. And it becomes part of your music vocabulary, your style, your way of playing. I notice certain things that I do on the guitar that weren't there three years ago. They developed just from actually doing the playing.

PR: When did your solo career actually start? And did you think you were taking a risk by walking out there onstage with just a guitar?

JP: When I play solo I get the feeling that I'm playing for an audience like they were sitting in my house and we were together and they asked me to play, which is the way I started playing solo guitar. I mean, I've been playing solo guitar for a long time. Every time I have guests at the house or I am visiting someone, it is always "Bring your guitar." They never say "Bring the drums and the bass" [laughter]. So I'm always sitting there, and then they say "Play," and I play for an hour. And they say, "Play this tune" and "Do you know this tune?" and somebody starts humming, and so I'm playing the guitar, and I've been doing that for years. And someone once said to me, "You ought to go out and play on the stage, you know, solo."

But I always felt like, no, people wouldn't dig it. They're going to say, "Well, jazz—where's the bass and where's the drums and where's the rhythm?" So I was always hesitant to do this, and occasionally in a club I'd play one or two tunes solo, and that would be it. Like waiting for the bass player to come away from the bar or something. Now that I'm doing it, I feel a little more comfortable about it, and the response has been nice. Nobody has said "It's not loud enough" or "There's not enough excitement." But I don't think I'm doing anything special.

PR: Your solo concerts feature a large variety of tunes. How do you decide what to perform?

JP: I try to pace my music—try to play what I feel but try to change tempos, changing keys I especially think is important. I like to communicate with them—I like the feeling. Sometimes you get a feeling that they're not with you, and then you have to make a change. I might play eight bars of a tune and just stop and go into another tune because I don't feel that it's what I want to play.

Maybe you start a tune, and you can't get into it, and you're trying to get into it, and you see it is not working. That's just the way it is. Usually when that happens, that's it. No matter how hard you try to get into it, you're doing what you can do with that song at that time, emotionally and mentally, and whatever—I don't like to use the word *creative*. So generally I take the tune out. I try exploring it a little bit, but I just finish it and try something else.

What happens when you're playing a solo is it's different, because one night you go up and play tunes and they all work out and they all sound like they're brand-new, and you're really having a ball with them; and the next night you go and play some tunes—say maybe a couple of the same tunes—and they feel and sound like you've never played them before, and they're like the hardest thing in the world to play, and you are struggling from the time you start. Sometimes it's free and loose and easy and it's a lot of fun, and other times it's a lot of work.

It's hard to sustain your interest—not to sustain your interest, but for things to come off like you want them to. You'll be a note off here and there, and that's just enough to throw everything off. I mean, lots of times the audience can't tell, or many times they say that they liked it, and you didn't like it, but that may be the difference in what you are communicating.

And you never know what it's going to be like before you sit down and play. Many factors enter in, like the sound of the room. If the room that you're playing in doesn't sound in the spectrum of what you want to hear, that can make you play different. The acoustics of a place change. I found that if my seat is a little bit too high or a little low, it changes things. I should actually have a stool made or a seat made for myself and carry it around, but I'm too lazy.

I noticed one time when I was doing some concerts and when the stage people set up my amp on my right, I didn't snap to it. I was so nervous about doing a big concert. I was with Ella Fitzgerald and Oscar Peterson, and that was the big time, and I had run out there to play and the amp was on my right. I never play with my amp on my right, and I couldn't figure out what sounded so different, and I had a hard time playing. Well, after about four concerts I noticed that, being quick to notice things [laughter]. I said, "Wait a minute, this should be on my left," because that is the ear I listen out of.

So lots of little things change—the temperature, if it is warm or cold. Air conditioning blowing on the guitar affects the strings, makes them tight. I played half of a concert last night, and there was no air conditioning on, and everything was loose. Then they put on the air for the intermission, and they left it on, and I was onstage, and all of a sudden the strings got tight. But you can't say "Please turn the air conditioning off."

A lot of things affect the way you play—how you feel when you wake up. I like maybe not to take what I'm doing seriously. I don't like to feel like I am doing some really important thing, but sort of have fun, relieve the pressure of playing and allow ideas and things to come through without censoring things. I like to take chances when I play, too, that is, make mistakes or whatever.

WE: We've been talking a lot about your solo work. But you still enjoy working with other musicians, don't you?

JP: Yes. There comes a time when you feel like you want a rhythm section for a change, or you get the thought, "Joe, it'd be nice to have a bass and a drummer." Lots of times I play with Oscar [Peterson]—we play duo—and just the mere fact that there's another instrument playing and another person's ideas stimulating me and make you work and think . . . Every once in a while I think about it.

Of course, I play sometimes in groups put together by Norman Granz for jazz festivals, and this would have bass and drums. Not a lot of it, but four or five times a year I'm playing for a week or so with a rhythm section—with horns, jam-session style—which is good, which is really different and stimulating. But mainly I've been doing solo. The next thing I've been doing is playing duo with Oscar, which is hard and demanding but exciting and challenging, because trying to keep up with him and be where he is, sometimes I have to play and dance at the same time [laughter].

PR: Signing on with Pablo Records was certainly a pivotal move in your career, to put it mildly.

JP: That label really is to me sort of the start of my career. Even though I made records before, and I had some kind of a little notoriety in *Down Beat* from other records. But I stayed in Los Angeles, and I have a family, and I started doing studio work, and I would always play jazz gigs around Los Angeles—Dante's, the Lighthouse—but I never left. I did a short tour with George Shearing, and then I came back because I had children.

But I met Oscar Peterson through Herb Ellis and other musicians, and Oscar once said that he might start a trio up again with a guitar, and if he did would I be interested? I said yeah.

Norman Granz is his manager, and I'd forgotten all about Norman Granz and Jazz at the Philharmonic, and Oscar called me and asked me if I'd work three weeks in Chicago with him and Niels-Henning Ørsted Pedersen, the bass player from Denmark, and we went, and Norman Granz decided to start his record company, Pablo, in about 1973, I think. The first recording he made was a live recording of the trio with Oscar. So I met him, and he said he was starting a record company and would like to record me. I don't know if he said he'd record me or if I said, "Hey, record me!"

I did a record with Oscar and then one with Duke Ellington before he passed away, and that sort of snowballed, and I did one with Ella, but—I don't particularly like any records I make. You hear everything you should have done and your mistakes. I'm striving to make that perfect record, but the way with Norman is that the more you repeat a performance the more sterile it becomes. You may not make any mistakes, but you've lost all the spontaneity because you are so busy waiting for that spot where you goofed, and you do it, and you get it all right, and you are not taking any chances. The sound—it comes off not real, you know, at least that's what they say. And I kind of believe that too. Maybe I should change my ideas about not liking the things that I do. I think that maybe after a year or so, I may listen to something and say, "Well, it wasn't too bad." But that's the kind of attitude I have.

WE: One of our favorite records with you as a sideman is *Duke's Big 4*.[6]

JP: That was really one of the high points in my musical—I hate to use the word *career*, but now I have a career, because first of all I didn't know that Duke Ellington ever made any records with a small group or quartet. I always identified Duke and always heard his music with a band or orchestra or on solo piano, but later I found out that he had made some with Coltrane. So when I was called to do this by Mr. Granz I went down to the studio, and there was Duke Ellington sitting at the piano. I thought, "What's going to happen here?" There was Louis Bellson on drums, Ray Brown, and me. And that was the group.

The strange thing was that it was all a rhythm section, but Duke's

6. Duke Ellington, *Duke's Big 4*, Pablo Records, 1973.

playing piano, and I play electric guitar, which means I'm not *just* a rhythm player, it's understood. So that meant that it would be like me playing solos with Duke Ellington, you know. I was really kind of taken aback, careful, but he was really easy. He just sat down and started doodling on the piano—doodled out a little thing, and we started to play that. I mean, we didn't rehearse or anything. He just started playing "Sophisticated Lady," and then we just said, "OK, let's make a record. Let's do it," and that was it. No beginnings, no endings, and we did the whole album in three or four hours. I was really honored to be on a record with Duke Ellington. Man, that was a good start.

PR: We understand that you're not a big fan of some other guitarists of note, like Jimi Hendrix and John McLaughlin.

JP: First of all, I never heard a Jimi Hendrix record that I listened to thoroughly. I don't know what he did. I don't even know if he *was* a guitar player. He made a lot of noises, and he did a lot of things. I heard one or two tracks of his, and I couldn't tell if it was him or what was playing, because it was so loud. I never made a study of him.

And McLaughlin—I know for a fact that he was a jazz guitar player. I heard a record of his recently, from England, where he was playing a kind of bebop, and so he could play the guitar before he went into whatever he is doing now. He actually knew how to play the guitar. So the music he is into, I don't particularly listen to it, but I figure he knows what he is doing, because he can play. That's what my criteria is: if a guy knows how to sit down and play music like we all know it, and if he goes into some bag where he's going to play Indian music or spaced-out—I mean, if he knows what he's doing, and he's not shucking—I figure he's maybe trying to find something, so I think that's OK. But I think that the great many guitarists are overrated through the media.

PR: Rock players?

JP: Yes, rock players. I don't know how to say it, but a lot of them can't play. Put them down in a room and say, "OK, here's Joe the barber. Play something so that Joe the barber knows what you're playing. Take the amps and fuzz tones and wa-wa's away, and just play some music for me or my friends, and let's see if you can play some music." I think a lot of them wouldn't be able to play anything.

There's a lot of them—for instance, this thing came up—the *lead* guitarist. There's a lead guitarist, and there's another guy. The lead guitarist doesn't do anything but play lead [laughter]. That's his whole thing.

Right? I think that's funny, myself. Why do they have to have a lead guitarist and another guy? The other guy knows three chords [laughter]. The lead guitarist knows—I hate to sound bad, because some of the music is good, and some of the players are good, but not the majority of them. They're all bending strings and using all the fuzz and wa-wa and Echoplex and everything. So if you could take all of these guys and put them in a room and each guy will take a chorus on the blues or something, you wouldn't know which one was which. They all sound the same.

WE: Are there any younger players who impress you?

JP: I never heard him, but I hear he's very good—Steve Khan. I like Larry Coryell—he's not too young—and there's Ralph Towner and John Abercrombie. Both of these guys are from Berklee [College of Music]. They are good players. Philip Catherine, I know him. He's a good player.

When you are talking about guitarists like that, you are talking about guys who can play the guitar in front already. So now what they're doing is trying maybe to find their identity, or a style, or an approach to playing what they like. And you must remember that these are guys of another generation, and they would no more go into the bebop thing or whatever is traditional jazz. They have to play from the point where they started just like I did.

For me to change now and say "OK, all these guys are doing this new thing, so I should jump right in there and do the new thing." Well, I listen to some of it and try to incorporate some of the sounds that strike me, and I put them in my music. But to deliberately go and say "I have to change all this and play different kinds of chords and different kinds of tunes because that's what's happening" is—I could do it if I practiced and studied, but it wouldn't be real for me. Because I am from a different time—music time. It doesn't mean that you are old or new; it just means that you do the music that you grew up in. That's your music.

So I like the players that know how to play. Regardless of what you are doing, though, you have to have the basic fundamental ability to play the instrument, and people like Catherine and Towner have that. I mean, they could play "Stardust," maybe in a little different way, but they do know what they're doing, and they know music. That is different.

WE: Among your guitar contemporaries, whose playing holds the most interest for you?

JP: Jim Hall, Barney Kessel, Pat Martino, and Kenny Burrell, too. Tal Farlow, naturally Christian, Wes, naturally. My favorite guitar player was

Wes Montgomery. I feel that Wes was really a jazz guitar player regard-less of what he did on the records. He just did everything the way he always did. They just sweetened the records. But I thought he was really *the* innovative, swinging jazz guitar player.

PR: Joe, are there musicians out there whom you'd like to work with?

JP: Gee, I never thought of that. I like to play with anybody who can play. It's always good to play with people that put demands on you. A good thing for a player to do is put yourself in situations where there's a lot of demands on you so that puts a challenge to you and brings out your abilities. I like to play in all kinds of different contexts.

One time I played in a rock context for two nights. I used the wa-wa and a big amplifier. These guys were pretty good, good blues-rock play-ers, and I played with them just to see what it was like. I had the volume up, and I was right there. The only thing I got out of it was excitement, and it came from the sheer volume. It got so rhythmic, so heavy and loud that actually it'd lift you right off the floor. By the end of the night I was so tired I said, "I don't want to play in here."

SELECTED DISCOGRAPHY

Sounds of Synanon. World Pacific Jazz 48. 1962.

With Gerald Wilson's Big Band. *Moment of Truth*. World Pacific Jazz PJ-61. 1963.

Catch Me! World Pacific Jazz PJ-73. 1964.

The Best of Joe Pass. Pablo PACD 2405-419-2. 1972–85.

With Duke Ellington. *Duke's Big 4*. Pablo 2310 703. 1973.

Virtuoso. Pablo 2310708. 1974.

At the Montreux Jazz Festival. Pablo 2310752. 1975.

With Zoot Sims. *Blues for Two*. Pablo 2310912. 1982.

Whitestone. Pablo 2310912. 1985.

Appassionato. Pablo PACD 2310-946-2. 1990.

SONNY STITT

Photograph by David D. Spitzer.   Used with permission.

E normously talented in his own right, saxophonist Sonny Stitt had the misfortune to develop a sound and approach that were uncannily similar to those of his slightly older contemporary Charlie "Bird" Parker, one of the pioneering figures in twentieth-century music.

Stitt never wholly escaped the comparison with Parker. Even after Stitt's death in 1982, one obituary writer noted that he "was respected for independently developing a Parkeresque bop style in the 1940s." Parker's ghost loomed over Stitt's career for more than a quarter century after Parker's death at age thirty-five in 1955; this is a tragic irony, since Parker reportedly held Stitt's playing in high esteem.

Edward "Sonny" Stitt was born in Boston in 1924. His family life placed a premium on music: his father was a music professor, and his brother eventually launched a career as a concert pianist. Stitt was playing gigs in his early teens and was on the road in Tiny Bradshaw's band before he was twenty. He moved to the center of the modern jazz movement when he joined Billy Eckstine's band in 1945 and then, a year later, replaced Charlie Parker in Dizzy Gillespie's sextet.

Stitt made his first recordings as a leader in the late forties and early fifties in the company of Bud Powell, Max Roach, Art Blakey, J. J. Johnson, and longtime collaborator Gene Ammons, with whom Stitt co-led a band. Playing with such nonpareil musicians, Stitt, then in his twenties, was spurred to mature flights of improvisation that, more than fifty years later, sound as fresh and inspired as they did the moment they were conceived; *Genesis*, a hard-to-find anthology on the Prestige label, is an indispensable document of those sessions. It was also during this time that Stitt quit playing the alto exclusively and included the tenor and baritone saxes (some say he did this to quiet the charge that he was imitating Parker).

Having established his reputation as a bebop player of great prowess, Stitt began leading a variety of small combos, a format he preferred until his death. After the breakup of the band he fronted with Ammons, Stitt toured with Norman Granz's Jazz at the Philharmonic aggregation, rejoined Gillespie in the late fifties, and increased his visibility among the young lions of jazz by replacing John Coltrane in the celebrated Miles Davis Quintet of 1960.

In the early sixties Stitt renewed his partnership with Ammons, engaging in classic tenor battles both onstage and in recording studios. Their association, although intermittent, lasted until Ammons' death in 1974. During the seventies Stitt toured with the Giants of Jazz, enjoying a reunion with former bandmates Dizzy Gillespie and Art Blakey.

Sonny Stitt, one of the most prolific recording artists in modern jazz, recorded scores of albums, and he was on the road incessantly. Extremely popular in Japan, he first took ill there, on his final tour, and he later succumbed to lung cancer in Washington, D.C., at the age of fifty-eight.

Recorded 1980

PR: Your playing seems to be steeped in jazz traditions from the thirties and forties. Could you comment on this?

SS: I'll tell you the truth. The way I see it, there's only one way to go, and that's the true way. You've gotta play the melody, you've gotta stay inside the limits, or you'll be what you might call [an] "outlaw."

But it goes deeper than that. It goes to what goes through a man's mind. You see, to me a musician is an artist, and he is painting a portrait or a picture with musical notes, with time which has gotta be there, or you've lost all continuity, the whole aspect of playing jazz. It's gotta have a pulsating rhythm, it's gotta have soul-feeling, colors, and you must be able to keep the audience's interest. That's what it boils down to. But when you play somethin' way over the people's head and they say, "Where is he? He's on Mars," you know [laughter].

PR: Didn't Charlie Parker leave his audience behind at first?

SS: Not really.

PR: You mean that even early on people were in tune with his innovations?

SS: Oh yes. I've seen him play to audiences—have you ever seen a mother bird feed her young? With their mouths wide open? It took them a half a minute to applaud. He mesmerized them; he hypnotized them, you understand? No, he didn't confuse his audience at all. He was too clever for that.

WE: Let's turn to your early years. Was there a music scene in Saginaw?

SS: They had clubs when I was comin' along. They had a place called the

American Legion. That was like an after-hour place [where they'd] have their jam sessions. I lived around the corner. I could hear them playing all night. I'd open my window.

WE: Did you ever take part in those jam sessions?

SS: Well, they finally let me in. I asked my mother's permission, and she let me go 'round, man. I never forget, his name was Mr. Kansas City. And he said, "Does your mother know you around here, boy?" I said, "Yes, I told her. I asked her to come around here." And he said, "Well, you can come in for a little while," 'cause everything was goin' on, you know.

WE: Would you participate or just listen?

SS: Well, they finally let me play a little bit. So I played a few choruses on the blues, and one old drunk, he called me a bunch of dirty names and said, "Get outta here. You can't play that thing."

PR: That sounds like that story about Charlie Parker when he first started out and the audience would throw things at him . . .

SS: And he went home in tears, yeah. And then he practiced, and that's exactly what I did.

WE: Were you aware of some of the giants playing at that time, like Coleman Hawkins?

SS: Well, when I got to be about sixteen or seventeen, I started listening to Lester Young quite a bit. And there were a few records—78's around, you know. And I would hear Benny Carter, Johnny Hodges. I remember Tab Smith, and I remember . . . I used to always live with a *Down Beat* magazine like all the kids did. And then there was Jimmy Dorsey and Toots Mondello, and Benny Goodman—he was my favorite clarinet player, Benny Goodman. I liked Artie Shaw and some of the other guys, but Benny Goodman. Really! Can you imagine—when I was a kid there was Gene Krupa, and Roy Eldridge, and I heard those records and things, and I end up playing with these guys? On the jobs at the Philharmonic.

PR: When did you first leave Saginaw?

SS: I didn't finish high school, and I went on the road with a band called Cornelius Cornell. This was summer, and we got stranded down in Tennessee. Bookings were bad. And Thad Jones was in the band and George Nicholas, "Big Nick," and several guys that could play—nice band. It sounded like Duke Ellington's band. This was about '41. Then I went to another band—Claude and Clifford Trenier. They had a band like [Jimmie] Lunceford. I stayed with 'em about six months, and I went back and finished school. So I had two summers out on the road.

I had maybe six months to finish school, and Ernie Fields came through town with his band. He wanted to hire me. They were a third-rate band; that's what they call them. The second-rate bands were people like Andy Kirk, Tiny Bradshaw, and Les Hite, I believe. And they were all good bands, you'd be surprised. First-rate bands were like Duke Ellington, Lunceford, Count Basie, Cab Calloway. There were a lot of second-rate bands and a *whole* lot of third-rate bands, and this band was a third-rate band, you know.

So my mother said, "You gonna what—you gonna quit school at this late date, you gonna quit, and I worked so hard to get you where you are?" I said, "I'm gonna play jazz, baby. I'll see ya." "Oh," she said, "you are?" She took my clothes and threw them on the floor. "You take your clothes, and good-bye. And don't come back anymore." Well, that struck a nerve, you know what I mean? I said, "Wait a minute, we can talk this over." So I said, man, I can't go, my mama won't hold still for this.

So I graduated, and I sure am glad I did. I'm a distinguished alumnus at my high school, and my picture hangs in the library with all the judges and the doctors and lawyers and so forth; and I got the proclamation from the mayor. The proclamation gives me a day, May 16, and he gave me the gavel.

So when I graduated a war broke out, and there was a vacant spot in Tiny Bradshaw's band, and he sent for me, and I did my first stint in Chicago at the Rum Boogie—Joe Louis' Rum Boogie, then. And we spent ten weeks there.

WE: Didn't you live for a while in New York with Bud Powell, his mother, and his brother?

SS: Sure, but they didn't have enough room for me. To show you how things happen in this business—bread cast on the water. When I was a boy we didn't have enough room for Wardell Gray, but there was no hotel for black people then. Only had one hotel, and we weren't allowed to stay there.

WE: What city are you talking about?

SS: Saginaw. Didn't have but one hotel. In those days it was very preju-diced, you know. And I found him, you know. I have a knack for that. I said, "My mama got a room you can stay in when I go to school." I was up at five, you know. So he'd be gettin' home about 4:30, and he'd sit there and have a cup of coffee, some breakfast, and then he'd sleep, 'cause

I'd be gone all day. And by the time I got home he's up and playin' his horn or something. Wardell Gray.

He and Big Nick were really my teachers, 'cause you can't learn much from records. Nowadays you can, because they're more extensively played. The solos are drawn out; at least I think mine are, like kinda laid out.

PR: Different than a three-minute 78, right?

SS: Yeah. And they'd play a chorus, and you wonder, "What should I play now after that?" [Laughter.] Well, the same thing goes for that too, you know. Like in Japan—I heard the kids play over there, and they can really do it just like the records, but after the record's over they don't know which way to go. And that goes for over here too. They transcribe a lot of my solos to find out and analyze. But see, I can't play it twice the same way, not identical. The structure and chords will be there, but the notes fall in different places because of the hearing and the thought.

I'm saying there is no way you can depict an individual; you can only be yourself. Now I advise them to study what was played and memorize some of it, but you got your own personality to live with. And you'd be like night and day: you'd play this solo, and then you start playing yours, and you sound like a different person. So why not be that different person, you dig?

WE: Dizzy sounded a lot like Roy Eldridge when he came up.

SS: Well, that was true, but he had more than Roy to deal with. He had people like Jonah Jones, Charlie Shavers, Louis Armstrong, Hot Lips Page, Red Allen, Bunny Berigan—he was a bad cat, now, Bunny could play, man. And Harry James, he could play too, you know. Well, just musicians, man, you know.

See, and another thing—one of my pet peeves is this: music is not bent on what color you are; it's what kind of music you play. Because I'm black and you white, that doesn't make you better or me better. It's the musicianship that counts. It's what you're gifted with by the good Creator, God in heaven. See, because everybody can appreciate music, I think most people do, but musicians are not made, they're born. Athletes are born. You've got to develop your gift if you are bending towards that in life. Like lawyers—they're really born. Yeah, they know how to talk. You know, some people can't get it out; that's why they hire a lawyer [laughter]. Some people can play.

PR: Speaking of younger players, do you get around to hear many of them?

SS: I don't have a chance to see 'em. But they come around me, like they're my children almost. I never give them a cold shoulder. No way, man. I remember when I was young how that feels. 'Cause I got the brush-off too, and I just can't do that to people. See, they want a chance to show their wares too, and I give 'em a chance.

Sometimes I just take 'em under my wing and teach 'em. Like one little boy in Pittsburgh, he's blind. When I first met him he was about ten years old. Maybe you heard of him—he made some records too—Eric Kloss. I'm his teacher. He still calls me Uncle Sonny. He was a little tot. His father, Dr. Kloss, would bring him up to the Crawford Grill, and he'd take his lessons on Saturday. 'Cause I played there quite a bit in those days—Midway Lounge, Crawford Grill, Louis' Hotel over there. You know, around town.

WE: From your prolific recording career, it seems like you've played with just about everybody.

SS: I have had the honor to play with almost everyone, yes.

WE: Did you work with Don Byas?

SS: Don and I were great friends, but we never played together. And Ben Webster, we never played together. We were great friends, man. They called him the Brute, but I called him Uncle Ben. And another great tenor player, in my estimation—I have the highest regard for him—his name is Budd Johnson. He was with the Earl Hines band. Boy! Boy! Boy! Man, he's a gas. He's a beautiful man. He can *play* rings around a whole lot of youngsters. They think that because he's up in age he's an old man, you know. And I'm lookin' for fifty-seven. See a lot of people run from the numbers—I'm just glad I'm here. I hope I make fifty-seven [laughter]. I'm lookin' toward ninety.

You know there's a man, Eubie Blake. Well, I almost fell on my face. Mike Douglas had him on his program, and I got a lot of phone calls right away. Mike asked him a question like this, he said, "Mr. Blake, the big bands are coming back, and if you ever had a big band who would you get in your big band?" The first name he mentioned was *mine*. Man, I'd like to die. Phew. I say, "Oh, my goodness, what a tribute to pay to me." He knows what's happenin', man. Earl Hines is another dude, man. I could work with cats like that, you know, but, I mean, those people are so outstanding. I just look up to them as musicians that are untouchables. They last that long they gotta be untouchable.

PR: We mentioned Dizzy Gillespie a few minutes ago. Don't you have a special relationship with him?

SS: Dizzy Gillespie? There's my favorite trumpet player. He's like a father to me, Dizzy is. When I stopped drinkin' booze, man, we was playin' at the Wolftrap. I said, "Dizzy, I stopped drinkin'." He said, "Thank God!" I heard him all over the stage. He used to come up to me and says, "Hmph, terrible. You smell like alcohol." I said, "I just had a couple of beers, Diz." He said, "No, I saw you with a cognac glass." And I said, "Well, you're right there too." I never argue back at him, you know. Oh no. That's disrespect. And that's what we must have among ourselves. If you [offend] someone you respect, man, you're lost. You know, I'd hide my booze from Dizzy. Yeah, I would. Because anytime someone loves you that much, thinks that much of you that he doesn't want to see you go down the drain with a bottle of booze or whatever . . . so he was up there praisin' the Lord for me.

WE: You played with Miles for about a year too.

SS: Yeah. I knew Miles when Miles was about—hmm, I think Miles is a couple of years younger than I am—he was about sixteen, and I was eighteen.

WE: Did you meet him in New York?

SS: I met him where he lived, in East St. Louis. I was playing with Bradshaw.

WE: Did he sit in?

SS: Oh no, man. No, I taught him some little licks, you know. Yeah, I played in his band though. I took Cannonball [Adderley] and Coltrane's place. He cried like a baby when he couldn't join Tiny Bradshaw's band. He wanted to go on the road so bad. His mama said, "You too young, you gotta finish school," like my mother did. Which was the best thing for him to do. A lot of guys mistake Miles as being real mean. He's a nice little cat, man. And they get the wrong impression about Stan Getz too. He's my friend too, *very* good friend, man. We were born on the same day. I love him really. Boy, he's a master musician, believe me he is. They're like my brothers: Dexter Gordon, James Moody, Illinois Jacquet.

PR: James Moody's played Las Vegas for several years. Have you ever considered going that route?

SS: No, I don't feel like sitting in anybody's pit band. I like to travel. I feel free to just give my message. And now Moody's doing the same thing. He's happier like this. Now see, you can't confine a cat like that, man. Dexter Gordon—he loves just to travel and blow; he's happy, you know. In fact, I just left the Village Gate playing with Dexter Gordon. Me and Dex played in Billy Eckstine's band together.

WE: With Art Blakey and Sarah Vaughan?

SS: Yeah. Fats Navarro. Dizzy was in the band. And Gene Ammons, and Leo Parker. We had a good time together. Billy talks about that a lot of time on TV. "Yeah, I remember Sonny. Sonny was in my band." We had a band, man. Would you believe, man, after three nights if you looked at your music everybody looked at you funny. You had a music stand there, but the music was under the stand, baby.

WE: You wouldn't even refer to it?

SS: No, you just felt kinda ashamed that you didn't memorize your part within three days. There's a whole lot to remember, too. Man, everybody in that band could play. Yup, he [Eckstine] picked them all, you know.

PR: Were there other memorable groups you could tell us about?

SS: I'll tell you a band I really enjoyed playing with, Gene Ammons and myself. Oh, we had a wonderful time. I remember all those days. Now he was what you might call a timid soul, big as he was. I remember one time we had a manager, and they got in some kinda argument. Jug said, "Don't grab me." Teddy Stewart [our manager] was scared of me. But Jug was deathly afraid of the manager. Well, he [Stewart] was a big fat cat. But I mean, you know, that don't mean that you gonna win the war. He'd get tired quicker than I would. I'd run a block first and let him get real good and tired. So he threw a rock at Jug one time, I remember that.

I remember when my buddy died, you know, and I went to the funeral. That's another thing that's very displeasing—to see my friends go. I was on my way in my car, going to a job, I think in Ohio, and I read the paper, and it said Charlie Parker had died. I just turned around, put my stuff in the house, you know, and I went up to the church on Seventh Avenue, parked my car. And the first one I saw was Dizzy, and then Charlie Shavers and umpteen of my buddies, you know. And Dizzy say, "Hey, Son." I say, "Hey, Dizzy, I ain't gonna work this week." He said, "Here are your gloves." I said, "Gloves for what?" He said, "You gotta carry him, man." He said, "I got mine on, here yours." Phew! It sure was a bitter pill. Because I had never felt like that before. After you put the gloves on and you—I didn't see him in the casket. I was on my way down to see him, and they started closing it. So I remember him like he was. I'm sure glad I didn't see him. And so, as we carried him up the stairs I felt like all the blood in my back was draining out through my legs and stuff like that, you know. And everybody's cryin' or singin'. I say, *man!*

So Milt Jackson and I happened to go to Coltrane's funeral—in Chicago, I believe. And so they was asking us. I said, "Man, I done put on gloves once. I'm not gonna do it anymore. But we were great friends too. They'll have to find somebody else. No, not me."

PR: Who played music at Coltrane's funeral?

SS: A fella named Albert Ayler. And he was way up in the balcony, and he had on this white suit, tuxedo or somethin'. And the first I seem to remember, a weird chant—well, he belonged to somethin' like Arabian or whatever it was—and all this hollerin' and chantin'. I don't know what faith that was, but it sounded very Arabic. And so then I heard this weird saxophone . . .

WE: Tell us more about Gene Ammons.

SS: I knew him very well. Like if he had a problem—well, he had a nickname for me, in fact all the cats, Dexter right now, they call me String. Like I always been lean. I'm not really skinny—I weigh about 170, 175—but I was kinda lean and lanky, you know. So if he got somethin' on his mind, if he broke his horn, "Go get String." I'm no repairman by any—I take some chewing gum and some rubber bands and some cellophane or somethin' and probably wire up somethin' for him so he could play that night, you know.

We were playin' Madison Square Garden, and somethin' happened to his horn. Boy, he had a fit: "You gotta find String." And I just got there, you know. So he went to the other dressing room and found me. I says, "Just cool it, Jug. I'll see what I can do." And so we got the horn together, and we played. And we used to have a lot of fun.

But Gene's funeral was a whole lot different. When I came into the church they said, "You gotta play 'Goodbye.'" He made a record, you know, *Goodbye.*[1] I said, "No, I won't play 'Goodbye.'" I said, "I'll play 'My Buddy' for my buddy, though." And after I played "My Buddy," you know they made a record of that? It's out on the market, "My Buddy." And everybody start boo-hooin', you know.

---

1. Gene Ammons, *Goodbye*, Prestige Records, 1975.

Oh man. Most of my friends are dead, while I'm still tryin' to play. I'm still trying to play. I really enjoy playing. I don't know what to do if I couldn't play. That's all I ever wanted to do. That's all I've ever done.

PR: Your alto and tenor saxes are sitting beside us.

SS: They both have different flavors, you know.

PR: Is it true that you once had a couple of your horns stolen?

SS: Funny thing about that, man. They still have an epidemic. You know, I advise all saxophone players to watch their instruments when they lay 'em down. I won't mention the hotel's name—I was in the hotel lobby. They had three exits to this hotel in Philadelphia, and this thief ripped me off with inside of two or three minutes. I just turned my back lookin' for my ride to work in, and I looked around, and the chair was empty. I almost had a stroke. I couldn't believe it. Had my name all over 'em too. I mean, not the horn itself, but the case.

OK, so I get to work with no instrument, but there's a saxophone player standing in the door. I said, "Man, I just got ripped off of my horns. Can I use yours for the night?" He said, "Sure, Sonny. I came to play with you, but I understand." I played his horn, and man, I gave his horn a workout, buddy. I was mad; I was unhappy. So I go home empty-handed, no saxophone. My wife said, "Where your horns?" I said, "I got ripped off." So I made a phone call to Selmer, who I advertised for the last twenty-five or thirty years. They said, "I know how you feel, Sonny. Don't worry about it. We'll get you some more, and you'll get 'em to-morrow." That's them, right there.

PR: When did this happen?

SS: About two or three years ago.

PR: Each horn has its own personality, so when you lost two it must've really hurt.

SS: *Man*, I almost had a stroke. And I was just gettin' used to 'em. I'm gettin' used to these now, you know. After their first overhaul job, they'll have a different kind of sound, because, you see, you do grow into the horn. Yes, you grow *into* the instrument. I mean, it's almost human.

WE: Tell us something about the record *Stitt Plays Bird*.[2] Was it your idea?

SS: No, that's the company's idea. I made another one too—a tribute to Charlie Parker. But they are commercializing. I don't resent it, but I

2. Sonny Stitt, *Stitt Plays Bird*, Atlantic Records, 1964.

really think that they are putting a feather in my cap that I don't deserve. I don't think anyone can fill his shoes. Nobody. To me he was the epitome of being a saxophonist. They write a lot of nonsense about things that was said back years ago about my getting the keys to the kingdom. That was a bunch of bunk. I don't get it. You got to play your saxophone the best you can and your way and your way only. Can't nobody provide the entrance to any kingdom for anybody, you know. You're lucky if you get a piece of the action, OK? [Laughter.]

WE: When was the first time you heard Parker in person?

SS: That's funny you asked that. I was playin' with Bradshaw. I think it was in '43, and I had two overseers—the bass and drummer. They used to watch me, 'cause this was my first time on the road, and they didn't let me have a breath of fresh air. They thought I was gonna fall into some kinda pit or somethin', you know. Well, they asked me where I was goin', and I said, "I'm goin' to find Charlie Parker." I had heard so much about this guy. They said, "You haven't been to Kansas City before. How you gonna do that?" I left my bag in the hotel room and I'm going to Eighteenth and Vine, and I stood there about twenty minutes to a half an hour just looking at people and things, you know. And I saw this guy come out of the drugstore. He had on two overcoats and dark glasses and an alto in his hand. And I say, "That's him." Just like that. I asked him, "Are you Charlie Parker?" He said, "Yeah, how did you know?" I said, "I don't know, don't ask me." Well, that's my first adventure or experience with clairvoyance. It's funny, you know. It was him. So we went up the street to a place called the Gypsy Tea Room.

WE: So the two of you got together and played music.

SS: Just the two of us. But he didn't like the club owner, or the club owner didn't like him. And he said, "Let's go, man, 'cause this guy, we don't get along" [laughter]. So we packed up and left.

WE: You don't remember what songs you played?

SS: No, I don't remember too much about that. Because it didn't last but about fifteen minutes. We didn't spend the whole day. And I just went back to the hotel. I saw him from time to time after that, you know.

PR: You've done recordings and appeared with dozens of other saxophonists. Is it the challenge that motivates you?

SS: No, it's fun. It's like any other game. You watch that on television about the games people play? We play a game too. Years ago, though, the game was much more vicious. Cutthroat. Can you imagine Lester Young,

Coleman Hawkins, Chu Berry, Don Byas, and Ben Webster on the same little jam session? They had a place called Minton's Playhouse in New York. It's kaput now. And these guys, man, nothing like it. And guess who won the fight? That's what it was—a saxophone duel.

PR: Lester Young?

SS: Don Byas walked off with everything [laughter].

PR: Were those sessions like marathon physical contests?

SS: No, no, it's everything. It's physical, it's mental, and it's creativity. It's all you know. It's a free-for-all.

PR: Are you supposed to leave the session when you stop coming up with ideas?

SS: You don't *have* to leave. The audience is the judge, and they applaud, and they are not lying as to who won the fight. You know the slickest and trickiest won. See, there are a lot of tricks to music. You open your bag of tricks, that's all. That's why when the youngsters sometimes have a habit of challenging an old-timer, I give them one word of advice. It does not pay to sell an old professional down the river and call him, you know, "old-fashioned," or man, some of the old cats will eat you alive. That's right. You better show a little respect.

PR: Do you meet guys in small towns who want to come up on the stand and show you up?

SS: I give 'em a welcome mat. I'm a strong believer in giving you enough rope to hang yourself. But that isn't fun anymore. I'd rather encourage them to be more proficient at their artistry, you know, and then I can be proud and say, "Well, I was a part of that." Rather than discourage them by just waxing them for real, which it can be done easy enough. But that's not my goal. I like to see music survive and become more legible to the average listener so he'll appreciate it and understand it more. That will give the little guys coming up—see, I only can play one job at a time, you know what I mean? So there's room. In fact, it's only crowded at the bottom. A lot of room on top.

SELECTED DISCOGRAPHY

Kaleidoscope. Prestige 7077. 1957.
Sonny Stitt Sits in with the Oscar Peterson Trio. Verve 8344. 1959.
Only the Blues. Verve MG-V-8250. 1960.
Sonny Stitt and the Top Brass. Atlantic 1395. 1962.

With Gene Ammons. *Soul Summit*. Prestige 7234. 1962.
Stitt Plays Bird. Atlantic 1418. 1964.
With Booker Ervin. *Soul People*. Prestige 7372. 1965.
Giants of Jazz. Atlantic 2-905. 1971.
Constellation. Cobblestone 9021. 1972.
The Last Stitt Sessions. Vols. I and II. Muse MCD-6003. 1982.

GÁBOR SZABÓ

Photograph by Chuck Stewart.   Used with permission.

The jazz mainstream absorbed a rapid succession of musical forms during the sixties, from Indian ragas and the bossa nova to fusion jazz that incorporated elements of rock, soul, and pop. Accompanying this eclectic bent, an unprecedented number of non-American jazz musicians gained international reputations. The ranks of jazz guitarists were swelled by the likes of Mahavishnu John McLaughlin, Laurindo Almeida, Bola Sete, Attila Zoller, and Hungarian-born Gábor Szabó.

Gábor Szabó received his early musical training behind the Iron Curtain in Budapest, where he was born in 1936. He fled his homeland for the United States during the Hungarian revolution twenty years later. With the help of sponsors, he attended the Berklee College of Music, a famed jazz conservatory in Boston.

Szabó's first major appearance in the United States was in 1958 with the Newport International Youth Band. His four-year association with Chico Hamilton's band (from 1961 to 1965) brought him wider exposure, and winning a 1964 *Down Beat* magazine critics' poll award solidified his position as a rising new star in jazz. In 1965 Szabó joined the band of Charles Lloyd. A year later he left the popular Lloyd outfit to form his first group with the unusual instrumentation of two guitars, two percussion, and bass.

Szabó's bands were distinguished by their exotic aural colors. The music they played was infused with ethnic Hungarian strains and the influence of Indian ragas, and Szabó's guitar playing had definite gypsy overtones. Some critics compared him with Django Reinhardt in this regard. Although Szabó was not born a gypsy, his studies as a youth with gypsy guitarists left impressions that later were hard to ignore.

Szabó's position as an expatriate musician gave him a unique perspective on the American jazz world. *The Man from Two Worlds*, a Chico Hamilton recording made when Szabó was in the band, aptly described his cultural duality.[1] In the mid-sixties he became convinced that modern jazz had reached a dead end and desperately needed the influence of popular music to restore its vitality. He therefore introduced blues and

---

1. Chico Hamilton, *Man from Two Worlds*, Impulse Records, 1963.

rock material into his repertoire and adopted arrangements that toned down the jazz attitudes of his earlier work. In so doing, he succeeded in capturing a broader audience for his music, but jazz critics charged that he had succumbed to commercial pressures.

During the seventies Szabó was recorded in glossily produced settings by the CTI and Skye labels. This formula was abandoned occasionally in favor of a straightahead blowing session, as on *Skylark*, a Paul Desmond date that contains some of Szabó's best playing from the period.[2] Szabó also was active as a writer. His credits include arranging Chico Hamilton's score to Roman Polanski's film *Repulsion* and composing the popular tune "Breezin'," which was turned into a megahit in 1976 by pop-jazz musician George Benson.[3]

Based in Los Angeles, Gábor Szabó worked in television during the later seventies. In 1981 he returned to his native Budapest to produce recordings. Within a year, this former freedom fighter and distinctive jazz guitarist died of kidney and liver ailments at the age of forty-five.

❡ ━━━━━♪

Recorded 1976

PR: Gábor, how easy was it for you to hear jazz during the Cold War in Hungary?

GS: Jazz wasn't a very easily accessible thing in those days, because when I got interested in music, it was possibly the darkest days of Stalinism, and even after Stalin died, you know, probably the worst part of the Cold War was going on in the mid-fifties. It was against the party ideology and all that to be involved with so-called decadent Western [art] forms and cultures, so therefore there wasn't anything available on those lines in the Hungarian radio or the music stores or anything like that. The only way to keep my interest satisfied to some degree was to try to get on my radio some stations from West Germany, Italy, France, and many of those were even jammed.

So I was very limited, and in a way I guess it made you more of a fanatic: like we would listen practically twenty-four hours a day. We would be searching on the radio for different things. And we were very fortunate

2. Paul Desmond, *Skylark*, CTI Records, 1974.
3. George Benson, *Breezin'*, Warner Brothers Records, 1976.

to have—there was one radio program, "Voice of America," which was [on] every night from eight 'til ten. Willis Connover is the head of that. He's possibly the most popular American in the entire world except [in] the United States. Nobody knows him here, but his voice is all over the world, from Asia to Africa to Europe. He had this marvelous program—the first hour was kinda popular music, the second hour was jazz, and that was really our bible. That's where we found out what was going on in the world. And in those days even tape recorders were kind of scarce. If some of us had a tape recorder then we would try to tape as much as we could possibly get from the radio and analyze those things, enjoy, listen, and I guess that was about the only source, because albums were not available. I was one of the lucky ones; I owned about six or seven albums which—to buy it from people who had relatives in the United States, and they sent them as gifts. But I remember that one album under those conditions would cost me about two weeks' salary.

PR: Which amounted to what?

GS: Five or six hundred florins, which would be the equal of, I would say, about thirty to forty dollars for an album. In the fifties that was still preinflation time, so that meant for a great deal of money over there.

WE: In your last answer you referred to others with whom you listened to jazz. Who were they?

GS: When I say *we*, I mean about a dozen musicians and people who were crazy about jazz. We had a club called the Hot Club, the Hungarian Hot Club; we had regular meetings, and all of that done illegally really, because even an organization like that would have gotten us into trouble in those days, because they would have considered it a kind of a conspiracy. And immediately they would have labeled it as political, even though it was [for] purely musical purposes, but still the nature of the music—because it was American—they would have labeled it a political gathering, and we would have gotten into a great deal of trouble.

I was twice taken in and questioned by the secret police—once because I had a pack of Camel cigarettes on me which I got from the American legation, and the second time because they saw me coming out of the American legation. We were very fortunate to have a vice-consul [in Budapest] who was American-born [of] Hungarian parents, and he was a great jazz fan. As much as he could help us without getting us into trouble he would try to supply us with some albums or *Down Beat* magazines, things that were like incredible treasures for us in those days, because those were the only links to the outside world which we felt so far away from that it was just pitiful.

WE: How old were you then?

GS: Seventeen, eighteen.

PR: Do you think that the Communist party would have reacted more favorably to dixieland jazz because it put more of an emphasis on a collective sound rather than individual soloists?

GS: No. You're just talking about a technicality, but still the overall sound they considered decadent. They did not consider it an aesthetically acceptable musical sound. They called it "sensuous" and "sinful." You see, the moral values—except that it's all phony, really—but the moral values in Communist countries are very strictly enforced and practiced. For example, those were the days [when] there wasn't a kiss in a movie from about 1949 until about 1956, the time when I left, because that also had no redeeming social value. If they caught young kids kissing or let's say on the street at night embracing, the moral patrol—there was a unit in the police department like that—would take them in, and I guess scare them; then they let them go. The parents had to come and get them. Things were terribly puritanical. I guess just like a heavyweight fighter who's training for a fight: any distraction, let it be flesh or anything that hasn't got anything directly to do with the purpose, is considered a threat, and therefore it has to be avoided.

WE: What prompted you to become a musician? And who first influenced you to play jazz?

GS: I'm going to tell you something that's probably going to surprise you. It wasn't a musical influence. It was more like a young boy with a fantasy. The person who actually got me to play the guitar was Roy Rogers. When I was eleven or twelve, at the end of 1949, they still had a few American movies coming in. That was just before the total communications breakdown between the East and the West. And I did get to see a couple of Roy Rogers movies, and I was just fascinated by [the] exotica of cowboys and the Sons of the Pioneers singing in harmony; I just thought that was great. So that was my main motivation for getting a guitar.

I would say the first real great impression on me was probably Gerry Mulligan, even though I'd heard Dizzy and Duke Ellington and a few of the more progressive sounds before. But Gerry Mulligan did actually happen at the same time when I was getting interested in jazz music. He'd just started his first quartets in those days, so I discovered Gerry at the very beginning.

PR: Could you relate the events that led to your exodus from Hungary in 1956?

GS: They [the Hungarian government] wanted to show it to the Western world that in Communist countries it is possible to have demonstrations and you can actually show your disenchantment if you wished to, so they had an organized kind of token demonstration put on by the college students, who were just simply demonstrating for better conditions in the dormitories or something like that. Nevertheless, what they didn't figure on [was] that this got people together, because gatherings were out, too, unless they were the kind that was to glorify the system and the regime.

So this allowed the people to get out on the streets in big groups, and we found out about each other that, well, "He's not a Communist, he's not a Communist," and just like wildfire, it spread. And it started getting out of hand, and they realized it. So they were trying to stop the whole thing, but it was just getting worse and worse, and then all of a sudden we started hearing slogans: "Get the Russians out of Hungary. The troops, the army, and the tanks, get them out of Hungary" and stuff like that. And it was getting to be more and more serious.

Now, come five o'clock in the afternoon, all the workers from the steel mills and these places, the ones who were really hurt the most by the system, who had to work terribly hard and making very little money, they joined in, and then it really started. The whole thing started about one or two o'clock in the afternoon, and by nine o'clock it was a full-fledged revolution, taking over the radio station, and by that time guns were around, and next day the revolution was won. The government was overthrown. Imre Nagy, who was a very well-liked personality who was not Communist—they just had him in the government to pacify people—we elected premier of Hungary, and it was just euphoria for two or three days, while it lasted.

Then of course it was no revolution anymore; then, all of a sudden, the Soviet Union decided to invade Hungary. It became a war between Hungary and Russia, which of course was quite ridiculous. As it turned out, with the little primitive weapons, like molotov cocktails, it was estimated at one time that for each Hungarian about twenty Russians were taken care of. But still it could only go on so long, because they attacked us with air force, tanks, and if we had an ocean, maybe the navy, too!

PR: Were you in the midst of all this?

GS: Yes. Then of course it lasted and lasted, and we were hoping, because we were constantly encouraged by Voice of America and Radio Free Europe to hang on, you know, and we thought if nothing else, that the UN would maybe drop some weapons, if no troops at least some sort of help, but nothing happened for two reasons. I think Eisenhower was very much against any kind of a friction, and, number two, the Suez Canal crisis was happening at the same time, and it took away the attention from the Hungarian business, and it was, I guess, more in the Western interest to straighten things out at Suez. So by the time anything could have been done, the Russians put back their puppet government. Up to this day it's [János] Kádár; he's the party leader now.

As soon as that was done, they called back the UN representative and sent the new one, who officially was not requesting anymore the help from the UN, because he was saying that there was some antirevolutionary elements sabotaging the glorious Hungarian revolution, but with the help of the Soviet Socialist Republic and the good people of Hungary, we got rid of that counterrevolutionary element, and things were back to normal. Of course when I realized that, I knew that for the next hundred years or so that there's no hope for change, and that's when I packed up. Number one, for music I had always wanted to be in the West; and number two, it would have been dangerous for me to stay there.

Because as I found out two years ago when I went back home, thirty-five thousand people of my age just disappeared. They were taken away from college dormitories in the middle of the night. My generation you don't see on the streets of Budapest today. The only ones you see are a few of them who are in wheelchairs or missing a leg, but mainly people of my generation are not seen. They either left the country and came out to the West or they disappeared. The ones that stayed home were massacred, alone.

PR: Did you travel straight to New York?

GS: The first stop was actually Austria. That's where I arrived on foot. The Red Cross took over there; they took us to Salzburg. Over there you had to fill out an application for what country you would like to go to, which of course I filed United States. Oddly enough, the gentleman that

I mentioned before, the vice-consul in Hungary, who was called back to the United States about two months before the revolution and [for whom] we had a big good-bye party, we never going to see him again in our entire lifetime, because it looked so hopeless, and he showed up because he spoke Hungarian. It was a great reunion, and he helped us speed it up a little bit to come to the United States.

Then we went to Camp Kilmer, New Jersey, where again we had to wait for sponsors, because they wouldn't let you out of the camp until somebody took responsibility for you, you know, to put you up or look for a job for you. When that happened, then I left Camp Kilmer, and after about a year of just odd jobs—I was a janitor at an air force base—I saved enough money to go to Berklee school of music in Boston.

WE: What did you study at Berklee?

GS: Well, unfortunately, then they didn't offer a degree, but now they do that, too, and the whole school was based on a so-called Schillinger system. Joseph Schillinger was the creator of a compositional method, and that was their meat and potatoes. I would say that would be the equivalent of a classical training.

Aside from that they would have the fun classes, like big-band writing and big-band ensemble playing. Then of course you took lessons on your own instrument. Also jazz history. To me that was like being in heaven after dreaming about all this the better part of my teen years in Hungary. To be dropped into the middle of a musical mecca like that was just the greatest thing that had ever happened to me.

WE: You didn't meet Roy Rogers there, did you?

GS: No, by that time I had forgotten about that [laughter].

PR: Another student at Berklee when you were there was composer-arranger Gary McFarland. He died very young—a stunning loss. Since you were close friends, could you estimate his stature for us?

GS: Well, as a writer, to be very frank with you, I think there's just nobody like him since his death. Aside from the fact that he was a contemporary writer and a very open-minded person about music and everything else, he had such a definite character to his writing which I don't think I've witnessed in anybody else ever since. I think once Duke Ellington, before Duke died, even mentioned that Gary had in a way reminded him of himself when he started.

Gary had a way of voicing things, for example, with the clarinet and the trumpet. He got away from the sectional writing, you know; everybody was writing for five saxophones, then five trumpets and four trombones or whatever. Gary kind of introduced the orchestral kind of writing, more like Gil Evans. He would put a trumpet with a mute and a clarinet and maybe a vibe together in a unison line and get a marvelous, new, different kind of sound out of it. He was able to create such colors, which was quite neglected in jazz writing.

Most people, most jazz arrangers and players for that matter, made that mistake in those days that anything that was a bit on the sensitive side or a bit too colorful they felt that it was a little too gimmicky and it was not rough enough for a jazz personality. Gary, on the other hand, did not have this insecurity about him. He would search for aesthetically beautiful sounds, and he did not care whether it had that basic, you know, gutbucket sound to it. He would just look for all the colors that were available in a situation where there were more than one instrument together.

And I think that's the main strength that Gary had, that he made again a jazz band sound like an orchestra rather than just a band. In a way he reminded all of us that jazz is music just like classical music is music, and there are colors to be found, and it can still swing its behind off, you know.

WE: One of our favorite albums of his is *America the Beautiful*, which was also one of his last.[4]

GS: That's right, it was. That's a typical example, because he incorporated from rock to Latin to just about everything, and still it remained Gary McFarland, and it was definitely jazz, and those colors that we were talking about, they were just magnificent in that piece.

WE: Considering your formative years in Hungary where the life-style was nonindividualized, was it at all hard for you to take solos in the bands of Chico Hamilton and Charles Lloyd?

GS: That's a very good observation. Even before communism there were the Nazis, and we were always made to do things. We really didn't have any kind of individual freedom to speak of, even before communism, because if for no other reason [than] for economic reasons, you constantly were faced with things that you just simply have to do. And when I came out here, not just in jazz music, but in my personal life too, the hardest thing up to this day to me is to make a choice, because you do have the

---

4. Gary McFarland, *America the Beautiful*, Skye Records, 1968.

freedom of making a choice. And my first eighteen years of my life I lived that way, that I never questioned anything. In jazz also it was the most difficult thing for me to get out there and take a solo, because I had all the options, and it was up to me to decide what I was going to do with the freedom available for me.

So you're right. I'll never forget it. When I first started playing with Chico Hamilton, and that was probably the first musical assignment that I had where—especially those days, in the early sixties, extended long solos were in style, like Coltrane and these people in those days, they would take half-hour solos sometimes. And after the second or third chorus, I panicked. I didn't know just how to extend my ideas, and I didn't have the confidence that they were good enough to be extended.

Oddly enough, musically, I don't have this problem anymore. In fact, if anything I'm trying to simmer things down and crystallize and simplify things more and more. But in my personal life up to this day the most difficult thing I find is that I have options, that it's up to me what I'm going to choose. I see all the different possibilities, you know, and to every coin I see the two sides, and it's terribly difficult for me to make decisions many times. Sometimes I do wish that certain things were made a little more mandatory for me, like I just have to do this . . . And of course you only have to blame yourself, nobody else, if you made the wrong decision.

PR: According to *Down Beat* magazine, in 1967 you made some provocative comments alleging that jazz as it had been known was dead. Was this true?

GS: It is correct. There were some times that they quoted me somewhat wrong, because I was quoted as saying that jazz is dead, and actually what I said was "Jazz as we knew it is dead." And especially those years . . . I just called them the "post-Beatle era," because I think that changed so many things in our lives, the Beatles did. I mean, not just music but in social behavior, in the clothing, everything. They affected all society.

Anyway, the Beatles changed my mind about nonjazz music—I won't even say rock music or pop music, just nonjazz music—because up to that point I was a fascist about it, too, until I realized that I had more do nots than dos, you know, like I cannot do this because if I do that it won't be jazz; I cannot play that tune because that's not a jazz tune, and so on. All of a sudden I realized that when the Beatles came out with some of their songs—like "Michelle," and there was an album particularly that shook me up, that was the *Sgt. Pepper* album—that I felt that their music was getting to be so deep that it was really getting to be simply ridiculous to write them off as commercial music or rock music, and that's something a decent jazz musician won't get involved with.

I started sounding some unpopular notes by the simple fact that I recorded some Beatle tunes on my first album, *Gypsy '66.*[5] On that I recorded some Beatle tunes, and I recorded Burt Bacharach tunes and a few other things. It sounds silly now, because everybody's doing it, but believe it or not, it was a very unpopular move and kind of outrageous to record Burt Bacharach tunes, like "Walk On By" and a couple of those things. Some people started saying that I'm a traitor to the profession. On one of these occasions, in an article, I said that let's face it, jazz as we knew it is dead, because you cannot keep it in such an incestlike form any longer.

I felt that's what was happening to jazz: that we only listened to each other, we only played each other's tunes, and it was coming to the point when only jazz musicians would go out to jazz clubs, because we were cutting ourselves away from people so much by this nihilistic attitude, which was that if people liked you, then you felt insecure, because you must be commercial, and if they didn't like you, that meant that they were just really hopeless, because they'd never understand art. I found that there was an attitude developing in jazz that was almost thriving on this masochistic thing—like it can't happen anyway—and we were just licking each other's wounds.

That's the reason that at that time I made that statement, that [jazz] as we knew it was dead, and if we keep it the way it was, then it really will be dead, because we must let some fresh air in from the outside. I personally was very much impressed by the Latin music that was happening, which was bossa nova of course at the time. Even before that, I liked Afro-Cuban music a great deal. I was probably one of the first people—Charles Lloyd actually turned me on to Ravi Shankar way back in 1960 or '61, so I felt that that had a great effect on me, and I was incorporating some of that into my music as well. And of course the thing that I cannot help, the Hungarian tradition, that was just there to begin with.

So of all the people, I really couldn't afford to be a chauvinist about jazz, because to begin with I had some other influences in my playing.

5. Gábor Szabó, *Gypsy '66*, Impulse Records, 1966.

When I made that statement, of course, all hell broke loose, and then they really got after me: "Who is he to say that? He's not even American!" and all that. But up to this day I mean it, and I back up that statement, because if you look around today, all those things are happening that actually I started doing in those days.

WE: Jazz critics will sometimes contrast what they refer to as an uncompromising, pure jazz played by figures such as Cecil Taylor, Anthony Braxton, and Charles Mingus, with crossover jazz or jazz rock, which is considered by these same critics to be a diluted form of the music. How do you react to this sort of comparison?

GS: Look, they cannot help it any more than I can what they're doing. Really, sincerely, it's not speculative what I'm doing. I am 100 percent believing in the way I'm playing. I couldn't even possibly try to fabricate a sell-out sound, because usually people are hipper than that. Even things that really become big sellers usually are things that people who are doing it believe in 100 percent.

Now it is a simple fact of anything in life, I guess, that if what you're doing and what you believe in appeals to more people, you're going to enjoy a greater amount of popularity. But I wouldn't call it any more pure form of jazz music than what I'm doing. I imagine Cecil Taylor believes 100 percent in what *he's* doing. And I'm a musician, and I find it difficult to enjoy Cecil Taylor. So just the simple fact that economically he's not doing as well as, let's say, some others does not make an artist pure, or that doesn't make it pure jazz. That's still that old overtone that the more you suffer the purer you are. That's not true.

At the risk of sounding cold about it, it might just be that the man's [Taylor's] talent is distorted somewhat, and therefore he will only appeal to a certain, limited amount of people. So I'm just saying this as an argument that it could even be the opposite, that maybe he's fabricating something to a greater degree than those of us who are so-called doing a little better commercially. And what he's doing is about as close to traditional jazz as what I'm doing. You know, it's categorized as avant-garde, but his music is about as close to New Orleans or Louis Armstrong as mine is. So even just talk about pure jazz, I don't go along with that either. It's something the critics like to write about sometimes, especially when they feel a little bit mean [laughter].

PR: How long were you with CTI?

GS: Three years.

PR: How was that experience?

GS: It was frustrating, I must say, for one simple reason: because all the time I was with them I felt that I should be very happy and [feel] very lucky that I'm with the greatest, classiest jazz label in the world, [but] as much as we liked each other personally and individually, Creed Taylor and myself, still I was never able to communicate with him in the studio. He's a terribly difficult person. He knows what he wants. He hardly ever talks; when he's got something out of you that he likes, you know it, because he says, "That's it," but up to that point you really don't know what he wants of you.

On the other hand, you're not quite secure in doing what you want to do, because he's terribly opinionated, you know, so like when you're displeasing him, you know that, too, even though he doesn't say anything. So all the albums I did for CTI, I feel like they were kind of highly polished, very cold, ice-cold works of art, or whatever you want to call them, and they were all Creed Taylor, you know. It's Creed Taylor who makes an album, and the artist is just another means to, you know.

PR: Did you have to compromise your way of playing?

GS: It's not even that. I never even got to the point with any of the dates that I did for him where I would have even known what I was shooting for, because before I would have arrived at that point, he usually either asked me to go on to another tune, or he was already happy, when I didn't even feel that I started playing yet. And once he's happy with a take, it really doesn't mean anything to him that you're not happy with it, because he tells you it's great and it's marvelous and you can do another one if you *must*, but it's really silly because he's got what he wanted. So in an *innocent* way, it was a horror story, you know.

WE: Let me enlarge this discussion by focusing on two other guitarists. First, Wes Montgomery. Creed Taylor succeeded in making him popular by having Montgomery put unusual emphasis on the way he played octaves, but did this strategy water down the integrity of his music?

GS: I knew Wes quite well. It is very possible that Creed sort of stopped his growth as an artist to some degree, except for the simple fact that Wes, before Creed got to him, had several albums out, marvelous albums on Riverside Records and things like that. He was a musician's musician. Very few people knew about him. He was probably one of the most underrated musicians. I'll never forget, in L.A. once I went to see him, and there were six people in the audience, and four of us were guitar players.

Creed recognized the great attractiveness of that sound that Wes got from the octaves that he played. Look, on a recording I wouldn't say that he really hurt Wes, because we're talking about songs, and Wes was a great melody player. He got just as much kick out of playing a melody with his very charming and seductive way. And in live performances Wes did just as much of all his craft. In other words, he wasn't only doing the octaves and the chords; he was still playing like a demon, just like he always used to.

So we have to make a distinction between two things here—Creed got him to make certain kind of records, true, and eventually I guess Wes even could have stopped doing that, except that he died so suddenly, and he was just riding high on the top of success, really. So we don't know, he probably would have eventually stopped playing that one particular way and would have eventually again mixed things up, and he could have afforded to do so because he was becoming so popular.

So I would say that in Wes's case Creed did a great deal of service to all of us and to Wes, of course, because I know Wes was terribly happy about his success. Because as much as he could play some very intricate things, he was just as happy playing a nice melody. And that's why they sold, because you could feel that happiness in that simple approach that he had, and it was just the most infectious kind of thing.

WE: How about George Benson, who just left CTI?

GS: In the case of George Benson, on the other hand, and to some degree with me, too, I think that Creed did an exact opposite. He did not recognize that certain thing that might have been for us what the octaves were for Wes. Because I know, for example, that Creed probably wanted to do the same thing with me and with George Benson, too—not the same way, but he probably wanted to make us more popular and sell records. And for some reason or another, the exact opposite happened.

All my records for CTI were the deadest kind of clean, very neat, clean records, but even the individual sound was killed in it, because he overorchestrated all my things, and the same thing with George Benson. See, George went out, and the first album he did for Warner Brothers he used his own musicians, the people he wanted to use, and he made a human record. In other words, instead of all the New York Symphony Orchestra and Don Sebesky's arrangements and everything behind you, he made a George Benson record. That record, I feel, is pretty much George Benson, the *Breezin'* album, you know, because that's just how George would play in a club. There's a very minimal overdubbing on it, and what comes through, really, is George Benson, the player, who's sitting in a club and sings and hums along with his guitar, and he certainly exhibits some fancy playing as well.

WE: He plays it as tough as he can on that album?

GS: Well, maybe not *as* tough as he could if he just really wanted a hard-core jazz album, but again, in his case, he enjoys singing. He always did that. And I think he plays enough on that album. By the way, I wrote "Breezin'," and I recorded that too about four years ago.[6]

PR: I wondered whether or not you might have some advice for guitar players about playing or breaking into the business or hanging in there.

GS: Well, it's easy to give good advice, and I don't want to do the other extreme either—like "Get out of the business." I don't want to say that either, but I'll tell you one thing. Looking back on the things that happened to me, I don't think there was ever, ever any question that I was meant to be a musician. In spite of all the low points in my career and my personal life and everything, I think it was unavoidable that I become a musician. I could do well, or I could do badly, but I knew that it's going to be music one way or the other.

SELECTED DISCOGRAPHY

With Chico Hamilton. *Transfusion*. Studio West 102-CD. 1962.
————. *Man from Two Worlds*. Impulse A-59. 1963.
With Charles Lloyd. *Of Course / Of Course*. Columbia CL 2412. Mid-1960s.
Spellbinder. Impulse 9123. 1965.
Gypsy '66. Impulse 9105. 1966.
Jazz Raga. Impulse 9128. 1966. (Szabó plays sitar.)
More Sorcery. Impulse 9167. 1967.
High Contrast. Blue Thumb BTS28. 1972.
With Paul Desmond. *Skylark*. CTI 6039. 1974.
With Charles Lloyd. *Gábor Szabó Live*. Blue Thumb BTS6014. 1974.

6. Szabó's version of "Breezin'" appears on *High Contrast*, Blue Thumb Records, 1972.

CLARK TERRY

Courtesy Concord Jazz, Inc.

Trumpeter, flugelhornist, and big-band leader Clark Terry is a powerfully benign force in contemporary jazz and an ebullient elder statesman of the music. His life and work represent a major link between modern jazz and the towering achievements of the early pioneers of the idiom, especially his hero, Louis Armstrong.

Born in St. Louis in 1920, Terry grew up in a city that has spawned some of the finest trumpet players in jazz, including Miles Davis, who repeatedly cited Terry as an important early influence. Terry honed his jazz chops on the St. Louis trumpet competition, then left his native town for a stint in a United States Navy band. Before the forties were over he had worked with bands led by Charlie Barnet, Charlie Ventura, and Eddie "Cleanhead" Vinson. Terry capped off that decade with a three-year stint in the Count Basie Orchestra.

Clark Terry's tenure with Basie was followed by a nine-year matriculation in what he affectionately refers to as "the university of Ellingtonia." Terry's virtuosity made him a key soloist with the Ellington band, and his sparkling style is featured on such seminal works as *A Drum Is a Woman* and *Such Sweet Thunder.*[1] After Ellington, Terry toured Europe with Quincy Jones's band in the Harold Arlen blues opera *Free and Easy.*

In the sixties Terry worked the New York commercial recording studios. He joined NBC television as a staff musician, but his world-class gifts as a complete trumpet player often were overshadowed by the glitzy show-biz antics of "Tonight Show" bandleader Doc Severinsen. Terry continued to play commercial jobs and did television work to make ends meet, but his jazz life remained intact. During this period he was a regular on Verve label big-band recording dates, he cut classic small-group sessions with jazz legends Thelonious Monk, Coleman Hawkins, and Ben Webster, he co-led with trombonist Bob Brookmeyer one of the finest mainstream quintets of the period, and he introduced, on a superb recording with the Oscar Peterson Trio, the hilarious, muttered scatting he dubbed "mumbles."[2]

1. Duke Ellington and His Orchestra, *A Drum Is a Woman*, Columbia Special Products, 1956; Duke Ellington and His Orchestra, *Such Sweet Thunder*, Columbia Records, 1957.

2. *The Oscar Peterson Trio plus One*, Mercury Records, 1964.

Feeling stifled in the early seventies by the commercial studio scene, Terry launched two formidable projects almost simultaneously—a big band and his own recording company. Although Etoile Records is now defunct, Clark Terry's Big Bad Band has been sustained by a variety of excellent sidemen and straightahead, extroverted arrangements by the likes of former Basieite Frank Wess and Ernie Wilkins, formerly with Ray Charles.

Clark Terry is a versatile and sparkling stylist whose immediately identifiable puckish sound exudes contagious joy. Moreover, he has long been one of jazz's primary advocates for perpetuating the fragile traditions of the music. Aside from his brilliance as a performer, Terry's influence as a jazz educator has been deeply felt through the textbooks he has authored and the workshops he conducts regularly across the country. One of his most recent recordings, *Portraits*, his first as a leader in five years, provides a forum for Terry's passionate remembrance of things past.[3] *Portraits* features Terry's brasswork and vocals in a combo setting while paying tribute to some of the most influential trumpet players in jazz history.

Recorded 1975

PR: Clark, could you trace for us the instrumentalists that had a major influence on your style?

CT: Well, that's very easy to do. I think anyone who is my age, and I'm past fifty, if they didn't admit that they were inspired by or influenced by Louis Armstrong they would be telling a falsie. So in answer to your question, Louis Armstrong was my man in those days.

PR: We just happen to have a Louis Armstrong record ready to play in the studio.[4] When it's finished we'd enjoy hearing your responses.

CT: Beautiful. Fantastic. You know, I think everybody who gets involved in jazz and improvisation should be forced to listen to that cut, because there's a great lesson in theory, harmony, and music history there. If you listen closely to that, you'll notice that Pops [Armstrong] was involved in what we sometimes refer to currently as "doubling-up" in passages. He played against the quarter note. And that was *unheard-of* in those days.

3. Clark Terry, *Portraits*, Chesky Records, 1989.

4. "All of Me," recorded in 1932, appears on *Louis Armstrong V.S.O.P.*, Columbia Special Products, 1974.

And if you notice, he sang on that track exactly the way he played. The same linear message that he would give forth when he played, he did that when he sang. If you'll notice also, the rhythm sections in those days, they only played with the heavy four, "chomp, chomp, chomp, chomp." And as time progressed and jazz got a little more involved, it became a little more swinging, like "um, chomp, um, chomp," more on the two and four. But back there it was "chomp, chomp, chomp, chomp." And I listened to Pops in that context and in later years where the rhythm sections were a little more popping on two and four, and he still was a phenomenon up to the very last note he played.

When he got sick he was off for a number of months, and then he came back to play. He came on the *Tonight Show* once while I was on, and he played, and even though his embouchure was a bit weak from having laid off for a long period, he was just a phenomenal person—that warmth and that message. And that true jazz feeling was there.

I always think how amazing it is for a man like Pops to be as creative as he was in that period when there was nothin' for him to gather his thoughts and things from, except from what he felt and what he lived and what he had within. He was to me like the pioneers in the old days who came through this territory [the West] with axes and saws and chopped down the ways and made paths which later became the highways along the mountains and valleys. This is what we think of Pops. He paved the way for all of us, you know.

WE: When you go to clinics, do you find that young trumpet players are aware of Louis Armstrong's importance?

CT: Very sad to have to report this, but many of the young people who are involved trumpet players, they don't even know that Louis Armstrong ever existed. They're a few that do. But it's quite typical of some of our youth today that they wanna get involved sort of like building a house; they wanna start on the fifteenth floor and build a skyscraper and forget all about the fact that you can't go up there unless you dig *down* there, you know. In order to go high, you gotta dig deep and go low. So you gotta have a good foundation.

And many of the young people are missing the boat completely by not getting involved to the point where they study this type of playin' from people of this sort like Pops and Jabbo Smith. Jabbo was another gentle-man who played the fast, double-up passages. And if they don't get into that, then they don't know from whence it comes, you know. They don't know what they're involved in and the evolution of the whole thing.

WE: Do you think the media is at all responsible for that?

CT: Oh, why of course it is! Definitely, definitely. Absolutely. That's a sad note there, too.

We need to know the truth. And for those who are gonna get involved and *stay* involved and really master their crafts—they're gonna be involved in jazz—they *need* to know what it was all about. Because it didn't all just start with Coltrane, you know [laughter].

PR: Miles Davis has named you as an early favorite. Since you both came from the same town, do you have any special recollections of him?

CT: Oh yeah, definitely. First of all, I knew his teacher very well—Buchanan—who later became principal of a few high schools in East St. Louis, which is where Miles was raised up. His father was a dentist, Dr. Davis, and Miles at this time was a fledgling kid on the horn. And Buchanan used to tell me, he says, "Come over and hear this kid. You gotta hear him, man." So I went over one day and met this little, timid, skinny kid, you know. And he played pretty good, but his only problem at that point was that he always wanted to use a vibrato, and Buchanan would sort of rap his knuckles and say, "Play that without that shakin' sound. You sound like an old man," he said. "You'll shake enough when you get old; just play straight." And I think that this is the thing that directed Miles to the pure, ice water clear–type sound which he developed. That straight tone, you know, which is so beautiful in jazz and so lyrical in his type of playing.

WE: Miles's music in the seventies, his so-called fusion innovations, have been particularly controversial. Do you have an opinion about that?

CT: Yeah, I do. Miles, as you know, is a very good friend of mine, and he's a person who's a rather difficult person to get to talk to and to get beyond a certain invisible shield which he wears. And I don't know exactly why he turned out to be that type of person, except that jazz people have always endured such difficulties and hardships tryin' to get an opportunity to do their thing, as you well know, so it could be that a little bitterness and resentment on the part of the powers that be as far as lettin' them get to do what they wanted to do.

But he's a very *warm* person once you get to know him. And Miles is also an enterprising person. He's from a wealthy family. And Miles likes money. And Miles is very aware of the fact that the type of music that people are buying today is not the kind that he was accustomed to playing—which would naturally give vent to, you know, his feelings and produce what he felt was good music.

So I think it's a matter of economics. He found that it was fashionable, as far as the buyers and the media is concerned, for this kind of music to be played and to be accepted, so he got involved. And as it turned out, he took a stab at it just for a trial, and *one venture* turned out to be probably much more successful than his whole previous year, during which he was involved in playing *his* type of music, so to speak. And I think he just went over that way to sort of survive. A lot of us have had to do many things that we haven't really loved doing. I worked in the studios in New York for twenty years, and I had to play an awful lot of things that I didn't particularly go home humming [laughter]. But I went home with my pockets jingling [laughter].

WE: Are you saying that Miles's music during this period lacked integrity?

CT: Well, not necessarily a lack of integrity. He's a very smart person, and I think he knows what he can do. And I wouldn't be surprised if in the next year or two Miles will turn around and make a wailing jazz album, sort of like things he used to play before, and people will say, "Wow! listen to that," you know. And he'll win back some of the fans that he possibly may have lost.

I could never put a person down. I don't think it's fair for anybody to put another person down for doing what they see fit to do. Who knows what motivates this person to do this thing. Could be maybe that he even enjoys doin' what he's doing, you know. So who are we to put one down. There's an old Indian prayer that says "Never criticize your neighbor until you have walked a mile in his moccasins" [laughter].

PR: Both you and Armstrong share a credo of joyousness. But much of the jazz in the sixties and seventies has a tragic air about it. How do you feel about that?

CT: Well, I have mixed emotions about that. It's kind of tragic in a sense that a person who has been oppressed—it may be a little difficult for you to understand the situation, because possibly you've never been an oppressed person. Maybe you've been free to do all the things you've wanted to do; maybe you've never been considered to be a second-class citizen. And when you feel that you can do whatever it is that you can do as well as anybody else and then you're hampered and stymied in your efforts to do this, it has a tendency to make you a little bitter, and if you allow it to seep deeply enough into your being, your personality becomes a part of that. And naturally if your personality becomes a part of that, your music, if you're a musician, your jazz is gonna reflect that.

So a lot of the music that you hear today is a music of resentment, and a lot of the activities and the bandstand habits that you witness are results of these things. People who are involved have been kicked around a bit, and they wanna just say, you know, "Why can't I do what I wanna do?" And as a result they get a little calloused, and their music comes out that way.

I've reason enough to be the same type of person, but I have the capacity for maintaining a great love for people and for beauty and for love, period. And I try to let that seep through and take over and sort of squash the would-be hatred that might be within. And when you've been attempted to be lynched two or three times and if you've been taken advantage of on several instances and all sorts of injustices have been flung your way, which has been the case with me, you would definitely have a justified cause to feel that way.

But I suppress all that, because I feel that if I turn bitter it's gonna make me ugly and make me frown. And I love to smile, I love love, and I love life and I love people, so I try to forget about those things. I don't think that I should allow myself to be lowered to that degree, you know. Of course, I don't *forget* those things that those people did to me. There are ways and means of, you know, retaliating. But I think you can catch more flies with sugar than you can with vinegar.

WE: In the past, racist obstacles were common for black jazz musicians on the road. Has this situation improved?

CT: Some of the situations are far better, and the living conditions are far better now when you're traveling in the South than they were years ago. We were relegated to stay in Miss Jones's house, Miss Green's house, across the tracks. I've slept in places that were so filthy and damp I wouldn't dare take off my clothes. I slept with my hat, overcoat, shoes, overshoes, everything on just to try to make it through the night. Get up in the morning, catch the bus, and go to the next place.

Also to play in areas where you were definitely faced with the type of segregation that would have a tendency to make you bitter, if you would succumb to that. Such as a place where you're playin' and the whites would be dancing down here, and the blacks are sittin' up in the balcony watching; and in some instances it was reversed, and the blacks were dancing, and the whites were up watching. And you're supposed to play your best, you know, give vent to your feelings. Create! You're a jazz musician, you know. You're an artist, so you got to create. So in order to keep a clear mind for creating you have to stamp out some of that would-be hatred.

PR: Back to a fun topic. You've made famous a kind of bluesy, wordless patter that you call "mumbles." How did that come about?

CT: Well, mumbles is sort of a put-on of all the old places in my home-town of St. Louis where they had sawdust-covered floors and the dens of iniquity, as they were referred to in those days. But actually, they were just places of refreshment where you could go in and buy a beer or what-ever and relax and listen to, generally, a piano player who in most in-stances played in the key of F-sharp. And if you ever felt like you wanted to sing—he usually played on an upright piano with the top of it which was triply laminated to withstand the weight of several steins of beer—and if you bought him a nice big cold beer he would be very happy to oblige you and play for you as you sang.

It didn't matter how good you sang, how bad you sang, nor what you sang about. But the minute you got into your song if you decided you were going to be extemporaneous and create somethin', which was the case in those days, you'd sing about how you felt in the mornin'. You'd go, "Well, I got up in the mornin'," and by the time you got to the second measure of whatever it was that you intended to sing about, it didn't mat-ter what was being sung about nor how good nor how bad. You could see the sawdust bouncin' from the floor about a foot high and the finger-poppin', and as Ellington would say, "the earlobe-tiltin' and the head-shakin'," you know, and the frivolity and the happiness just exuding throughout the whole place.

So it was my put-on of these people, and I did it for a party record. We'd finished this date with the Oscar Peterson Trio in Toronto, and we went through the date—when you've got a rhythm section like Oscar Peterson, Ray Brown, and Ed Thigpen, you don't usually fool around with too many takes. With that kind of background it's pretty easy to get it right in one or two takes. So we did the date in sort of record time, and we had more than enough for an album. So I asked them if they would do this for me. I always wanted to do it for a party record. Just to put it on in my home, you know, just for laughs and reactions. I asked Oscar and Ray if they'd do it, and they said, "Sure." When we got halfway through it, I looked at Oscar, and he was on the floor crackin' up. So he stopped and said, "Let's start over again. Let's do it. Let's put it in the album." So I says, "Well, there's not really . . ." and he says, "Oh, we'll take out something and put it in." So I said, "Well, I've got a slow version too." He said, "We'll put that in too" [laughter]. That's how the mumbles was born.[5]

WE: You are currently fronting a big band, and a recent recording of that band took first place in an international critics' poll.

CT: I didn't know that. Did we?

WE: Yeah. It won in the category Talent Deserving of Wider Recognition in *Down Beat* magazine.

CT: I never read those things. Half of those people don't know what the heck they're talking about anyhow [laughter].

WE: So this isn't a very coveted award?

CT: It's nice to be liked, but you gotta do what you gotta do, anyhow. If it hadn't won the award, I wouldn't have gone home and cried, you know. But I'm very grateful that it did, and I'm happy to hear that. I didn't know that. I really didn't.

PR: In a sense, you were prepared to lead a big band by playing with Basie and Ellington. Could you relate something about the experiences you had working with those two giants of the music?

CT: Yeah, well, I spent a little more time with Ellington than with Basie, and I think it's general knowledge to everyone who knows anything at all about the two gentlemen that Ellington was, as we say colloquially, a little "heavier" than Basie. Although Basie was endowed with a certain thing about swing in jazz that's just natural. Basie taught us all something that we use in clinics an awful lot—the importance of the utilization of space and time in improvisation.

You know, we get a lot of kids who want to play jazz and feel like they have to [play like crazy and fill up all the space] from the time they start to the time they finish. Basie taught us to slow down and play a note and use the space. Use the rhythm section. All that space in between is still a part of your solo. So Basie was very, very influential to me and to everybody who was associated with him and to jazz, period.

---

5. The album Terry is speaking about is *The Oscar Peterson Trio plus One.*

So in answer to your question, I usually refer to my stay with the Ellington band as having attended "the university of Ellingtonia" for nine years, and Basie was, of course, prep school leading up to that. I enjoyed very much working with both bands, and I became very close friends to both of the gentlemen. Basie and I are still very good friends, and Duke and I were very good friends until his untimely death.

PR: What did you think of Ellington as a man?

CT: Fantastic person. If I had to name a person who inspired me the most and the one man in this world whom I figured to be the *most* important, the most influential, and the greatest person that ever lived, I would say Duke Ellington. And I've read an awful lot about a lot of great people, and I've met an awful lot of great people, but Duke Ellington would win my vote.

PR: What kinds of things were special about him?

CT: There were things about Ellington that were just unexplainable but were just fantastic. Just a certain chemistry and electricity about him that sort of exuded and became a part of you, once you were around him, through the process of osmosis. And he had a way—you've probably heard the old saying that "Duke Ellington's band was his instrument." That's quite true. He had a way of utilizing guys in his band to the extent that they weren't even aware that they could give out themselves.

For instance, we did an album many years ago called *A Drum Is a Woman*. And in this suite he was depicting different roles of great jazz people from way back from the origin of jazz through the medium of music, and the parts were portrayed by different guys in the band. So he says to me, "Clark, you're going to do Buddy Bolden for me." I said, "Well, maestro, I don't know anything about Buddy Bolden." You know Buddy Bolden never recorded. He was off the scene before records were being made.

But anyhow, he says, "Oh, sure, you know Buddy Bolden. He was very romantic, and he loved the ladies. Every time you saw him he had a lady on each arm, and he was very suave and very debonair and very kind and very gentle, and yet he was very robust and very manly and very strong, and as a matter of fact, when he tuned up in New Orleans across the river in Algiers he used to bust glasses on people's tables over there." While he's talking to you, you imagine all these things, and he said, "Oh, he bent notes; he was very masterful at bending notes," which is a very important ingredient in jazz, you know. You have to vary the pitch from its origin to below or above the pitch and back and forth, etc.

In telling you all these things, he knows you're going to absorb them and listen. So he says, "Go ahead, give it a try." He hit some chords, and I played with a big, fat, full sound. He says, "That's it! That's Buddy Bolden!"

So he had a way of doing things like that. And he could write a passage, and he would pick certain sounds . . . For instance, when Rex Stewart was with the band—Rex had a knack for being able to do sort of a half-valve bubbly-type semitone with a third valve. Well, whenever he wrote a chart, whenever that E-natural came up in the section, he would give that part to Rex. You could always hear Rex with that little thing; nobody else could do that. Duke knew that, so he took advantage of it. Again it was proof that the band was his instrument.

Aside from that, he just had very suave and debonair ways with people, you know. And it was just a joy to be around him and to observe. He could mingle with kings and queens and ordinary common people. Everybody loved him. He was a beautiful man.

WE: You have the reputation of being a fine teacher, and you're in great demand at school workshops and clinics. What urged you in that direction?

CT: Being involved in the studio scene I noted a gross amount of complacency among the professionals. They would naturally have reached the point where they could play everything perfectly; they could read beautifully and flawlessly. So they would pass out a piece of music, zip right through it, and say "Next." And in the meanwhile they've got their racing forms out, or "Hey, I just saw a new house on sale, think I'll sell my boat." And it really got to be such a drag 'til it bothered me, you know? These people were great musicians, but they were no longer interested in jazz and music from the [standpoint of] feeling and from the standpoint of the perpetuation of our craft.

So I got out of that and got involved with the young people, and it's been very, very rewarding. And I hope that I shall always remain with young people, because it keeps you fresh and young. For a fifty-four-year-old cat, you know, I like to think that I'm still young, that it keeps you fresh, keeps you alert, and keeps you buoyant and keeps you on top of things, 'cause kids will ask you questions, and they make you think back for the answers.

And many of the answers are not in books, you know. You have to really figure out ways and means of getting these things across to them that we used to learn by osmosis. Years ago there were bands in every hamlet and township and city in the world, and as a kid became a musician, one who was able to play in these little territorial bands, he graduated as his talent grew from one to a higher degree to another, on up until he reached the status of what was generally referred to as "the big-band plateau."

And we find that some of the things, as I said before, are not in the books, and those of us who were there with the older ones, who sort of helped create the whole scene, we're able to pass it on, sort of like masonry was taught years ago from mouth to ear. It's very difficult to write four or five measures of music for a kid and expect that kid to be able to play it in a manner that a jazz player played it twenty or forty years before he was born. So it's up to us to sort of link the gap, you know, and void that vacuum that ordinarily would be there.

PR: Not only are you leading a big band, but you also formed your own record company, Etoile Records. Why?

CT: Well, sooner or later a person who is conscientious about what he's doing and believes in his craft, he just gets tired of people telling him when he walks into an office that "it doesn't have that Madison Avenue marketability." Well, you get tired of that. They're trying to tell you in other words that you gotta do it like *I* say do it, because this is what I'm gonna expose to the media. And what you're sayin' and what you're doin' doesn't fit into my program.

So you get a little bit sick of that sometimes, and you want to put out a record because you *believe* in it. You know it's good music, and you know it's what you have lived all your life, that's what you want to pass on and leave here for posterity, so you put your money where your mouth is, that's all.

So to the tune of eighteen thousand dollars—I made a few mistakes, because this was a live concert at Carnegie Hall, and I know that they had a bum crew there for recording, so I had to pay that crew plus bring in my own crew and pay for all the rental of both sets of equipment, and I had to do a lot of editing to weed out certain sounds that weren't conducive to the record.[6] So it cost me a lot more money than I should have paid, but at least I got it out.

6. *Clark Terry's Big Bad Band in Concert—Live*, Etoile Records, 1970.

So as I said, you put your money where your mouth is. It cost me eighteen grand, and this was put out about three or four years ago, and I've gotten back about nine grand, so I'm halfway back. And if it takes me ten more years, 1 don't care. All 1 was interested in was provin' to the people that you don't have to do what everybody says you gotta do. You don't *gotta* do nothin' but stay the way you are and pay taxes and die [laughter].

SELECTED DISCOGRAPHY

Introducing Clark Terry. EmArcy 36007. 1955.

With Duke Ellington. *A Drum Is a Woman.* Columbia Special Products CL951. 1956.

Serenade to a Bus Seat. Riverside SMJ-6209J (Japanese import). 1957.

With Gary McFarland. *The Jazz Version of "How To Succeed In Business Without Really Trying."* Verve V/V6-8443. 1961.

With Oscar Peterson. *The Oscar Peterson Trio plus One.* Mercury 60975. 1964.

The Clark Terry–Bob Brookmeyer Quintet. *Gingerbread Man.* Mainstream 6086. 1966.

Clark Terry's Big Bad Band in Concert—Live. Etoile CPR1A. 1970. (Recorded at Carnegie Hall.)

Clark Terry and His Jolly Giants. Vanguard VSD 79365. 1975.

Memories of Duke. Pablo Today 2312-118. 1980.

Clark Terry–Red Mitchell. Enja 5011. 1986.

Portraits. Chesky JD2. 1989.

HENRY THREADGILL

Photograph by Jules T. Allen.   Used with permission.

M ulti-instrumentalist Henry Threadgill is one of the most important musicians to emerge from the jazz avant-garde of the late sixties. A gifted soloist on the alto, tenor, and baritone saxophones, flute, and clarinet, Threadgill is also one of the finest living composers in jazz. He has taken top honors in the composer category in *Down Beat* magazine's critics' poll every year from 1988 to 1991; he won the same award in the *Down Beat* readers' poll in 1988 and 1989. Equally at home writing luscious ballads, pieces without key centers, basic blues, or wide-open big-band charts, Threadgill uses sources that are similarly kaleidoscopic: ragtime, traditional New Orleans, bop, rhythm and blues, West African forms, and Indonesian gamelan have all found their way into his music.

Born in 1944 in Chicago, Threadgill started on the piano at nine, switching to the tenor and alto saxophones in high school. He attended Wilson Junior College and later earned a degree in flute and composition from the American Conservatory of Music.

Threadgill entered the army in 1967 and served a year in Vietnam. After his discharge in 1969, he joined the Chicago-based Association for the Advancement of Creative Musicians (AACM), founded in 1964. In the sixties the AACM was preeminent among jazz organizations established in metropolitan centers around the nation. Musicians affiliated early on with the AACM included Muhal Richard Abrams, Chico Freeman, George Lewis, Douglas Ewart, Rufus Reid, Anthony Braxton, and the five members of the Art Ensemble of Chicago.

The AACM received very little domestic critical attention during its first five years. In 1968, however, several of its leading figures toured Europe and recorded prolifically for small continental labels. This exposure prompted the scrutiny of the international music press and greatly enlarged the stature, if not the pocketbooks, of the AACM players. In the mid-seventies Threadgill and many of his AACM cohorts moved to New York City. Their presence inspired solidarity among musicians indebted to the works of John Coltrane, Ornette Coleman, and Cecil Taylor, among others. It also helped catalyze interest in the history of black music in this country, as well as in many of jazz's often-neglected pioneers, whose music was frequently quoted by their AACM descendants.

After moving to New York, Threadgill played for more than a decade in the celebrated trio Air, formed collaboratively in 1972 by Threadgill, bassist Fred Hopkins, and percussionist Steve McCall. The unit was dissolved in 1985, but over its thirteen-year existence Air recorded a dozen excellent albums that showcased this small ensemble's finely crafted and complex, yet accessible music. Perhaps their most popular record was *Air Lore*, a 1979 release on Arista Novus that featured the trio's updated versions of Joplin rags and blues and stomps by Jelly Roll Morton.

More recently, Threadgill has concentrated on writing and arranging for larger ensembles, such as the critically acclaimed Sextette, which he led for five years, and its 1990 successor, an expanded combo called Very, Very Circus, with the unusual instrumentation of two tubas, two guitars, sax, trombone (or french horn), and drums. Aside from Threadgill's continued achievements as a jazz writer and bandleader, since 1984 he has written several nonjazz works, such as his first and second string quintets, both premiered at Carnegie Recital Hall in New York.

Throughout each stage of Henry Threadgill's remarkable odyssey, from inner-city Chicago and the core of the jazz avant-garde to a position of increasing stature as a contemporary American composer, his music has been earmarked by a keen sense of dramatic development, a rhythmic volatility that seems to propel his works into constantly changing directions, and a reverence for the past with a view toward the future.

Recorded 1979
PR: Henry, how did you get started in music?
HT: I've been playing music just about all of my life. Professionally, I've been playing since about 1962. I've played all types: the usual thing—learning music, music school, music lessons, hanging out, playing the music in the street, marching bands, veterans' post bands, polka bands, blues bands, the whole thing.

In about 1961 I came in touch with Muhal Richard Abrams. At that time he and Eddie Harris and some other people were running the Experimental Band in Chicago. Eddie Harris was the first person to start this band. Then Muhal Richard Abrams kind of took it over a little bit later; I think Eddie's other commitments pulled him away from it.

There was a band set up where they were doing a vision of music, and you could take things in there and get them played. That's what I did. I went in there initially not to play, but I took some of my material there that I had written for big band to hear it, to get a reading on it. Later I began to play with the group. It was a very good group; a lot of very important older musicians were some stable elements in it, where you could really learn something.

In 1962 I met Joseph Jarman, who later became a member of the AACM, and Roscoe Mitchell. We got together and had a group for a couple of years and did a lot of work together. The AACM sprang up at that time—the early sixties. Parallel to that was a group running in St. Louis, Black Artist's Group, and there were some people there, the Bowie Brothers. We had a relationship established with Detroit at that time— with Marcus Belgrave and others up there. Actually I was coming out of the service at that time, so I was stationed around St. Louis. I stayed a lot with Oliver Lake, and I got to play with a lot of players in the particular idiom I was working in.

Leo Smith and I had a group together for a long time, called Integra, with Lester Lashley. He's a bass player, trombone player, and a very fine artist—painter and craftsman. He's a musician in the AACM. We had a group together with a dancer and an actress. In the late sixties going into the seventies, Leo and I went to Europe, about 1970, '71, something like that. Lester didn't go with us, so we picked up Leonard Jones. He's another bass player out of Chicago that had been associated with AACM. He had been living in Europe, so we worked around Europe together.
PR: When did Air come into the picture?
HT: When I got back from Europe, the group that [Anthony] Braxton, Leo, and Leroy Jenkins had broke up, and I'd heard Steve McCall play with them—actually I had heard Steve McCall play previous to that, on Joseph Jarman's first record date, *Song For*—and I was really impressed with his playing.[1] So when they broke up, I was interested in getting with him. I was working with different size groups—quartets, sextets—trying to get a working group and get some kind of direction in terms of what I wanted to do. So when Steve was free, I got in touch with him and Fred Hopkins, who was living next door to me at the time. And we started working together on a show called *Hotel*. It was a show based around the

1. Joseph Jarman, *Song For*, Delmark Records, 1967.

music of Scott Joplin. I did a lot of writing for that show, and the three of us just continued to stay together after that. We formed the group Air out of that.

We've been together about seven years. And running parallel to that, I've worked with Muhal Abrams' sextet, with Roscoe Mitchell, who's done a lot of saxophone things, and with Braxton, Jarman, Leroy Jenkins, Arthur Blythe. I'm still constantly learning things, you know, the longer I live and keep working at this music, and learning about the creative energy involved in it. And that's just in the way of music. I'm learning quite a bit from dance and theater. I've spent a lot of time working with theater people—doing shows, writing and conducting for shows, things like that. So it goes on and on that way.

WE: Growing up in Chicago must have had its advantages, at least musically speaking.

HT: Where I grew up in Chicago, on Thirty-third Avenue and Thirty-first Street, was really the cradle of the entertainment community, because Bird and all of them played up and down the street. Lester Young, Charlie Parker, Fats Navarro, Johnny Griffin, Dexter Gordon, played right there. I was a kid, but it was in the community. There was no separation. It wasn't a matter of going out to Mill Run or having to travel twenty-five minutes to get to a place and then pay an exorbitant rate to get in. They were right there in the community. People like Sam Cooke, Nat "King" Cole, went to school and lived in that area.

Chicago is a segregated type of housing situation; they have Polish people here, and black people here, and Puerto Rican people here. So the black people were playing jazz and blues, and any time Bird and them were in town, you knew how they were going to be as far as the way music was being put out. People weren't being programmed as much; there were jazz programs on the radio, blues programs, you know what I mean. And record stores that piped music out into the street would play everything. I mean, one minute you might be listening to the Clovers, walking down the street coming out of the record shop, and the next minute a cat might play something by Lester Young, then turn around and play something by Muddy Waters, then Rosetta Tharpe, Mahalia Jackson. So as a kid you were constantly exposed to it. Now it's a different matter.

WE: What's different?

HT: Well, the programming has changed. The monolithic type of idea of making a single thing pay off 1000 percent is a much greater force today. It's funny how people think we've attained a certain liberal view-point. It's a much more controlled situation. You listen to radio today, you don't hear the variety we know exists. There's no reason in the world you should hear the same thing all day long on the radio from station to station. There's no real creative programming going on. People are pro-grammed to buy, feel, and to act certain ways on the basis of what they hear, what the industry puts on them.

PR: Do you blame the media for the current state of affairs?

HT: Yes, well, this type of irresponsibility can be traced to several places. When one studies the history of the world, what part art plays in all the major empires, how Hitler used music to control the masses in a cere-monial and ritual way, how it's used in church situations, how art is used to set up an emotional and psychological fabric in which people are then impressed and led. This is the same type of thing that's been happening more in America since the late sixties, this type of programming. People don't really make their [own] decisions. It's like we read about in psy-chology, a type of control behavior where you can make people do a certain thing with music, and believe me, it's completely understood by people in political positions, people in capitalistic positions, people that affect this economy.

PR: Isn't it a matter of choice, to either go a commercial route or to make music that's more personally rewarding?

HT: I don't know if it's more rewarding. I know it's more rewarding for me. Everyone has to determine for themselves what the treasures are, what the benefits are, what they reap in life. I think the mere fact of the time that I was born, and the time that I started developing as a musician, had a lot to do with me making that type of decision, and who I am, too, you know.

Like I said, I started playing music in high school around 1959, and one should understand what was happening in America at that time in terms of clubs and things. The club thing was changing; they were dis-appearing, and Charlie Parker had died in 1955. By the time we got to 1962 or 1963, it had been a whole other turnover in the music. Brand-new elements had surfaced. I was very young at that time and could relate to those elements because it expressed what I felt, and it seemed to ex-press what I saw in front of me in terms of the world.

The things that Charlie Parker set up, he did in response to the socio-logical, psychological, and spiritual background that was prevalent at that time—in the forties. What he did was valid in reference to the backdrop, and it was an expression of his emotions. But when you get to the sixties, a lot changed in terms of what one was going to relate to. Different things was happening. People were talking about "God is dead," the whole drug movement jumped up, everybody wanted more license to do things in their individual lives, so that started to be a part of your total expression. I didn't feel that I could really use the music of Charlie Parker to go on to the late sixties and seventies and express myself. I had to learn that, of course, but to continue that, no.

WE: But you didn't start on the saxophone, did you?

HT: The first instrument I played was the piano. When I was a kid I took piano lessons for a long time. My aunt would teach; she was a pianist and singer, and she married a very fine bass player who was with Ahmad Jamal for a long time. So I got into piano because it was in the house. When she got married, she married a jazz musician, so I fell in love and wanted to play the bass, but I was really too small to play it. Later I decided I wanted to play the drums. I didn't know what it was that I wanted to do with percussion, but I used to mess around with drums, congas, different things like that. 'Til I *really* heard Charlie Parker, and I decided that I wanted to play the saxophone [laughter], there wasn't no more doubts about what it was gonna be. Nothing was vague anymore, you know.

WE: Because of Parker, did you start on alto?

HT: I started on tenor. It was a long time before I played alto. I played tenor, then I started playing clarinet, and then I started playing baritone saxophone. Then I became interested in bass clarinet by the time I got to junior college, which was a very interesting time in my life. In 1962 I met Bob Pulliam, a very fine musician in Chicago, and that was the time I met Jarman and a number of other people who were very important. Writers, poets, dancers, artists were all gathered at this one junior college.

It was strange; there was just a host of "outside" creative people—Jack DeJohnette, the list goes on. It was called Wilson Junior College; now it's called Kennedy-King Junior College. Malachi Favors was there, Eddie Williams, Eddie Harris, Bunky Green, Louis Hall, the late Christopher Clark, and Charles Gaddy, Dracia Khalid—it was almost impossible to believe.

That was in the period that the AACM was being formed, '61, '62,

'63. All these people would come up to Chicago, like George Coleman, Frank Strozier, Charles Lloyd—there was a whole group of cats who came up from Memphis—Essex Rainer, an alto player; Billy Dupree, an incredible bass player. The level of involvement in what was going on, the music courses, I just couldn't believe it. We were studying like mad-men. We would really take things to the extreme. For instance, say an instructor assigned some homework to a student. We just wouldn't do a homework assignment one time; we'd do it maybe fifty different ways. That would be a regular thing. Because we were really out to find out what was going on. It was that way in terms of the writers, the poets, the painters who were there.

WE: And from this setting, the AACM was born, correct?

HT: The AACM got together for the same reason most people get to-gether. They had some problems; the musicians were having some prob-lems. Cats didn't like to be told on a gig they couldn't play their music. They came together to play their own music, not to change anything. I don't think that anyone was even thinking of something new or of what kind of force they were going to be.

The one reason the AACM stands out, and I'm not playing the AACM down, is the fact that they were organized. What was in the air in Chicago was in the air every place. The difference that Chicago made was that they got organized. And any time you organize, the effect is felt much more strongly, and it's a much more lasting effect. There were plenty of musicians walking around in lots of cities that was feeling and thinking the same ideas, because if something is in the air, it's in the air. When they organized, that was one of the main things, to encourage musicians to play and write their own music. It grew like that.

And they had a built-in study situation where musicians worked with each other trading ideas, learning each other's techniques and different ways of dealing with music. And there was a music school for students, so you had some kind of bond there that you could lean on. You had a num-ber of brothers you could lean on—your comrades. They weren't isolated from you. If you were hungry and out of work, you could get your fill anyway.

We used to go out in patrols in the AACM. We bought us a Xerox machine, and we ran off flyers and cards. And we sent a group of guys over to this El stop, and a group of guys over to this El stop, to pass out stuff. And then we'd go out with big posters and wire and put posters up on poles all over the city. We did every step of the work, every step of the work, every step of it.

PR: Were you getting help through grants?

HT: It was a long time before the AACM began to get any type of granting money from the federal government. You know, the National Endowment for the Arts hasn't even been set up that long to supply money to jazz musicians. That's a new category. Before, you had to apply to the music category, and your works were dismissed because they weren't, quote, "classical." We were going after small grants from business and granting organizations, and they weren't giving us anything.

But as a matter of fact, we weren't interested initially in grants. It was such an excitement about the music and involvement in it at that time. That was enough. But as the organization grew and had more business to take care of, we had to get some type of funding. So we have been working on that level through the seventies. It's been about trying to be funded, because you can't seem to do enough unless you're funded. The larger organizations are funded—the operas, the ballets, et cetera. All these things are funded, and this music is the only real indigenous music out of America. We felt that should be funded too.

PR: Could you find work in clubs?

HT: The clubs weren't into hiring us. If we were going to come in and play standards, you had a better chance of being hired, and still, the chances were slim. The club situation had just diminished so terribly in the sixties. We started playing in galleries, churches, storefronts, things of that nature. Wherever we could set up, in some community center, anywhere, and produce our own concerts. We might have one or two concerts going each week, every week. We'd also be having a big band working in some club if we could get them to give us one night. We'd work off the door or something like that. They'd never give us any outfront money. It was out of the question.

WE: Labeled a free jazz player, did your fortunes change as the sixties ended and the different era of the seventies opened up?

HT: I think by the time you get into the late sixties and early seventies people had matured, and the whole period of the charlatan had really come to an end. Either people had now learned their craft and really knew something about what they were doing, or they were fooling people. Anyway, the musicians that were working in the area that we were working in had been so badly labeled and abused, not only by the press, but by older musicians who were working in other styles. We had been slandered something awful, you know. "They don't know scales. They don't know how to play 'All the Things You Are.' They don't know all the previous things." That wasn't true, but of course nothing is born without a price. You have to pay the price for that music coming on the scene.

So by the time you got to the seventies, with all these things having gone against you, the people who lasted were people who really knew what they were doing. Sure, there were a lot of cats who got up and couldn't play. I mean, they used the times as an excuse not to learn the craft and to learn their instruments correctly. A lot of people got up there in the bandwagon screamin', hollerin', and got famous for different things, you know. But they didn't last, and like I said, only those people who knew what they were doing lasted.

That community of Chicago alone could not support what we were doing. Those initial years of putting an organization together and setting up concerts—you couldn't do that for the rest of your life and support families, or even support yourself, working infrequently. The support of your comrades, that works for a while, but you can't go through ten years of that. You got to have money to live. You know, the same thing everybody else has. The cat that works at the post office, you got to have the same thing he has.

PR: Speaking of those older players, some of those guys still are your musical heroes, aren't they?

HT: I have a lot of respect for people like Dexter and Griffin. I love their work, always have loved it. They are true to what they believe in; they've stayed with the type of ideas they wanted to stay with. What I'm doing now, I'm staying with that—someone's gonna replace me. The large group of people I circulate among—Braxton, Oliver Lake, all of them—it won't be long before their names will be thought of in a more stylistic tradition and won't seem so radical.

We're not really radical at all. There's really no such thing as being radical, I don't think. You can't be that new. We're not doing anything new—it's just an extension. Your children are going to start using words differently; they're going to add more meaning to them. The jargon is going to change; the colloquialisms are going to be changed and added to. That's all we're doing. Nothing just jumps out of space. Things just don't appear. You don't even catch a cold that way. It's a continuum.

People think, "What's this have to do with it?" Well, I understand the type of programming that's going on in America, where there's been a break in information to the people. So you get this cultural lag, because people haven't been exposed to what's going on—the newer developments in the music. So I'm never offended by that, you know. All I can say about it is "Well, they don't have that book in their library."

WE: You've spent a lot of time in Europe. Did you find European audiences more responsive to your music?

HT: The Europeans have been involved in art for years. This is a young country. It's only two hundred years old. We're just babies. The Europeans have had a chance to be corrupt and go back on their ways, practice Christianity and all forms of it, exploit every nation on the planet, and look at their wares. In 1900 they had the first Indonesian orchestra, gamelan, in Paris. That's all part of their life-style.

The large influx of black American artists in the twenties and thirties to Europe completely indoctrinated those people to the value and worth of what the black artists in America were doing. Then, their world interest in art goes back to the Greek and Roman empires. America—we talk about it lots of times, but we forget exactly what it is we're talking about. We're talking about someone who is in puberty, two hundred years old. God!

PR: How well did the older expatriate jazz musicians accept what you and other younger players were doing over there in the early seventies?

HT: Johnny Griffin, he's been over there a long time. We played opposite Griffin over there, and I was with Griffin here in the States—in New York and in Chicago. I never felt so much that the musicians that became expatriates were the ones opposed so much to what was going on as much as a lot of musicians that stayed in the States. I really felt they put down the developments in the music. It's really amazing. It's kind of hard to talk about without calling people names, and I just can't do that. It seems a strange thing to put down someone who's been spending ten or fifteen or twenty years practicing at something. Putting that person down simply because you don't like what they're doing and can't assimilate what they're doing in terms of your own thinking!

When one has become stylistically set in one's ways, it's hard to reconcile what other people are doing. Once you get stylistic, you stop. There's no more development. I believe what Coleman Hawkins was involved in. He always said, "Just keep your mind open." A lot of people close their minds to the developments that go on. You have to stay abreast—that's your job if you're a musician. It's your job to learn how the language is changing.

SELECTED DISCOGRAPHY

Air Song. Why Not 7123. 1975.
Air Lore. Arista Novus AN 3014. 1979.
X-75. Vol. I. Arista Novus AN 3013. 1979.
Air Mail. Arista Novus AN 0049. 1980.
When Was That? About Time 1004. 1982.
Just the Facts and Pass the Bucket. About Time 1005. 1983.
Air Show #1. Black Saint 0099. 1986.
You Know the Number. RCA Novus 3013-1-N. 1986.
Easily Slip into Another World. RCA Novus 3025-1-N. 1987.
Spirit of Nuff . . . Nuff. Black Saint 120134-2. 1991.

BILL WATROUS

Courtesy Selmer Corporation

T rombonist Bill Watrous is considered one of the supreme virtuosos in all of jazz on an instrument that is among the most exacting to play. His speed and control are impeccable, and his execution is vivid at even the most blistering tempos. But above all there is his sound, big and burnished at all levels of his astonishing range.

Born in Middletown, Connecticut, in 1939, Watrous seemed destined from the start for the jazz trombone. His father, Ralph, was a fine trombonist who played with several bands in the thirties and forties, including Paul Whiteman's. Watrous' exposure to jazz was widened by hearing big bands on radio broadcasts and by catching touring bands led by the likes of Count Basic, Lionel Hampton, and Benny Goodman at the nearby Ocean Beach Park Ballroom.

In the late fifties Watrous did a four-year stint with the navy. In 1959, a transfer from San Diego to the Brooklyn Navy Yard enabled him to jam with a variety of dixieland bands in New York City. When he was twenty-one and just out of the service, Watrous joined the band let by famed trombonist Kai Winding, an unusual aggregation composed of four trombones plus a rhythm section. Later Watrous studied harmony with ill-starred pianist-composer Herbie Nichols. Nichols, grievously underrated during his lifetime, served as an important early mentor for Watrous.

Watrous' abilities as a straightahead, swinging melody player helped him get extended gigs in the late sixties with television bands on the Merv Griffin and Dick Cavett shows. A sought-after studio musician by day, Watrous at night found work in big bands led by Johnny Richards, Quincy Jones, Woody Herman, and Thad Jones and Mel Lewis. He also played for a brief period in the jazz-rock bands Ten Wheel Drive and Eclipse.

In 1973 Watrous hit the mother lode when he formed one of the tightest and most fiercely swinging big bands in recent memory, the Manhattan Wildlife Refuge. Its debut recording won rave reviews from the critics, as did its second album, which earned a Grammy nomination.[1] By 1977, however, this band had fallen on hard times financially.

1. Bill Watrous, *Manhattan Wildlife Refuge*, Columbia Records, 1973; Bill Watrous, *The Tiger of San Pedro*, Columbia Records, 1975.

In 1976 Watrous resettled in southern California and organized Refuge West, a touring big band that remains unrecorded. During the eighties he did a series of small-group sessions for Famous Door Records that exploited his bebop roots, and he became a fixture in Los Angeles recording studios. More recently, he has collaborated with composer-arranger Patrick Williams on two mainstream big-band dates. For the first recording, *Someplace Else*, Watrous was recorded in live performance backed by an eighty-nine-piece orchestra.[2] The follow-up, *Reflections*, was a 1987 Grammy Award winner and featured Bill Watrous' debut as a vocalist on "Dear Bix," Dave Frishberg's wistful homage to the legendary cornetist of the twenties.[3]

Recorded 1980
PR: Bill, what prompted your interest in music?
BW: It's actually quite simple. I started out playing trombone as a child. Having a father around who was very prolific musically on the trombone, and you know how kids are, your main goal if you are really brought up decently by your parents is to emulate them. I picked up the trombone very easily and went through grade school. I was sort of a prodigy on it at the time because I could play anything I heard.
PR: Did you have formal lessons?
BW: No, I never did. I just listened to *him* play, and I listened to music in general. I was a sponge when it came to music, and there was very little that escaped me that was worthwhile.
WE: What kind of music was around the house?
BW: Oh God, everything. First of all, when I was a little kid we didn't have a television set 'til I was around nine or ten, so up to the age of ten we listened to a lot of radio. And I remember a lot of the great evenings where they would have all these coast-to-coast hookups that were sponsored by the musicians' union. And you'd hear all the great bands, and some of the stuff that I heard impressed me so much that I really got deadly serious about the music. And then I equated it with what I heard my dad involved in, and it suddenly rescued me from a rather oblivious childhood.

2. Bill Watrous, *Someplace Else*, Soundwings Records, 1987.
3. Bill Watrous, *Reflections*, Soundwings Records, 1985.

I didn't exactly know what I wanted to do, you know, and suddenly I found there was something that I could just *do*. I mean, not perfectly, there was lots of things I had to learn—there is still a lot of things. But it was something that "Hey, I can do this, and I can make sounds," and it was exciting, and it bailed me out of a rather mundane childhood. So after I got through grammar school and played in a high school band . . .

PR: No lessons up to this time?

BW: No lessons.

PR: Did you know how to read music?

BW: No, not so you'd notice [laughter]. There was an awful lot of moments of nervousness, but usually after I heard it and saw the notes as it went by, I would begin to associate with it. Thanks to Dick Van Venuti, my band director in high school, he saw to it—he put me to work on theory for a whole summer before I finally got into the band, so that when I got there I could at least identify what key we were playing in and notes on the staff and lines and spaces and all. So you pick it up fast. Really, when you come down to it, the actual science of music, such as the theory and all, is not that hard.

PR: So your academic training came after you were proficient on the horn?

BW: Yeah. I sort of worked my way into the academic area to the point where I've amassed quite a store of musical knowledge, you know, all these years. It's just by osmosis, not necessarily setting out to do it, but it happens. But I was encouraged, and I got the opportunity while going to New London High School in Connecticut—God, it was a stone's throw from the city, and we used to bop down to the city all the time to hear bands.

I got to hear an awful lot of people, and I got to talk to Sonny Rollins outside Birdland one night. I never thought I'd ever see the day. I just was awestruck. I was talking to him about—asking him about tunes and stuff, and he was *very* nice, man. He stood there and talked to me about changes and stuff. And I was really impressed. I talked to Maynard [Ferguson]; he'd come through with his band. And it wasn't about two years later that I was standing on that same bandstand with Kai Winding's band, as a matter of fact.

WF: You were in your early twenties?

BW: I was twenty-one and had joined the Kai Winding Band. I couldn't read a note of music, and it bugged the hell out of him, 'cause I could *blow* like a maniac, and he couldn't figure out how I could play that well and not really have anything down. But as it came along on that band I got my reading chops together; then when I got off that band and got into the studios in New York, then I *really* pulled it together doing live TV. And I trained that element of me to try to go for the best take I can whenever I play. If you do it correctly and concentrate and are not all drunk and juiced out when you get there, it'll come to you.

WE: When you made those trips to New York, who else impressed you?

BW: You know who really more than anyone killed me and that was Phil Woods. I just went ape the first time I heard this guy play, and this continues to this day. Every time I hear the man play. He is probably the most perfect jazz musician alive.

WE: Have you worked with him?

BW: Oh yes. Many times. On recordings in studios, in jazz parties—we played "Quick-Silver" together out at Dick Gibson's jazz party about a million miles an hour this past year. He's perfect, and he's exciting at the same time. If you can be perfect and then have something to say, too, that's a rarity. Jazz musicians like Woods come around about once every fifty years.

PR: How'd you get into Kai Winding's band?

BW: I called him up. I was just getting out of the service, and I called him up and said, "Hey, I play the trombone, and you got a spot for me?" And he didn't, but he said, "Look, I'll hear you if you wanna come by. Come on by to Lynn Oliver's." And I came by Lynn Oliver's. Geez, my car broke down on the way there, and I ran the rest of the way, with a trombone in hand. Up two and a half flights of stairs.

I got up half of the first flight, and I heard them playing. And they were playing great, and I thought, "I'm not going in that room. I'm not going in that room. I'm leaving now." And then I realized I had nowhere to go. My car was broken down around fourteen blocks south of Lynn Oliver's studio, which was up on Eighty-ninth Street and Broadway. So I said, "Oh, geez, I better go up and face the music." So I straggled up the stairs and sort of slipped in the room and sat down against the wall and listened to this thing.

At the time they were playing "Round About Midnight," a Monk composition, and they finally got through with that, and they played another tune. And then he came over and introduced himself and said, "Well, look," he says, "we'd like to hear you." And then he had this one trombone player, Eddie Green, step out for a minute and let me go in and play. He says, "Well, what would you like to play?" Which was nice of him. I said, "How about 'The Preacher'?" because I had taken the parts off the record down at the Navy Music School by this time.

And we played it, and he let me play around fifteen choruses. He just let me play, and he says, "Oh, man, forget it, gotta have this kid." We played a couple more tunes, and then we sight-read something I hadn't seen, and then he knew the answer. That was the end of it. But the rhythm section dug it enough so that they talked him into going through with it and hiring me anyway. They said, "He'll pick it up." And I did.

PR: Was that your first big gig?

BW: Actually, my first big gig was with Roy Eldridge in New London, Connecticut, while I was still there. You know Roy came through town and wanted a trombone player to play with him, and I was the only one in town who could play. And I was playing quite well at the time, so he added me just for the night. And that was really exciting, man. Boy, he has *energy*. And then the next one was with Billy Butterfield, and that's the only main names I would say before Kai came on.

WE: We heard a story about you getting on the stage with Charles Mingus when you were young. Is that true?

BW: Yeah. That's a true story. It was down at the Café Wha. I was still in the service at the time. It was the bass player from Detroit, and he was after me. Bob Friday was his name. He says, "Hey baby, you gotta come on down, man." He sat around and taught me the tunes that I would probably have to know. He says, "Here's what they'll probably play." That was "Confirmation," "Quick-Silver," "Moose the Mooche," "Chasin' the Bird," "Constellation"—the standard bop repertoire, mainly Charlie Parker and Bud Powell tunes. With an occasional Horace Silver tune that would pop, you know.

So I checked myself out and had it pretty well down. We went down there, and at the time Mingus was up on the stage playin', and Lonnie Hillyer and Charlie McPherson were there. And I had played with them before with Bob Friday in a loft, and they saw me, and they said, "Hey, Brother, come on up, man, play, you know, blow." But bear in mind this was at the Café Wha; this was a *tight* scene, man. You didn't even step in that place with your horn unless you meant business. There was no games played in this joint. You went in there, and you either played or you got the hell out of there. If you went up on that stand and didn't play, you probably would get lynched if you left there, you know. You would never come back again if you went in and bombed out.

So Friday had me all primed up for this thing, and we go in, and Mingus is on the stand, and Barry Harris is playin' piano, and Clifford Jarvis is one of the tenor players. A whole Detroit crew—I do believe Elvin Jones was playing drums. It was a heavy-duty group.

So anyway, Lonnie Hillyer and Charlie McPherson, trumpet and alto player, were the front line, and they were playin' "Confirmation" at that time. In fact, they were into the trumpet solo when they said, "Hey, come on up." So I come up on the band, and I'm standin' there, and I'm aware of these evil, baleful glances from Charlie Mingus, but I was *so* anxious to play that I didn't give a damn.

So Lonnie got through playin', and Charlie got through playin', and then I started playin' on these changes of "Confirmation." And all of a sudden I hear this big Boom! Mingus had slammed his bass down—just set it down really hard—and marched off the stand yellin' and gesturin' back at the bandstand. He says, "Hey, man, there's only two cats on the stand when we started. Now we got three cats on the stand, man. I ain't here to accompany a whole bunch of soloists. I ain't no workhorse. Man, I don't have to do this. This is my own time, and I'm on my time bein' here, and I'll play with who I wanta. I don't want to play on the stand with that boy."

WE: Was that the end of the set?

BW: No, no, absolutely not. He left the stand, and we keep playin', without him. No bass player. In fact, I was in the middle of my solo, and I had two choices, either take the damn horn down, pack it up, and slink out of there or tough it out. And I chose to tough it out, and I toughed it out to the tune of about nine choruses.

WE: Did Mingus leave?

BW: No, as a matter of fact, Mingus was at the bar. Mingus had turned his back to the proceedings and refused to acknowledge anything that was goin' on. He never did speak to me. He never did speak to me at all. But Lonnie and Charlie McPherson did, and so did Elvin—Elvin loved it. He dug it, man. When I was playin' he was throwing kicks and doin' stuff and all. He dug it, man. He came over and gave me a great big hug like a bear. And I remember it to this day, he's sayin' "Hey, man." And then later on he gave me one of these things in the leg that I'm told he does to

everyone, just clownin' around, you know. And I took two steps and col-
lapsed. He just did it to me like, "Hey, you're one of the boys now, here.
Survive this, man." I had this big purple bruise on the side of my leg for
about a week after that.

PR: Did the Mingus incident happen about the same time you met
Herbie Nichols?

BW: Well, this is all just previous to the time that I met Herbie Nichols.
Now, Herbie at that time that I met him had a few albums out and had
gotten absolutely no response from the jazz public. They all thought he
was weird and spacey.

You know, in my estimation anyway, and anybody who wants to can
dispute this, but I consider Herbie the missing link between Monk and
Duke Ellington. He is the combination of Duke and Monk that seemed
to make both of them make sense somehow or other, you know. He fit in
there and just did lovely things. Some of the tunes he wrote, like "Hang-
over Triangle" and "The Lady Sings the Blues," "Houseparty Starting"—it's great music.[4]

PR: What was Herbie Nichols like personally?

BW: Herbie was kind, he was gentle, he was understanding, he never
really looked down his nose at anybody, never put anybody down, never
swore at anyone, never got into a fight. He was a *big* man. You know,
he looked like he might be able to break you with one hand, but he never
was into that.

I have a vague sort of sad story about Herbie from when we played at
this place called the Riviera, which was right across from Nick's, right
down in the village. A trumpet player who played drums a lot, and when
there was a trumpet player in there he would play drums, see. And we had
no bass, and Herbie used to play this dixieland piano, but he would always
be inventive. He was so inventive that he would never play quite the same
thing each time, and it used to bug this drummer, and he would be yelling
at Herbie horrible things like "Hey, Dave Brubeck, why don't you knock
off playing like Dave." He says, "Knock off the Dave Brubeck crap,"
"Hey, how about somethin' we can understand," and "Hey, play somethin'
pretty for a change, you knucklehead."

And I remember one night, it was about a month before Herbie died,
and it's a shame that a man like that would've had to do crummy little

---

4. These titles are available on Herbie Nichols, *The Third World*, Blue Note Records, 1975.

gigs like that for nine dollars for the night—the whole night—to make a living. And I mean, the man was such a genius musician, a *really* great player. And he had to do that kind of crap for a living and then take that kind of garbage from this drummer over the piano over the top of the upright. You couldn't really see his face, but he'd be makin' these awful remarks, you know. And I remember turning back and looking at Herbie. He would play sort of hunched over the piano with one ear down, and I looked at him close, and the light caught him right, and there's great big tears coming out of his eyes, man. And this idiot across the piano was shouting all this garbage, you know, at him.

And that night I waited until Herbie finished up and started trudging home, and I followed him back, and I think it's the most interesting evening I've had talking to anyone, 'cause he sat down and poured out all the stuff that—he didn't let on that he knew he was dying. In fact, I don't believe he knew that he had leukemia. He didn't have the money to go to a doctor to find out if he had it. He died of leukemia, at a very young age.

WE: Had you been studying with him?

BW: Studying—when we talk about studying, we are so into this formal-study bag these days, which I mean is good, actually. I'm not gonna knock it, because that's why we have these young monsters around. We didn't have that. It wasn't referred to in those terms; you hung out and absorbed what you were told. In other words, you found a musician, and you got into an intellectual and musical discussion about what it really was, and if he liked you and respected you, he would sit down and he would say, "Well, look, here is where it is."

What Herbie really did was teach restraint to me and teach me to play a little bit more melodically instead of so jagged all the time. Which he actually did with his little Ellington, quick little clusters and things; it was still melodic playing just the same way that Duke would do it. It would enhance what he was doin'. What Herbie really wanted to be was the entire Duke Ellington Orchestra in two hands.

One of the things he did teach me was turn-backs and how to connect the end of one chorus to another by the use of certain kinds of chords which we call "turn-backs." They revolve you back down to the beginning of the tune again where your statement becomes a *long* statement instead of a series of short ones. That's, I think, one of the most interesting things he taught me. And he also taught me to play more melody whenever I could and don't be afraid to play pretty. He said, "Don't be afraid to play pretty." He says, "We're goin' to be going through a scene pretty soon where the cats ain't gonna be gettin' into playin' pretty. They not gonna be wanting to do that. It's going to get cold for a while," he says, "but don't worry about it."

PR: He was right.

BW: Yeah, he *was* right. It's amazing how clairvoyant the man was. He had a lot of things already set in his mind that he knew were gonna come to pass, and they did. You know, as I look back—he said, "People are gonna forget, they're gonna forsake melodious playing in years to come." But he says, "In all walks of life it will eventually come back around to it again." But that was it, and when Herbie passed we all were very much surprised and grimmed out.

PR: That night you followed him home, was that the last time you saw him?

BW: No, we worked the Riviera a couple of more weeks—weekends, Friday and Saturday. And one week he just didn't come. He just didn't come to the job, and we had no piano player that night. A couple of days later we all learned that Herbie had passed away in his sleep.[5]

WE: Let's turn to trombonist Roswell Rudd. Weren't the two of you a team in the early sixties?

BW: Well, sometimes we would team. Sometimes when Ros or I had got the gig for that weekend, the other would just come along anyway. We'd either spell each other, or sometimes we'd go up and play together—it would get crazy. It got so, at one point, you could not tell which one of us were playing. We had molded our styles so much that it was like one. And it was a really rambunctious, kind of a searing style that we were playing. Very Bill Harris– and Dicky Wells–oriented. That's pretty much where we were all coming from at that point.

PR: How about Vic Dickenson?

BW: And Vic Dickenson—right. Definitely into that, definitely into that. We were having a grand time. Then Roswell took a whole different tack. He decided to forsake playing in any kind of key, at all. He decided that that was not hip. I think it had something to do with his association with Archie Shepp. I honestly think that association destroyed him, but then again I will get people who will debate that, you know. But I only am debating it because I knew Ros when Ros really could play.

---

5. Herbie Nichols died of leukemia in 1963 at the age of forty-four.

WE: Since then your styles have gone in opposite directions.

BW: Yeah, we've gone in opposite directions. I've gone and taken—I've adhered to a more melodic tack. I think that if I want to hear a computer play, I will buy one and program it and let it make all sorts of strange noises and everything. You know, I still make strange noises, but I don't make a whole evening out of it.

WE: Are you familiar with Rudd's 1973 *Numatic Swing Band* recording? [6]

BW: Yeah, it's very strange. It certainly does not swing, which is interesting. Which I thought that maybe it would, because I know Ros, or at least I knew him. I certainly don't know him now.

WE: When you say "swing," do you mean . . .

BW: I mean energy or whatever. First of all we're talkin' about jazz, all right? We're talking about a force; we're talking about an energy, a forward moving force that's conveying that kind of energy. If we're talking about just improvised music, avant-garde, or space, or whatever you want to call it, then it has to be taken as improvised music. You can't call that stuff "jazz." There ain't any way. I mean, they don't want it called "jazz" either.

PR: Isn't improvisation the heart of jazz?

BW: The heart of jazz is improvisation, yeah. But there's different kinds of improvisation. There's jazz improvisation, and there's just plain improvisation. Classical players can get around and do that very same thing and just take their instrument anywhere they want to for no particular reason. I can do it too. I enjoy it sometime when it's done in proper context. And no one could play any weirder than I can when anyone says to me, "Hey, man, play out." Forget it. I'll defy them to find out where I am or what I'm doin'. But to me, it solves no purpose in music.

I have my own personal preferences as to what I like to hear. Now, if you want to talk about goin' out, I'd just as soon listen to Sonny Rollins. Now there's a guy who goes out, but he knows where he is. And knows what he's doing. He's a jazz improviser, because he's taking that stuff out and he's saying somethin' with it, you know. But some of these people, I defy—I don't know what they're doin'.

PR: Have you ever played with Archie Shepp or someone else who plays in that style?

6. Roswell Rudd, *The Jazz Composer's Orchestra Plays Numatic Swing Band*, JCOA Records, 1973.

BW: No, and I wouldn't.

PR: It seems that they do know the idiom, the jazz repertoire and the standards.

BW: I know, but they put it down while they're doin' it.

PR: Verbally, you mean?

BW: No, mentally and musically, you know. See, there's no love in Archie Shepp's soul from the music that I've heard. I don't feel any real love. There might be a love for what he's doing, but actually he's speaking topically. Archie speaks about what is going on today. Archie's speaking about the hatred, the inhumanity to man, the unfairness, the bitterness. He's talking about a side of life which, sure it's there. It's always been there. It's been there since we've been put on this earth. There's always been man's inhumanity to man. But I am one of those idealists that feels that the good and the beautiful things will eventually prevail over this earth. Not the ugly and the bitterness. So if you're talkin' about what's gonna prevail, and if you're saying that that crap is gonna prevail, well, I don't want to be here when it does [laughter].

Listen, I'm trying to bring some melodic beauty into what I'm doing. I'm not trying to confuse the people I'm playing for. And I don't care who you are or how important you think you are. If you're a musician, and you get out on the stage in front of people, and people have paid their good money to go and hear you, and you stand up on a stage and insult them with that crap, man, you're a fake, you know. Once you get on that stage and people have paid to see you, regardless of whether you want to acknowledge it or not, you are what? An entertainer! You are there to provide some enjoyment for these people.

Now, if you can play avant-garde music and make it happen and make it exciting and make it interesting, then great. If you go out there with hate in your heart, it's not going to be exciting and interesting. It will appeal to people who are really into that bag, and I hope not too many folks are, because that, by God, is what's gonna turn over this country into a pile of garbage, sooner or later. There's gonna be an uprising, and no one's gonna have anything at all, you know.

WE: Do unusual or far-out sounds offend you?

BW: I don't get offended by sounds that are unusual or far-out, providin' they're unusual and far-out in a context that means somethin'. But I can tell all too easy whether somethin' is just noise. You know, you can't fool somebody who's paid his damn dues learnin' how to play his instrument.

You can't jerk them around. You may be able to fool John Q. Public, or a certain portion of John Q. Public, with honks and beeps and screeches and weird garbage, but when it comes to actually playin' the horn and playin' the music on the horn without going out and doing screeches, and howls, and blats, and honks, and squeaks, you know—when you stack up a player against somebody like Phil Woods, to me you're not even in the same damn ballpark, man. Not to *me*. Now you may to somebody else. But I kinda think—like to think—that I know basically what's good music and what isn't. I'm a damn good editor.

Dammit, I used to be in Thad Jones and Mel Lewis' band. Some of the stuff that we did within the context that we did got out, quite out, but you had something to come back to. If you're just out, man, if you're just out there, what do you have to come back to? What you're saying is "Hey, man, we don't want to come back to it. We're just out there." But you know the old fable of the emperor's new clothes? I rest my case [laughter].

PR: Aside from the Thad Jones–Mel Lewis unit, you've worked in big bands fronted by Quincy Jones and Johnny Richards, and now you have your own seventeen-piece group, Refuge West. Are you especially attracted to a big-band setting?

BW: I don't really have an attraction to big bands. My only reason for having a big band, my only reason for having one before, was to provide a place for some people to come and play and get to stretch out a little bit. All these bands around, you know, and there are really very few that are playing music on the level that this band is anywhere. And I'm just excluding myself; the band as a whole is a monster.

The reason after, you know, losing tons of money on my New York band that I would go back and do this thing again is because I've been doin' all these clinics and concerts in schools, and here are these super players, and there isn't one place for them to go. There are no gigs for them. And I made up my mind that I was going to provide at least one refuge for some of the best of these players to come and play some music. And boy, it has been hot.

WE: You mentioned economic troubles with your previous band. Are things any better with your current group?

BW: I'm losin' my shirt. That's what's happening. I don't know how long I'll be able to carry it on without some record company's support.

There's a monopoly on the bands by a certain agency, you know, that if you don't work through their agency, basically you don't work. I think it's damned unfair, but there's not too much that can be done about it by now. Unless someone gets off their butt and starts a new agency that can have the horsepower to push some new bands, what we're gonna get is just what we got. Lots of ghost bands—bands whose leaders died thirty years ago, and they've been through three different leaders on the band so far, and they're still bilkin' the hell out of the people.

I'm takin' a terrible bath. I'm going to apply for a grant. I'm not hopeful of getting it, when they see how much my past years' earnings have been on occasion, but I'm going to put in for it anyway. I'm gonna put in for it on the grounds that I'm running a youth band, you know, featuring young players that are just out of the school music systems. I think it'll work.

WE: What are the main problems of being a leader?

BW: The main problems for me at this point are gettin' work for the guys. I don't have any trouble gettin' men, 'cause that's always really straight, you know. I guess the main problem is finding a good field to play softball on, you know [laughter]. We could use a sound system, which we don't have; we could use various items that a bandleader should have. I gather 'em as I go along—lights, stands, you know. It's a pain in the neck.

You know what's the biggest drag of all? It's when the gig is over at 2:30 in the mornin', and everybody is split, and you got seventeen music stands and seventeen lights to wind up and seventeen books to put in this big heavy box and all that crap to lug out to the car.

PR: You don't have road managers to do that work?

BW: No, I don't. I can't afford 'em. And I don't want to put people on the dole. I got strong arms and a strong back and as long as I'm able to, I'll try to haul that stuff. You know, the guys come and play, and they don't get paid very much. *We* don't get paid very much. And as a result, I don't want them to have to do a lot of crap. I want them to enjoy being on the band.

WE: A very visible group these days is the Toshiko Akiyoshi–Lew Tabackin Band. What do you think of their work?

BW: Interesting from a mathematical point of view, and that's about it.

It's a cold band, man. It's a cold band. I read an article that she wrote, and I couldn't *believe* that a leader would have this to say about her players, but it was in, I forget which magazine it was in, but I saw it when I was up in northern California. I was lookin' it over, and she was being interviewed. And he says to her, "So what is your main source of frustration?" And she says, "Well, my main source of frustration is that I want a jazz band and I don't have one. They're *studio* players, and everything they play comes out sounding too pretty and too polite, so I write the charts with the roughness built in." I almost puked on it.

What she's sayin' is, you know, a bunch of bull! Because they're studio players! Some of the best jazz players I know in the whole world do a lot of studio work. It just so happens that they're excellent jazz players, but they can play any kind of music too. I think that down through these years we've been downplaying this aspect. You know, we'll look at a player who can make a lot of funny sounds in one area or so on his instrument, and he's regarded as a genius, yet you take that player and you set him down with a really great composer in a good section of great players, and that silly son of a bitch can't play a note in tune with any of the other players there. There's something suspect in that musician's whole outlook. And then they'll cop out and say, "Well, I'm not used to playing with other players." Well, *come* on, you're either a musician or you're not. What are you?

SELECTED DISCOGRAPHY

With Kai Winding. *The In Instrumentals.* Verve V6-8639. 1964–65.
Manhattan Wildlife Refuge. Columbia KG 33090. 1973.
With Red Rodney. *The Red Tornado.* Muse MR 5088. 1975.
The Tiger of San Pedro. Columbia PC 33701. 1975.
Bill Watrous Quintet, Funk 'n' Fun. Yupiteru YJ25-7024. 1979.
Best of Bill Watrous. Famous Door 147. 1980.
With Kai Winding, Albert Mangelsdorff, and Jiggs Whigham. *Trombone Summit.* Pausa 711. 1980.
The Bill Watrous Quartet. *Roarin' Back into New York.* Famous Door 144. 1982.
Reflections. Soundwings SWD-2104. 1985.
Someplace Else. Soundwings SWD-2100. 1987.

INDEX